TIDEWATER VIRGINIA FAMILIES:
A Magazine of History and Genealogy

Virginia Lee Hutcheson Davis, Editor

VOLUME 7, MAY 1998 - FEBRUARY 1999

HERITAGE BOOKS
2024

HERITAGE BOOKS

AN IMPRINT OF HERITAGE BOOKS, INC.

Books, CDs, and more—Worldwide

For our listing of thousands of titles see our website
at
www.HeritageBooks.com

Published 2024 by
HERITAGE BOOKS, INC.
Publishing Division
5810 Ruatan Street
Berwyn Heights, MD 20740

International Standard Book Number
Paperbound: 978-0-7884-5808-8

From Virginia...........

I have felt very humble and great sense of pride to have received so many appreciative comments about *TIDEWATER VIRGINIA FAMILIES: A Magazine of History and Genealogy*. I am also gratified by the number of loyal subscribers. You give me great encouragement in the face of increasing challenges in the publishing field. We have stayed the course together and all of us have derived a sense of satisfaction in the research accomplished and our heritage that has been found and saved.

It is always awkward to talk about money, and after the opening paragraph it is difficult to make this request; but perhaps that paragraph describes the philosophy of your editor and subscribers. So..... **If you are notified of a balance due because of underpayment of the subscription amount, please honor this request and send the balance due.** I have never had a policy of returning checks because of underpayment (this doesn't seem polite to me), but I am solely dependant upon subscription income to publish the magazine. **Please see that the correct amount is forwarded to me.** If a subscriber overpays by more than $1.00 a notice is sent that the overpayment is credited to the next volume for that subscriber.

Because of the hard work and dedication of a few of us, the archaeological survey of the Golansville Meeting House Cemetery and site is now in progress. A brief survey of the cemetery is being financed by the Virginia Department of Historic Resources under their Threatened Sites Program. The existence of the cemetery has been confirmed and also that there is evidence of a significant number of interments within the cemetery. A preliminary survey of the foundation site is being financed by contributions of a few interested individuals. Fay Parrish Wade has been the moving force behind this, with your editor also contributing a great deal of concern and effort.

Research in tracing family lines in tidewater Virginia has been made easier through the abstracts of some of the county records (especially the burned record counties) by the work of Sam and Ruth Sparacio, The Antient Press, 1320 Mayflower Dr, McLean, VA 22101. Cross referencing in the index provides the ability to trace the female lines with greater ease.

TIDEWATER VIRGINIA FAMILIES Web Site has been updated, check it! **www.erols.com/tvf** and tell your fellow researchers.

VLHD

Walk the Land Your Ancestors Trod

Virginia Lee Hutcheson Davis

Continued from Volume 6, Number 4, page 212.

Use your ingenuity and continue your search among the available records using the suggestions in the previous article, then get your walking shoes, your compass, and your road map and start walking..........

For the period of the Civil War there are maps that detailed the countryside for both sides. Virginia was closely mapped. There are *Confederate Engineers' Maps* (drawn by the Confederates) and the *Atlas to Accompany the Official Records of the Union and Confederate Armies* (commissioned by the federal government). *Gilmer's Maps, 1862-1864* of northern origin give place names and identify the names of landowners, the latter not always in exactly the right place, but good as a source of reference to the "lay of the land" and for further research.

For those researchers who have lived and searched in areas where the county court records of deeds and plats are extant, these puzzles may seem improbable. In tidewater Virginia, where so many of the early records have been destroyed, it takes creativity and ingenuity to reconstruct land ownership, location and neighborhoods. The custom whereby an original patentee gave his land a name that future land owners would continue to use as long as the tract remained intact provides the possibility of tracing an ancestor back to a named parcel. Some may have been named for the patentee and some given other names significant to the original land owner; a number of such names have survived today. While our interest is in identifying the land, conversely this may be used to reconstruct a family. See the *NGS Quarterly* article by William Carley, 1993, Volume 81, page 165.

County chancery court suits may have survived where little else has. Among these suit papers one may find a description of land owned, or better still a plat drawing with boundary land marks and neighbors described. It took this to finally be sure of the earliest land holdings of one ancestor. While a deed of the early 1900s of the transferal had survived, there was no earlier record to trace it back in time. Only through the plat of an adjacent land division a hundred years earlier located in chancery files, and the road surveyor lists of a still earlier date confirmed the same neighborhood. Ultimately this led to being able to stand on land that was in the same family for over 250 years. There was the family burying ground; with the periwinkle, the cedar tree and the indentations defining early graves. There was also a grave marker for a soldier of the Confederacy.

Newspapers in the late 1700s were scarce, the *Virginia Gazette* of Williamsburg, being the earliest and the one most consistently in publication, covered most of tidewater Virginia. Almost none of the Virginia newspapers began publishing before 1785. Most of them covered a larger geographic area than the name would imply. The book, *Genealogical Abstracts from Eighteenth Century Virginia Newspapers* by Robert Headley lists them. Not only are obituaries included, but estate sales. The plantation of a King William County resident was described in detail when it was offered for sale by his executors. All of the King William County records of the 1790s have been destroyed save the Land Tax Records, and they are frustratingly silent in this case. The plantation is there today, and called by the same name. The present house was built shortly after Thomas' death on the exact same site of his house. The sweep of the river is the same, and the adjoining land today bears the same name as the plantation of the next door neighbor of this resident. It was into this family that the son of Thomas married.

Fire insurance records may provide information, not only about the individual, but about his place of residence. Such records may be found with the company or with the State Archives or Historical Society. The Mutual Assurance Society, against Fire on Buildings, of the State of Virginia was incorporated by the General Assembly in December 1794. (For a complete description of these records see Conley Edwards, *A Guide to Business Records in the Archives Branch, Virginia State Library*, 1983). These records can be found in the State Archives, and give not only definitive information concerning the location of homes, but also a description of the buildings insured, and in many cases a sketch of the home and dependencies. Of course at this early date only those homes were insured where there was a relatively large financial interest. The records are worth searching for the expected as well as the unexpected information they contain.

The Works Progress Administration performed a valuable service in its *Virginia Historical Inventory* with its mission to identify and describe old homes, churches, cemeteries and records of various counties. The surveys were made in 1936 and 1937. While this has been called "make work", the people involved saved for posterity descriptions and records that would now be lost. Some of the information they recorded is word-of-mouth and not quite accurate, but old homes that are no longer standing and sites of homes and cemeteries no longer visible are identified.

Each entry gives the subject, and in the case of an old home, the name the home was known by. *Spring Garden* plantation was a legacy of an ancestor in the early 1700s, and is still identified by this name today. The location of the subject, whether home, church or cemetery, would include the community name, county road number and mileage. The date of the period of a home or establishment of a church is given with a description of the owners or founders and a description of the architecture. While the descriptions of old homes may be simplistic from an architect's viewpoint, they have in some instances been recorded no where else, and have survived today. In the case of the cemeteries, many of the early gravestone inscriptions, now gone, may be included.

There is not complete consistency as to the subject matter covered by the researchers in each county, and not all of the counties are included, so one should not expect miracles. It must be emphasized that the material included is written on an elementary level and needs to be rechecked, where possible, for accuracy. It just may provide the light at the end of the tunnel in some of the counties where the records are burned or incomplete; besides the inventories are fun to read!

Many of the techniques that have been described in identifying the land of ancestors may be used with printed or microfilm sources. Some require hands-on research among papers found in the Virginia State Archives, in county records, or historical society holdings. Access to the loose papers of the county court records in the various counties in Virginia is only with the permission of the clerk of the county court. The loose papers held in the Virginia State Archives also may be used only with the written permission of the clerk of the court of the appropriate county.

There are a number of personal papers or manuscript collections that are available to the public, but these must be used at the facility itself. A number of recognized genealogists' personal research papers, as well as a number of individual family papers, have been given to the Virginia Historical Society, the Virginia State Archives, and the Alderman Library at the University of Virginia. There are also holdings at the Swem Library at the College of William and Mary and the John D. Rockefellow Library of Colonial Williamsburg Foundation. The special significance of these holdings is that all sorts of information comes to light, not only from the family papers, but from copies of county court papers filed with them, that have been subsequently lost or burned.

One very recent technique that should not be overlooked is the ability to generate land plats with one's computer. The computer program *Deedmapper* allows one to enter the metes and bounds of a property and generate an individual plat, scaled to a US Geologic Survey Topographic Map. Even more exciting is that, not only can an individual plat be generated, but adjoining plats, and thus a whole community of neighbors can be assembled. And so the location of an ancestor's home may be identified. Several of the Virginia counties have had their original land patents platted by hand and some of these have been printed. Several counties now have organizations that are sponsoring the platting of their patents by computer programs such as *Deedmapper*. See also the works of LtCol James W. Doyle in *Tidewater Virginia Families*, Volumes 5 and 6 for some lands that have been platted.

By the 1870s, one can generally follow land ownership to the present, through deeds and plat books. Armed with a Virginia Department of Transportation Map of Virginia one can find the county seat, and thus the circuit court clerk's office at the county courthouse, where these documents are housed. With a description of the land and present owner, one can then walk across the hall at a county courthouse and present this information to a clerk in the Commissioner of Revenue's office. There one can be shown a contemporary tax and plat map of the area and specific parcel of land in which one is interested.

The plat is well-defined with all of the boundary lines and the roadways. A Virginia Department of Transportation County Road Map should complete one's necessary tools to sally forth.

This makes the transition to the present and the true significance of "walking the land our ancestors trod". County road maps are a must if you travel the by-ways. In Virginia there are other ways to travel also. Since the early settlers traveled almost entirely by water during the early days of settlement one should explore the various boat excursions that are available. See the land from the same perspective as your ancestors. Blot out the modern developments and see the shorelines and the wide expanse of the rivers. Think of your ancestors crossing the James, with the wind suddenly rising and everyone on the small craft frantically helping to row and praying to reach the far shore in safety.

It may have been the James, the Rappahannock, or the Pamunkey River, or the Potomac or Mattaponi. It may not have been in Virginia, but the same research techniques may apply and the same excitement may result in having found the land of your ancestor.

It is hoped that this article, *Walk the Land Your Ancestors Trod,* will inspire you to search; and to convey to you the feeling of "connectedness" that results. The exhilaration of standing on the very ground a colonial ancestor must have stood looking across the expanse of a river and at the sloop making its way up river, is payment enough for the search. Stand beside a creek where his own wharf secured the sailing vessel from England, or on a hilltop and gaze across the mountains, and know that it was your family that had also experienced this same feeling. Stand under the very tree that once shaded your great grandmother as she played in her front yard, or on the same rock that she used to mount her horse for a canter over the fields....and transcend time and the generations gap. It is an emotional connection with one's past and one's heritage. How does one describe the feeling of continuity that is felt when one travels the same pathways, and virtually the same roads that lead to a church or courthouse frequented by one's eighteenth century family?

One must experience this feeling for one's self, and it is hoped the insight offered in this article provides the opportunity. It is an experience so powerful that each family researcher must conduct his or her own pilgrimage and quest for this "connectedness". It is a continued wish to share this feeling with all who seek their heritage.

Research Sources for Identifying "The Land"

The sources presented below are samples of the types of information available, and may provide suggestions for further research in sources and references that relate specifically to the geographic area in which a researcher is interested.

County Court Records
- Virginia Land Tax Records, Library of Virginia, Richmond, VA (LVA)
- County Deed Books and Plat Books, Office of the Clerk, Circuit Court, in most counties in Virginia. Copies and microfilm of these prior to 1865 may be found in the LVA. Many of the early deed books have been abstracted at various times.
- County Circuit Court Chancery Suits, LVA and/or Offices of County Circuit Court Clerks.
- County Surveyor Lists, pre-dating 1865, County Court records, and scattered among Loose Papers by county, VSA.

Manuscripts and Personal Papers
- *George Harrison Sanford King Papers.* Acc. No. Mss1K5823aFA1. Virginia Historical Society (VHS), Richmond, VA.
- *Virginia Livingston Papers.* Acc. No. Mss1L7627aFA1. VHS.
- *Robert Alonzo Brock Papers.* Acc. No. Mss1B7825a. VHS.
- *Eggleston Family Papers.* Acc. No. Mss1EG396b. VHS.
- *The Ambler Papers,* Library of Congress, Washington, DC.
- See also collections of the Library of Virginia, Richmond, VA and University of Virginia, The Alderman Library, Charlottesville, VA.
- *The Roger Jones Family Papers, 1649-1896.* Library of Congress, Manuscript Division, Mss 18063. A microfilm edition of these papers in 15 reels is available through the Library of Congress.
- *Works Progress Administration of Virginia Historical Inventory.* (1936-1937), Film 509, Library of VA.

Books
- Virginia M. Meyer and John Frederick Dorman, eds. *Adventurers of Purse and Person.* (Richmond: Dietz, 1987).
- Nell Marion Nugent, *Cavaliers and Pioneers.* 3 vols. (Richmond: VSLA, 1974, 1977, 1979).
- Virginia Genealogical Society, *Cavaliers and Pioneers.* vol. 4 (Richmond: VGS, 1994).

- Gertrude E. Gray, *Virginia Northern Neck Land Grants*. 4 vols. (Baltimore: Genealogical Publishing, 1988-1993).
- Morgan P. Robinson, *Virginia Counties, Those Resulting from Legislation*. (Richmond: VSLA, 1916).
- Dr. Malcolm H. Hart, *Old New Kent County*. (West Point, VA: Privately printed, 1977).
- C. G. Chamberlayne, *Vestry Book of St. Paul's Parish, Hanover County, Virginia*. (Richmond: VSLA, 1973). As well as other published Vestry Books with processioner returns.

Maps and Travel Guides
- *Virginia*, K. M. Kostyal, Fodor's Travel Publications, (Hong Kong: Twin Age, 1994). Available for other states also.
- *Virginia Atlas and Gazetteer*. DeLorme Mapping Company, P.O. Box 298, Freeport, ME 04032. Available for a number of states.
- *Rand McNally Road Atlas, United States, Canada, Mexico*. P.O. Box 7600, Chicago, IL 60680.
- Topographic Maps. U S Geological Survey Map Distribution, P.O. Box 25286, Bldg 810, Denver Federal Ctr, Denver, CO 80225. 1-800-USA-MAPS.

Other Sources for Walking the Land
- Travel Information, Virginia Division of Tourism, Bell Tower, Richmond, VA 23219
- Travel by Land, Virginia State Maps (free), County Maps ($.25, each). Virginia Dept. of Transportation, Office of Public Affairs, 1401 E. Broad St., Richmond, VA 23219
- Travel by Water, *The Annabel Lee*, the James River, 4400 E Main St, Richmond, VA 23231

This article was presented as a talk before the Federation of Genealogical Societies in Richmond, Virginia, June 15, 1994.

More New Kent County Connections

by LtCol James W. Doyle, Jr., USAF, Ret.[1]

In the last issue, we looked at the area of New Kent County near the northern end of the boundary between Blisland and St. Peter's Parishes. We will now continue to explore some of the family and business relations of the neighbors in the region extending from New Kent Court House to Eltham.

Before venturing into new material, it would be in order to correct and amplify some items from the last issue. The tract which included Hogg Pen Neck, first patented by John Pouncey in 1652, was subsequently patented by George Gill, Jr on 31 Mar 1663. At that time Gill renewed his 1650 patent for 700 acres and added 400 acres of new land.[2] Gill had apparently bought the land from Pouncey, and held it for some time before it passed to William Bassett. It is not clear why Bassett, in his will, describes the land as that which he bought from Pouncey.

The incident regarding the above land is mentioned because it portrays a typical history of four owners, Pouncey-Gill-Bassett-Foster, spanning less than fifty years; documented by subsequent patents and one of the few wills to survive. In most cases, we have only the land patents to guide us. If we are lucky, a new owner took out a new patent, and perhaps mentioned the circumstances of his acquisition — whether the earlier owner had deserted the land or sold it, and whether there were any intermediate owners. All too often, the only record of ownership after the original patentee has been lost to the fires which destroyed the deed books and court records.

So, here we take a look at some more patent records to find what they may tell us about early Virginia families. First, let us consider the large 2300-acre tract granted to Lewis Burwell and Thomas Vause on 18 April 1648. There are several features about this patent worth some study.

First, this is the land claimed by the holders of the headrights of the *Mayflower* passengers. Readers may want to refer back to TVF 3:3, TVF 3:4, and TVF 4:1 for the story of how the forty-six colonists came to venture to Virginia, and how the headrights passed down by inheritance for some fifteen years before being exchanged for land. From those articles, the reader may also see that the Mayflower had a companion ship, the *Thomas*, and that one of the passengers on the Thomas was John Broach (numerous spellings of this name occur). Only about a half mile downstream from the Burwell and Vause land lay a 1800-acre tract patented by John Broach on 10 Aug 1647. Because both Burwell and Broach owned numerous tracts of land in several counties over a period of years, it may be presumptuous to assume that their proximity here in New Kent was very significant.

Between Burwell and Broach lay lands of Thomas Broughton and Francis Fludd/Flood. Broughton had another connection to Lewis Burwell in that he was listed among the headrights for a patent for 1600 acres in Northumberland County on 17 Oct 1650.[3] Whatever their reason for having patented adjoining tracts of land in New Kent County, Broughton soon sold his tract to Richard Dyer, who secured a new patent dated 23 Mar 1650,[4] less than two years after Broughton's original patent. Although no family or business connection among the three families is known, it is interesting to note that survey data for the three tracts are in unusually close agreement, both as to the length and bearing of bounds, and fit to the named terrain features. It would seem that the same surveyor laid out all three plots. The surveyor was obviously very careful and competent. If only every patent had such good data.

Immediately to the west of the Burwell and Vause patent was a 1000-acre tract granted to William Crumpe and Humphry Vaulx by patent dated 26 Jan 1656. One is naturally inclined to ask whether Humphry Vaulx might be related to his neighbor, Thomas Vause. The difference in spelling of the surname means little in writings of the seventeenth century, so we must look further. A conclusive answer is right at hand, and it turns out that they are almost certainly close relatives.

To prove this, we may refer to four patents. The first, a patent to Lewis Burwell, dated 12 Jun 1648, includes Thomas Vand/Vaus and Hump. Vand/Vaus.[5] This record not only links the two men, but shows that both were listed with a third variant of the name. Going on to a patent for land to Richard Wilchin in Gloucester County, it says that his land included 200 acres by a bill of sale from Mrs. Eliz. Vaus, atty for

Robt. Vaus, and confirmed by Hump. Vaus and Mr. Croshaw.[6] Then we have a patent to Francis Hammon, dated 1 Nov 1654, which lists headrights Robert Vaus, Eliz. Vaus, Susan Vaus, and Hump. Vaus.[7] Finally, we have a patent to Francis Burnell, dated 1 Apr 1661, which states that the land was "granted to Thomas Vaulx 20 Jan 1650 & by order dated 7 Jun 1657 granted to Robert Vaulx, heir to sd Thomas, and by sd Robert and Elizabeth, his wife, sold to Burnell."[8] So, we can safely conclude that all the people using the Vaulx, Vause, and Vaus surnames were of the same family. Further, we now know that Elizabeth was the wife of Robert. We may guess that Susan was the wife of Humphry, and that Robert and Humphry were sons of Thomas. I have looked into the International Genealogical Index (IGI) and do not find information to confirm or refute the above guesswork. The IGI includes fairly complete coverage of baptism and marriage data from British parish registers, and is a good starting point for any genealogical study. Those interested in the Vaus-Burwell-Burnell connections have only a starting point for further research.

The above exercise not only gives insight into the Vaus family, but establishes that the Vause and Burnell families had adjoining lands in both New Kent and Gloucester counties. This could be reason to look further for intermarriage or close business ties between them. So we come to another puzzle involving name spellings. Is Burnell just a variant spelling of Burwell? Again, we will limit the investigation to information which can be readily gleaned from the patent records and the International Genealogical Index..

In the above mentioned patent to Lewis Burwell for 2350 acres, the headrights included Francis Burwell. In a patent to Edward Wade/Waad on 18 Mar 1662, the land is described as part of 2000 acres belonging to Francis Burwell.[9] This is almost certainly the land granted to Francis Burnell about Dec 1660.[10] The patent for this land is badly mutilated, and it can't be plotted, but it probably includes the three tracts which he patented in 1655 and 1657. The most compelling evidence that Francis Burnell and Lewis Burwell were related is the fact that the 2300 acres which Burwell and Vause were granted for the *Mayflower* headrights passed to the sole ownership of Thomas Vaulx, who then sold the land to Francis Burnell. Burnell secured his own patent for the land, with identical survey language, on 1 April 1661.[11]

This would imply that the man who is usually known as Francis Burnell is very "close" to Lewis Burwell. Contrary evidence is contained in the International Genealogical Index, which lists no Burwells with the given name of Francis. On the other hand, there is a family of Burnells in Devon, and that family has several members with the given name of Francis. Perhaps one of our readers can shed some light on this little mystery.

Francis Burnell went on to secure patents for a total of 5800 acres. The 2000-acre tract to the north of the Burwell-Vause 2300 acres has been plotted here because it fits perfectly within the space available, with one adjustment. We discuss that adjustment to illustrate a pervasive difficulty in plotting the land patent data. In this case, the patent for Burnell's 2000 acres calls out the bounds as having bearings exactly on the N-S-E-W points of the compass.[12] The adjacent tract, originally surveyed for Burwell and Vause, calls out the bearing of the short north bound as "E¼S 88 chains."[13] Because the Burwell and Vause survey had all the marks of being done carefully and accurately, I made the assumption that the surveyor who worked for Burnell either was inclined to round off his measurements to the nearest whole point or perhaps had an inaccurate compass. With this in mind, I rotated the Burnell plot one-quarter point clockwise, and the whole set of tracts fits better. In another case involving Burnell's land, I left the bearings as stated, with the result that bounds do not coincide. Note that the bounds of Burnell's 700 acres[14] diverge from Burwell's 2300 acres. The difference here is ½ point, or 5.625 degrees.

In the plotting of almost all of the tracts, the author has introduced personal judgment in interpreting the data. Sometimes, hours of trial and comparison of results is involved in making a decision as to how to display the final results. The process is open to review and revision, but the author's results are presented for what they are: a best effort involving hundreds of hours of work. I suspect that my work will stand, it is too involved for replication!

There is one more example of a problem which has been left unresolved. The 1000-acre tract granted to William Crumpe and Humphry Vaulx simply will not fit into the space where it must be positioned.[15] So there it is, with the northern corner lapping over his neighbor's land. By plotting of tracts owned by Cox, Freeman and

Woodington[16] one might be able to establish a rationale for adjustments which would create enough space. Unfortunately, no survey data can be associated with these tracts.

Thomas Gibson was granted two patents for a total of 900 acres. Although there is no definitive survey data in the patents, the amount of land matches very well with open space between neighboring tracts which can be plotted, so hypothetical bounds for Gibson are drawn in dashed lines.[17] Thomas Gibson is the same man who bought 1000 acres from John Broach on 2 May 1648.[18] That land, lying south of Ware Creek on the York River, was plotted improperly in the article about Broach Neck and Hocady Creek in TVF 4:217, which showed the tract on the north side of the creek. Gibson's son, Nicholas was granted a patent for 800 acres to the east of Thomas.[19] It is shown on the map as being located to the north of Burnell's 2000 acres, although the description could place it directly over the northern neck of Burnell's land. The latter option may be preferable, since the location shown is all swamp, and would not be attractive. It is possible that young Nicholas died or otherwise deserted his land, but there is no mention of a previous owner in the Burnell patent.

William Blackey had two patents in this area.[20] Of interest here is that somewhere, I have seen a reference to a man named Blackey Terrell, but I cannot now retrieve that reference. It would tend to be in line with the custom of marriages between neighbors and giving boys the surname of the mother. William Blackey later joined the general migration to the north and west with his neighbors of New Kent.

The Vaus and Terrell families also had a significant connection revealed by the will of Robert Terrill of London, merchant.[21] Robert named "friend Mr. Robert Vaulx merchant" to receive a legacy of £10. The beneficiary listed after Vaulx was "brother Richmond Terrell," ten shillings for a ring.

The purpose of publishing these maps with comments about the interaction of neighbors is to emphasize the impression that Virginia was, for over 100 years, a single "small town," spread over hundreds of square miles. Friends and relatives were spread over the whole region, but marriages were usually the result of interaction between "close" neighbors — close being defined as the distance a young man might walk to and from in an evening. But marriages and other family ties were forever. As the restless population continued their hop-scotching around the colony, they never really got away from their old neighbors and kinsmen. However far one might journey, he was always near his kin.

It must have been easy to settle into a state of mind that all your friends and neighbors were also cousins. It was just a matter of taking time out for a cup of hot tea or a glass of fresh cider (in season), to discuss the family tree and identify the common ancestors. Lacking firm data, kinship could often be assumed on the basis of circumstantial information. Every stranger had to submit to a gentle grilling, on the assumption that he was a relative — it was just a matter of figuring out how he was related.

So it may be that the famed southern hospitality is based on the belief that family ties are very special. And, we're all cousins. Make your family welcome. Help them in whatever need they may have. They, in turn, may be relied on to do the right thing for you.

See New Kent County plotted land maps on following pages.

Notes

1. James W. Doyle, Jr., 2923 Tara Trail, Beavercreek, OH 45434. JWDoyleJr@aol.com
2. Land Patent Book 5, 338.
3. Land Patent Book 2, 250.
4. Land Patent Book 2, 309.
5. Land Patent Book 2, 181.
6. Land Patent Book 3, 284.
7. Land Patent Book 3, 306.
8. Land Patent Book 4, 35.
9. Land Patent Book 5, 351.
10. Land Patent Book 4, (449).
11. Land Patent Book 4, 35.
12.. Land Patent Book 6, 334.
13. Land Patent Book 2, 119.
14. Land Patent Book 3, 388.
15. Land Patent Book 4, 50.
16. Land Patent Book 4 (478).
17. Land Patent Book 2, 135, 304.
18. Land Patent Book 2, 145.
19. Land Patent Book 4, 183.
20. Land Patent Book 3, 88; Book 4, 261.
21. Emma Dicken, *Terrell Genealogy.* (San Antonio: The Naylor Company, c.1950).

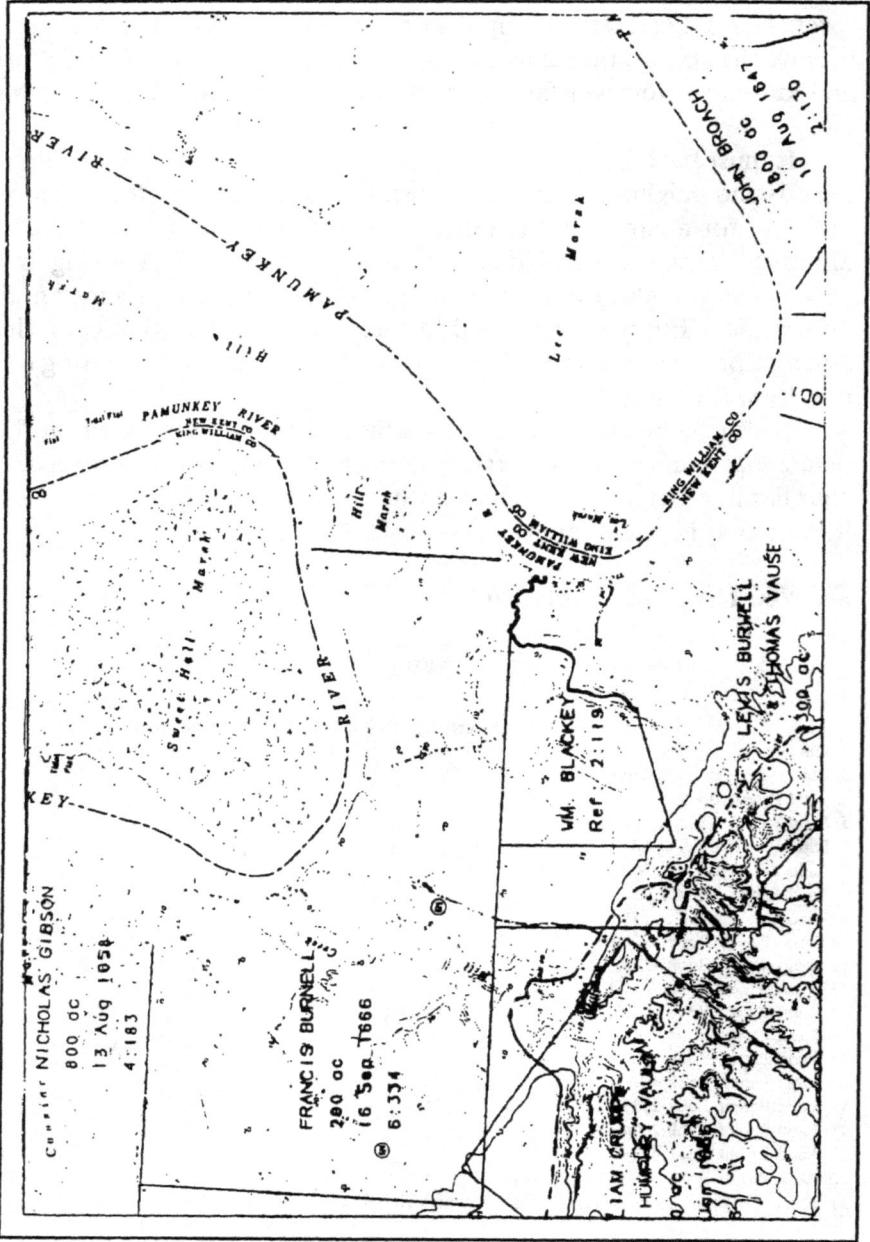

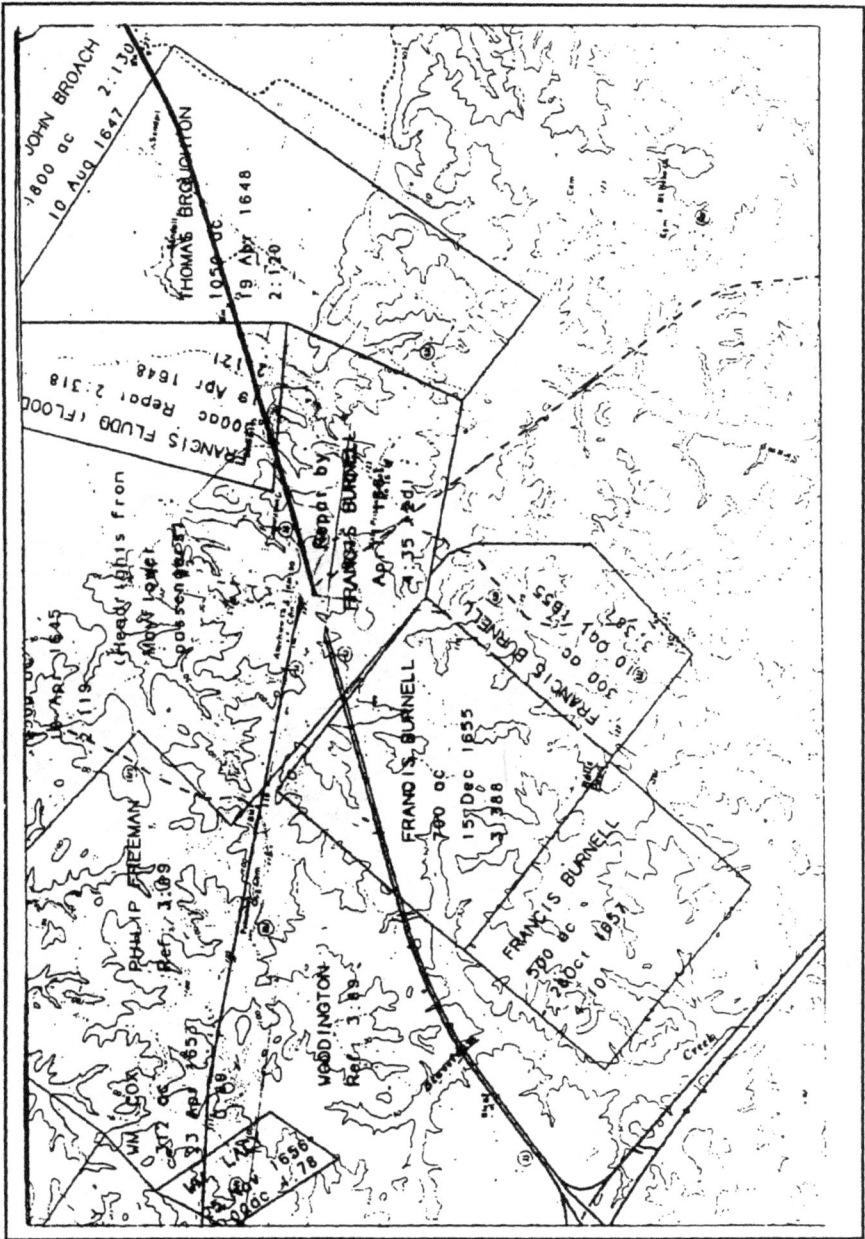

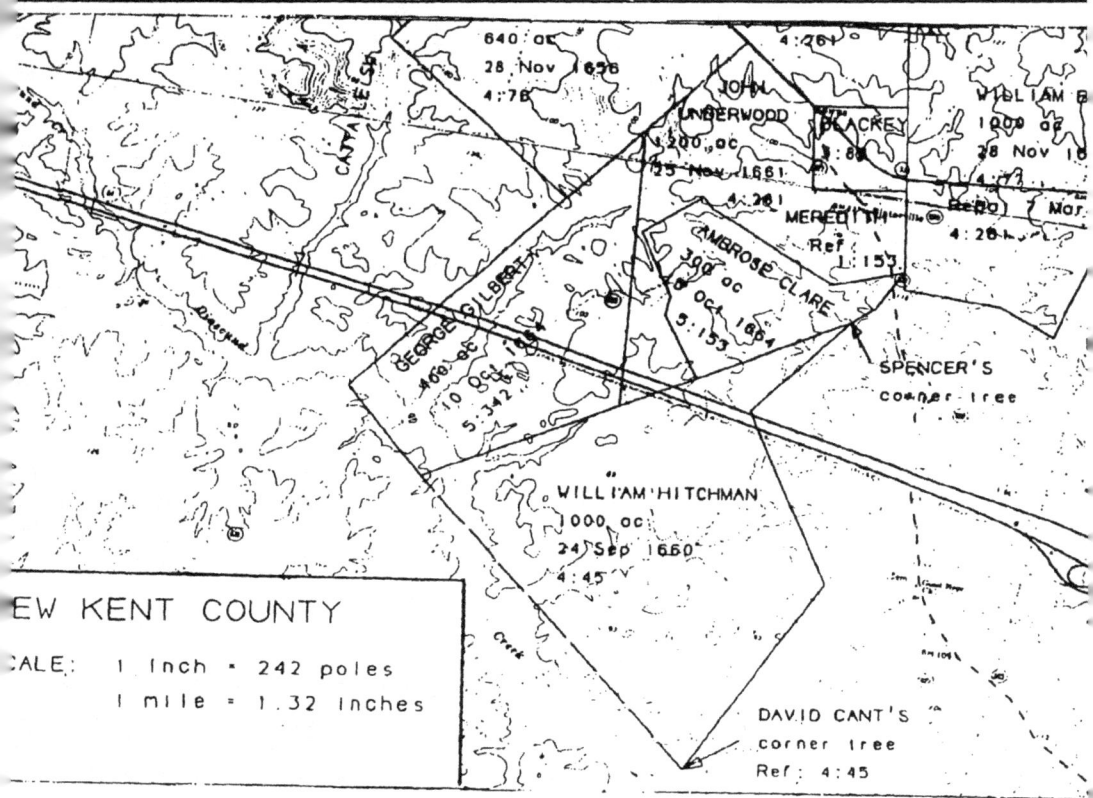

NEW KENT COUNTY

SCALE: 1 inch = 242 poles
1 mile = 1.32 inches

640 ac
28 Nov 1656
4:78

4:261

JOHN
UNDERWOOD
200 ac
15 Nov 1681
4:261

BLACKEY
3:88

WILLIAM B
1000 ac
28 Nov 16

4:77

1 Mar

MEREDITH
Ref 1:153

4:26

AMBROSE CLARE
390 ac
Oct 1664
5:153

SPENCER'S
corner tree

GEORGE GILBERT
400 ac
10 Oct 16
5:342

WILLIAM HITCHMAN
1000 ac
24 Sep 1650
4:45

DAVID CANT'S
corner tree
Ref: 4:45

CATALEE
Creek

Michael Talbot
Of Charles City County, Virginia

Carlos Maurice Talbott, Jr., D.Sc.[a]

The account of Michael and Peter Talbot through the second generation was presented in Volume 6, Number 3 of Tidewater Virginia Families (pages 154-159). This will continue the Talbot line.

Peter Talbot, the 2nd Generation

Although Peter[2] Talbot's will was proved in Charles City County Court in April 1742,[b] its provisions have not yet been found. According to a deed of John Middleton recorded in Prince George County on 10 November 1719, Peter[2] was married to Sarah Haley, daughter of James Haley. In this deed, Middleton conveyed the use of the Middleton estate to Sarah Talbot during her lifetime, and after her death, the land was to go to William[3], Jane[3] and Sarah[3] Talbot, children of Peter[2] Talbot and Sarah his wife.[c] An earlier Middleton deed dated 31 January 1714 is evidence that Peter[2] Talbot and Sarah Haley married sometime between 1714 and 1719.[d] John Middleton's son John left a will dated 20 November 1722 that named loving friend Peter[2] Talbot to be the Executor of his estate.[e]

James Haley, father of Sarah (Haley) Talbot, may have resided in James City County adjacent to and east of Charles City and southeast of Prince George counties. James Haley purchased 593 acres in James City County near Long Thickett and across James Town Road on 6 April 1676 from Lawrence Ash.[f] In 1704 he was on the James City County Rent Rolls for 310 acres of land.[g]

Sarah (Haley) Talbot survived her husband's 1742 death, married John Southall in May 1749, was widowed again by October 1750, and died 1764 in Charles City County. Several facts lead to this conclusion. In May 1746, the Charles City County Churchwardens bound James Morris, an orphan, to a Sarah Talbott.[h]

In May 1749, a marriage contract between Sarah Talbot and John Southall was proved in Charles City County Court.[i] Lucy[3] Talbot, orphan of Peter[2] and Sarah Talbot, chose John Dudley as her guardian at a March 1750 Charles City County Court whereas she had chosen

John Southall as her guardian six months earlier.[j] The will of John Southall was presented in Charles City County Court in October 1750 by John Southall, the executor.[k]

In June 1755, a suit in Charles City County Chancery Court between Lucy[3] Talbot, by John Dudley her guardian, versus John Southall, executor of John Southall (deceased) was revived subsequent to Lucy[3] Talbot's marriage to Richard Philips.[l] Finally, in 1764 the will of Sarah Southall of Westover Parish in Charles City County was filed naming son William[3] Talbot; and daughters Sarah[3] Dudley, Frances[3] Backhurst, Mary[3] Johnson, Lucy[3] Philips, Tabitha[3] Southall (deceased) and granddaughter Sarah[4] Southall.[m] Since Jane[3] Talbot was not mentioned in her mother's will, we presume she predeceased her mother without heirs.

William Talbot of Chesterfield County, the 3rd Generation

William[3] Talbot was born sometime between 1714 and 1719 as evidenced by John Middleton's 1714 deed which was modified in 1719 and named William Talbot as the son of Sarah (Haley) and Peter Talbot.[n] By 4 August 1730, William[3] had moved to Charles City County, along with Peter[2]'s family, and was a resident there in February 1745 when he proved the deed of Bowery Wood to Charles Collawn;[o] and in May 1748 when *deed of Mortgage John Middleton to William Talbot [was] recorded.*[p]

William[3] Talbot made his will on January 16, 1765 and died within the month. His will was presented in Chesterfield County Court on March 4, 1765 by his widow Elizabeth Talbot, Executrix.[q] This will designated Elizabeth and son Haley[4] Talbot as executors along with William West. William's will also identified three daughters (one of whom married William West), two more sons (Peter[4] and William[4] Talbot), and two grandsons, Richard[5] Worsham and his brother William[5] Worsham. Presumably, William had another daughter, Elizabeth[r] who married a Peter Worsham, the father of Richard[5] and William[5] Worsham.[s] Presumably, Elizabeth[4] died sometime between 1759 (when she relinquished her dower rights to land in Amelia County) and 1765 when her father wrote his will. In the 24 November 1768 edition of the Virginia Gazette, there is notice of sale of slaves and livestock from the estate of William[3] Talbott by William West and Haly[4] Talbot.[t]

21

In view of the pattern of his children's names (Haley[4], in honor of his mother's surname and William[4] and Peter[4], in honor of his paternal family), as well as the close proximity of Chesterfield County to Prince George County, it is reasonable to conclude that this William Talbot of Chesterfield County was the son of Peter[2] Talbot of Charles City County. In this regard, Chesterfield County, created 12 May 1749 from Henrico County, was adjacent to, across the James River, and due west of Charles City County.

In the Journals of the House of Burgesses, there is the November 3, 1762 petition of William Talbot who enlisted in the Virginia Regiment in 1755 and served as Sergeant. The petition stated that in 1758 he was wounded in the right arm during Colonel Grant's engagement near Fort Duquesne and in 1762 was incapable of hard labor. He was taken prisoner by the Indians at Fort Detroit and was in severe captivity there for fifteen months after which he was delivered up by the Indians. He rejoined the regiment and served until March 1762 when the Regiment was disbanded and he was discharged.

On 5 November 1762, William Talbot, by order of the House of Burgesses, was allowed £60/0/0 for wounds and hardships.[u] There is no evidence that this William Talbot is the same William[3] Talbot of Chesterfield County. However, this could explain the absence of William[3] Talbot from either the Charles City County or Chesterfield County records prior to 1762 when he witnessed a Chesterfield County deed by John and Jesse Bugg of Lunenburg County to John Hill of Chesterfield County[v]. William[3] Talbot was alive in 1764 because he was named in his mother's will. Moreover, Haley[4] Talbot, the son of William[3] Talbot, also served as a sergeant in Colonel Byrd's Regiment of Regulars during the war between Great Britain and France.[w]

Sarah (Talbot) Dudley of Charles City County

Sarah[3] Talbot, like her brother William[3], was born sometime between 1714 and 1719. It is probable that she married John Dudley of Charles City County before 1750 based on two facts. Lucy[3] Talbot, orphan of Peter[2] and Sarah (Haley) Talbot chose John Dudley as her guardian in March 1750.[x] Also, Sarah (Haley) Talbot Southall's 1764 will identified her daughter Sarah[3] (Talbot) Dudley.

Captain John Dudley, son of Thomas and Martha Dudley,[y] resided in Charles City County, where he died circa November 1782.

His inventory, made 5 December 1782, showed an estate in excess of £1250 with twenty-two slaves, twenty-four cattle, twenty sheep, twenty hogs, and four horses.[z] The administrator of his estate, James Southall Jr of Charles City County, was to sell his personal property.[aa] Another John Dudley, a possible son of John and Sarah[3] (Talbot) Dudley, is on the 1787 Prince George County Personal Property Tax List.

Frances (Talbot) Backhurst of Charles City County

Frances[3] Talbot was born after 1719 since she was not mentioned in the modified John Middleton deed. Her mother's will identified her married name as Frances Backhurst, and the following facts suggest her husband was James Backhurst of Charles City County.

James Backhurst, executor of the estate of Bolling Backhurst, made a trip to Williamsburg prior to 19 March 1790 on estate business. However, James Backhurst died prior to Dec 1791 when William Southall, his administrator, began accounts of his estate. Southall mentioned the Bolling Backhurst estate and the 20 December 1805 distributions to Thomas T. Backhurst and Ann B. Backhurst both *distributees for 12 years past* and their guardian John B.S. Backhurst another distributee.[bb] This William Southall was the brother-in-law of Captain John Dudley[cc] and, therefore, brother-in-law to James Backhurst; assuming Frances[3] Talbot had married James Backhurst.

Tabitha (Talbot) Southall of *Milton* in Charles City County

Tabitha[3] Talbot was born after 1719 and deceased before 1764. Sarah (Haley) Talbot Southall's 1764 will named granddaughter Sarah[4] Southall daughter of Tabitha[3] Southall, deceased.[dd] Tabitha[3] probably married James Southall of *Milton* in Charles City County.

The case for this argument is centered on James Southall's 14 March 1794 will.[ee] Therein James Southall gave his *oldest daughter Sarah T. Southall all my right and title in that tract of land lent by John Dudley to his sister Sarah, wife of William Southall, during her life, and then divised to Sarah T. Southall to her and her heirs forever.* He states *whereas I have acted as guardian for my two oldest daughters Sarah T. Southall and Elizabeth C. Willson [wife of John Wilson of Surry County[ff]] and have hired out their negroes devised to them by their uncle John Dudley* .... He also identified daughters Margaret Harwood Southall and Ann Bolling Southall. To his daughter Margaret Harwood Southall he gave his *tract of land whereon I now live known by the name of Milton* and to daughter Ann Bolling Southall *my plantation which I purchased of William Vaughan and generally known by the name of Vaughans containing two hundred and twenty five acres.*

Thus, the facts are that Tabitha[3] Talbot had a daughter Sarah[4] Southall; that James Southall of *Milton* had two daughters, Sarah T. Southall and Margaret Harwood Southall, whose uncle, John Dudley, was probably married to Sarah[3] (Talbot) Dudley; and that James Southall's other two daughters, not identified as neices of John Dudley, were likely children of a second marriage.

Genealogical Summary

Generation One

1. Michael[1] Talbot married John Nibblet's widow Mary, daughter of Daniel Washbourne circa 1679 and died in Charles City County before January 10, 1717. Known children of Michael[1] Talbot were:

    2. Michael[2] Talbot who died before February 10, 1718 in Prince George County, Virginia apparently without issue.

    3. +Peter[2] Talbot.

Generation Two

    3.+ Peter[2] Talbot (Michael[1]) married Sarah Haley sometime between 1714 & 1716 and died in 1742 in Prince George County. Sarah (Haley) Talbot, daughter of James Haley, married 2nd John Southall in 1749 and died in 1764 in Charles City County.

Known children of Peter and Sarah (Haley) Talbot were:

    4.+ William[3] Talbot.

    5. Jane[3] Talbot who was born before Nov 1719 and died before 1764. No further information.

    6.+ Sarah[3] Talbot.

    7.+ Frances[3] Talbot.

    8. Mary[3] Talbot who was born after 1719, had a child in 1745 by Edward Bryan of Charles City County,[66] and married a Mr. Johnson before 1764 when she was mentioned in her mother's will. No further information.

    9. Lucy[3] Talbot who was born about 1735, married Richard Phillips of Charles City County about 1755, and

died sometime after 1764 when she was mentioned in her mother's will. No further information.

10.+ Tabitha[3] Talbot

Generation Three

4.+ William[3] Talbot (Peter[2], Michael[1]) resident of Chesterfield County, married Elizabeth (_?_) and died January 1765. Known children of William[3] and Elizabeth Talbott were:

11. Haley[4] Talbot who probably married Frances Rudd and died circa 1798 in Chesterfield County, where his will is filed.

12. Peter[4] Talbot who died in January 1798 in Chesterfield County.

13. William[4] Talbot. No further information.

14. Sarah[4] Talbot who married (presumably Thomas) Ballard.

15. Mary[4] Talbot who married William West.

16. Rebecca[4] Talbot. No further information.

17. Elizabeth[4] Talbot who married Peter Worsham and had sons, Richard and William, both of whom served as commisioned officers during the Revolutionary War.

6.+ Sarah[3] Talbot (Peter[2], Michael[1]) who was born after 1714 and died sometime after 1764, married Captain John Dudley of Charles City County (died 1782). One child of John and Sarah[3] (Talbot) Dudley was perhaps:

18. John[4] Dudley. No further information.

7.+ Frances[3] Talbot (Peter[2], Michael[1]) who was born after 1714 and died after 1764 when she was mentioned in her mother's will. She probably married James Backhurst of Charles City County. The known children of James and Frances[3] (Talbot) Backhurst were:

19. John B.S.[4] Backhurst.

20. Thomas T.[4] Backhurst.

21. Ann B.[4] Backhurst.

10.+ Tabitha[3] Talbot (Peter[2], Michael[1]), who was born after 1719 and died by 1764, probably married James Southall and had children by him:
22. Sarah T.[4] Southall.
23. Margaret Harwood[4] Southall.

Notes

a. 641 Nor Oaks Court, West Chicago, Illinois 60185.

b. *Virginia Magazine of History and Biography* (VMHB), 21 (1914): 86.

c. Benjamin B. Weisiger,III, *Prince George County, Virginia, Wills & Deeds, 1713-1728 (PGCo 1713-1728)* (Richmond, privately printed, 1973) 46-47.

d. Ibid., 5.

e. Ibid., 72.

f. Louise Heath Foley, *Early Virginia Families Along the James River, Their Deep Roots and Tangled Branches,* vol III (Baltimore: Genealogical Publishing Co, 1990) 76-78.

g. Louis des Cognets, Jr., *English Duplicates of Lost Virginia Records* (Princeton, NJ: privately published, 1958) 174.

h. Benjamin B. Weisiger,III, *Charles City County Virginia Records 1737-1774 with Several 17th Century Fragments (CCCO 1737-1774).* (Richmond: privately published, 1986) 104.

i. Ibid., 112.

j. Ibid., 112-118.

k. Ibid., 115.

l. Ibid., 124.

m. Ibid., 2.

n. Weisiger, *PGCo 1713-1728* 47.

o. Weisiger, *CCCo 1737-1774* 102-103.

p. Ibid., 109.

q. *Chesterfield County Virginia Will Book 1.*, 455-458.

r. Gibson Jefferson McConnaughey, *Colonial Records of Amelia County, Virginia, Deeds 1754-1765* (Amelia, VA: privately published, now held by Iberian Publishing Co, Athens, GA, 1990) 50.

s. *Chesterfield County Court Order Book 5*, 58.

t. Robert K. Headley, Jr., *Genealogical Abstracts from 18th Century Virginia Newspapers* (Baltimore: Genealogical Publishing Company, 1987) 329.

u. Lloyd DeWitt Bockstruck, *Virginia's Colonial Soldiers.* Baltimore: Genealogical Publishing Co, 1988 175-176.

v. Weisiger, *CCCo 1737-1774* 59.

w. William Armstrong Crozier, *Virginia Colonial Militia 1651-1776* (Baltimore: Southern Book Co, 1954) 43.

x. Weisiger, *CCCo 1737-1774* 112 & 118.

y. Benjamin B. Weisiger,III, *Chesterfield County, Virginia Wills, 1749-1774* (Richmond: privately published, 1979) 102, 152.

z. *Charles City County Will Book 1*, 146-147.

aa. Headley 107.

bb. *CCCo Will Book 1* 610-613.

cc. James P.C. Southall, *"Concerning the Southall's of Charles City County"*, Judith McGhan, ed., *Genealogies of Virginia Families, vol IV*. (Baltimore: Genealogical Publishing Co. 1982) 529-530.

dd. Weisiger, *CCCo 1737-1774* 2.

ee. *CCCo Will Book 1* 169-172.

ff. Southall 532.

gg. Weisiger, *CCCo 1737-1774* 101.

Civil Appointments, 1781-1798
King William County

Contributed by Minor Tompkins Weisiger

These Civil Appointments from the Executive Department provide information of the lives and business of the residents of King William County. They have been selected particularly for those counties of tidewater Virginia for which the county court order books do not generally exist. There are not files for every year, or for all appointments made within a year. They are transcribed rather than presented as abstracts, to provide all of the information possible. In some cases the actual signatures of the persons writing the notation will be presented rather than a transcription of that signature.

King William February Court 1781
     Pursuant to an act of Assembly in that case made & provided. The Court doth recommend to his Excellency the Governor, Benjamin Johnson/ in the room of Liston Temple who is dead/ as a proper person to be Inspector of tobacco at Aylett Warehouse in this County under the same Inspection as Todd's in King & Queen ——.
         A Copy John Quarles jr D.C.

King William January Court 1782
     Pursuant to the Act of Assembly in that case — made & provided, this Court doth recommend to his Excellency the Governor, Joseph Fox as a fit able person to be Inspector of Tobacco at Frazer's Warehouse in this county & Mantapike in King & Queen County under one Inspection & William Alvey as an Assistance Inspector at the said Warehouses.
         A Coup Jnº Quarles D.C.

King William January Court 1782
     Pursuant to an act of Assembly in that case made & provided, This Court doth recommend to his Excellency the Governor Benjamin Johnson as a proper person to be Inspector of Tobacco at Aylett's Warehouse in this County, under the same Inspection as Todd's in King & Queen and James Powell as an Assistant Inspector at the said Warehouses.
         A Copy Jnº Quarles D.C.

King William June court 1782

Pursuant to an Act of Assembly in that case made & provided, This Court doth recommend to his Excellency the Governor Tho⁵ Littlepage, Geo. Braxton & James Ruffin Gent as proper persons to be added to the Commission of the Peace for the County there being several of the Gent. formerly recommended removed out of the County & others refuse to qualifie.

a copy John Quarles j D.C.

King William September 1782

        Pursuant to an Act of Assembly in that case made & provided, This court doth recommend to His Excellency the Governor Thomas Elliott, John Hickman & William D. Claiborne Gent as proper persons to Execute the Office of High Sheriff of this County.

A copy Jn° Quarles D.C.

King William September Court 1782

        Pursuant to an Act of Assembly in that case made & provided, This Court doth recommend to his Excellency the Governor, Nath¹ Burwell Gent. as a proper person to be added to the Commission of the Peace for this County.

A Copy Jn° Quarles D.C.

King William May Court 1784

        Pursuant to an Act of assembly in that case made & provided, This Court doth recommend to His Excellency the Governor, Holt Richeson & John Hickman Gent. as proper persons to be Sheriff for this County

A Copy Jn° Quarles D.C.

King William June Court 1784

        Drury Ragsdale Gent is recommended to His Excellency the Governor as a proper person to be one of the Coroners of this County.

A copy Jn° Quarles D.C.

At a Court held for King William County the 20ᵗʰ day of July 1786

        Pursuant to an Act of Assembly in that case made & provided, This Court do recommend to His Excellency the Governor, Holt Richeson, John Hickman & William Dandridge Claiborne Gent. as proper persons to be Sheriff of this County.

A Copy Jn° Quarles D.C.

At a Court held for King William County the 21th day of September 1786
Pursuant to an Act of Assembly in that case made & provided This Court doth recommend to His Excellency the Governor, Benjamin Johnson as a proper person to be Inspector at Ayletts Warehouse in this County under the same Inspection as Todds in King & Queen, and Reuben Turner as an Assistant Inspector at the said Warehouse.

A copy Test Jn° Quarles D.C.

King William.

Land			£117, 10, 2
Negroes	2402	at 10/	1201 — —
Horses	1790	at 2/	179, 16, —
Studs	6		10, 12, —
Chariot Wheels	20	at 36/	50, 8, —
Phaeton do	56	at 24/	67, 4, —
Chair do	110	at 12/	70, 16, —
Ord[y] Lic	4	at 5/	20, —, —
Phy[s]	4	at 5	20, —, —
			£2737, 14, 2

King William September Court 1787
Ordered that it be certified to his Excellency the Governor, that Joseph Fox & William Alvey, the Inspectors of Tobacco at Frazers in this county, under the same Inspection with Mantapike in King & Queen, are continued at the said Warehouses

A Copy Jn° Quarles D.C.

[obverse side, ed.]
His Excel[y] Governor [Beverley] Randolph & Mr W[m] Alvey
King W[m] Inspector Jan[y] 2[d] 89
Sir.

This will be handed you by Mr William Alvey who stand[s] recommended by King William Court as an Assistant Inspector of Tob° at Frazers & Mantapike Warehouse's and who for sometime past, has represented M^r
Joseph Fox one of the Inspectors, W. Fox has lately departed this Life, so that Mr Alveys Commissⁿ as an Assistant is at an end he therefore waits on your Excellency for a Commission as Inspector in the room of Mr Fox. If it is Practicable for Mr Alvey to Qualify to his Commiss, before our next Court wch is the fourth Monday in next month it would be a very great Conveniance to the people in the neighbourhoood of these Warehouses

                                                                        I am respectfully
Dec. 30th 1788   Your Ob Serv
                                                                        D. Ragsdale

I, John Quarles deputy Clerk of King William County do hereby certifie that Joseph Fox the Inspector at Frazers Warehouse in this County is dead.
                                                                        Jn° Quarles

At a Court held for King William County the 28th day of September 1789
                           Present Gent. Justices

John Roane	Christp^r Tompkins
Thomas Elliott	Nathl Burwell
Thomas Butler	James Hill
John Catlett	Isaac Quarles
William Harris	Francis Dandridge

                    Pursuant to an Act of Assembly in that case made & provided,
This Court do recommend to his Excellency the Governor, Benjamin Temple, John White, Robert Pollard, Thomas Nelson, William T. Gaines, Edward Pye Chamberlayne, John Roane jun^r & William Gregory Gent. as proper persons to be Justices of the Peace for this County.
                                                    A copy Jn° Quarles D.C.

King William June Court 1791
                    Pursuant to an Act of Assembly in that case made & provided,
This Court do recommend to his Excellency the Governor, Christopher Tompkins & William Smith as proper persons to execute the office of coroner for the said County
                                                    A copy Jn° Quarles D.C.

At a Court held for King Wm County the 27th day June 1792
                           Present Gent. [Justices]

31

Natha[l] Burwell   Benj[n] Temple
David Pannell   W[m] Gregory
Fra[s] Dandridge

       Pursuant to a Law in that case made and provided the Court doth recommend Tho[s] Robinson, William Harris and John Catlett Gentlemen to his Excellency the Governor as proper persons to execute the Office of Sheriff for this County for the insueing year which is Ordered to be Certified by the Court

                                    Ed Berkeley Clk.

King William July Court 1796
James Ruffin, Nathaniel Burwell and James Hill Gentlemen were recommended to his Excellency the Governor as proper persons to be commissioned to execute the Office of Sheriff of this County

                          Test. Jn[o] Quarles D.C.

At a Court held for King William County the 22nd day of January 1798
       James Ruffin, Nathaniel Burwell and James Hill Gent[n] are recommended to his Excellency the Governor as fit persons to be commissioned as Sheriff of this County, James Ruffin the present Sheriff wishes to continue in Office the Second Year

                   Test Edmund Berkeley 66

Transcribed by VLHD

From the records of the Executive Department, Commonwealth of Virginia. Virginia State Library and Archives. Box 3, A-E. Pre-1790.

Warwick County Court Records, 1683-1786

Abstracted below are some documents that were taken by Union Army soldiers during the Civil War, later were found at a trade show, and purchased and returned to the Commonwealth. Other records were confiscated and have not surfaced. Many of the Warwick County records were taken to Richmond for "safekeeping" and were burned during the evacuation of Richmond. ed. Since the record books have not survived the number following each entry will be the individual reference within the catalogue accession number.

Writ/Contract binding Thomas Avery of Warwick County to pay the sum of £8/15to George Reeves, Sept 20, 1683. Witnessed by Robert Avery and Mary Mitchell. Signed Thomas Avery. NN92.7.2AR

Account of horses and mares belonging to the orphans of Symon Daniall, deceased, July 22, 1687. Sworn by his guardian Tho. Merry in open court. Recorded by clerk Miles Cary. NN 92.7.3AR

Receipt of March 16, 1696 itemizing various bottles of alcohol; probably a tavern account for Mr. Andrew Cole. Also includes the purchase of a hat. Signed by Jurat Coram, John Gawen and Francis Page. NN92.7.4AR

Order to sheriff of Warwick County to summon parties in the debt suit of Henry Gibbs vs. James Selator (Sclator?), June 21, 1709. Signed by Miles Cary, clerk of court. Appears to have been executed by sub-sheriff Nath. Jones. NN 92.7.5AR

Writ/Bill of Complaint, August 3, 1715, by William Robinson, assigns of Joseph Tarrant against John Seymour in a plea of debt for the sum of 644 pounds of good sweet-scented tobacco, owed since August 5, 1714. Recorded by Miles Cary, the case was carried over to the October and December courts when it was dismissed for want of prosecution. NN 92.7.6AR

Writ/Bill of Complaint showing that Robert Midlston, late of Warwick County, is indebted for the sum of 430 pounds of good sweet-scented tobacco for which he signed a bill in 1715. Suit brought by Francis Jones, assigns of Matthew Jones, at July 5, 1716 court. Entries on the reverse side of the document show that the case was continued five times until the December 1716 court, when judgement was granted the plaintiff for his money. NN 92.7.7AR

Order to the Warwick County sheriff to summon Ralph Gough for May 2, 1726 court to testify in a difference between Thomas Cary, plaintiff & William Chanvoy defendant. Signed R. Gough, clerk of court. NN 92.7.8AR

Order to Warwick County sheriff to summon Servant Jones, William Jones, Albritton Jones and Matthew Wood to testify at December 1770 court in behalf of Cuthbert Hubbard in the suit of Allen Jones, plaintiff and Cuthbert Hubbard, defendant. Fine for not appearing 100 (?# tobacco) each. Signed by Richard Cary, clerk and executed by Richard McIntosh, deputy sheriff. NN 92.7.9AR

Petition/Writ of Thomas Finn of Warwick County requesting payment of £4/8/3½ due him by Dr. W. Cuthbert Hubbard and a summons to the Warwick County sheriff for Hubbard to appear at the next court. Witnessed by Richard Cary, clerk, March 20, 1771, and executed by deputy sheriff Richard McIntosh. NN 92.7.10AR

Order to Warwick County sheriff to take and safely keep Joseph Moore until the May 1771 court to satisfy Francis Tomkies for the sum of 148 pounds of tobacco and also for £16/3 costs for prosecuting a certain suit. Signed and witnessed by Richard Cary, clerk, March 20, 1771. NN 92.7.11AR

Writ/Bond of Replevin suing Robert Pulley and/or his security Robert Brown of Warwick County for legal costs of £7/18/4½ in processing a writ of *fieri facias* and judgement to collect £15/6/9 owed John Giles of York County. Payment to be made in three months. Signed and sealed by Robert Pulley and Robert Brown. NN 92.7.12AR

Accession No. NN92.7.1-12AR, Newport News Museum and Archives. Some scattered records may be found at the Swem Library at the College of William and Mary, Williamsburg and at the Library of Virginia, Richmond, VA.

Legislative Petition of
James Wright and His Wife Eve
York County, 1805

Contributed by Dennis Hudgins

A Petition will be presented to the next General Assembly, praying that an act may pass, relinquishing the right of the commonwealth in a tract of Land, lying in the county of York, whereof George Reid, died seized, to James Wright and Eve his wife, which Eve was the wife of said George Reid. Williamsburg, July 16, 1805. Virginia Gazette.

To the Honble the Speaker and Gentlemen of the House of Delegates The Petition of James Wright and Eve his wife — humbly sheweth — that the said Eve had a valuable tract of Land in the State of North Carolina —

devised to her in fee simple by her late Father George Anderson. deced. —

that sometime after the Death of her said Father — she was married to a certain George Reid of the City of Williamsburg in the Commonwealth of Virginia, and at the Request of the said George Reid, she agreed to sell the said Tract of Land in the State of North Carolina — the said Reid promising of her to vest the money arising from the Sale of the said Land, in land more convenient to her residence in the State of Virginia — that shortly after selling the Land & conveying the said same in the State of North Carolina — the said George Reid her late husband purchased a small Tract of Land in the County of York—very convenient to the said City of Williamsburg — Your petitioners beg leave further to represent to this Humbl House that the said George Reid died about the year 1792 in the said City & County of York — intestate as to the Tract of Land so purchased and without leaving any Child. but leaving a Brother & other Relations in the Kingdom of Great Britain and as your Petitioners are informed the Brother of the said George Reid deced. cannot inherit any part of the Real Estate which belonged to the said George Reid deced., being an alien — and that the Right in the Land so purchased by the said George

Reid in the County of York & State of Virginia — belongs now to the Commonwealth of Virginia —

Your Petitioners therefore pray that this Humbl House will pass a Law giving any Right which the Commonwealth of Virginia has in the said Tract of Land — lying in the said County of York & in this State to your said Petitioners — James Wright & Eve his wife (which said James Wright has intermarried with the said Eve late widow of the said George Reid, deced. and your Petitioners as is Duty bound shall ever pray.

Jas. Wright

Eve Wright

* * * * *

Will of George Anderson, 1757

In the Name of God Amen, the Sixth day of of [sic] July in the Year of our lord 1757. I George Anderson of St. Johns Parish and Granville County being Sick & Weake of body but of perfect mind & memory do make & ordain this my last will & testament in manner and form following

Imprimis That is to Say I Give and bequeath unto my beloved wife Mary all my estate Real & personall during her natural life and after her death to my Daughter Eave Anderson & her heirs and in Case She dies without Issue I Give my land & plantation to my brother William Andersons Son George Anderson and his heirs and assigns forever and the remainder of my estate to be equally Divided between him & Elizabeth Underwood Daughter of John Underwood and there heirs for ever and I doe hereby nominate and appoint my beloved wife Mary Anderson and Clabourn Croborn Jeffreys my whole and Sole Executors of this my last will & Testament uterly Revoking and Disav Disalowing all other former Wills or bequeath by me heretofore made Ratifying this to be my last Will & Testament In Witness whereof I have hereunto Set my hand & Seal the day & year above written   his

36

[signed] George Z Anderson
mark

Assigned Sealed published pronounced and Delivered by the Said Geo Anderson to be his last will & Testament in present of
his
James J Brazer
mark
William Anderson
Thomas Smith
At a Court held for Granville County 7th March 1758
This Will was ~~duly~~ proved in due form of law by the oathes of William Anderson & Thomas Smith two of the Witnessess thereto and was Ordered to be recorded   Teste [signed] Daniel Weldon C C
Truly Recorded A Copy teste   [signed] Reuben Searcy
* * * * *

Will of George Reid, 1792
City of Williamsburg

In the name of God amen this twenty day of October in the year of our Lord 1785 I George Reid of the city of Williamsburg being in perfect mind and memory do make and ordain this my last Will and Testament as follows I give and bequeath unto my wife Eve Reid after paying my just debts all my real and personal property requiring the sum of two hundred pounds sterling to be paid my brother William Reid for his and my Sisters use, the remainder of my estate for the use of my wife during her widowhood. Should she marry to pay within twelve months after three hundred pounds sterling to my said Brother William Reid and my Gold watch, at her death all the estate real and personal to be equally divided between my brother and my two sisters or their heirs forever — The loan Office Cert. it is my desire they shall not be disposed of but that the Interest rec^d on them. I appoint her my sole executrix of this my last Will and require of her to call on Mr. Benj^a Waller for any instructions on how to act for which he will be pleased to receive payment for his services — Should she continue a widow to make what remittance she can after three years to my brother.

At a Court of Hustings for the City of Williamsburg
held the sixth day of August 1792

This instrument of writing purporting the last Will and testament of George Reid dec[d] was produced in Court whereupon David Miller and Alexander Kevan being sworn declared they are well acquainted with the hand writing of the said George Reid and verily believe the said instrument of writing to be wholly written by himself and the Court being satisfied therewith the same is ordered to be recorded. And on the motion of Eve Reid widow and relict of the said George Reid dec[d] who made oath according to Law and together with William Lightfoot (of Sandy Point and Wyatt Coleman of the City of Williamsburg) her securities entered into and acknowledged their bond in the penalty of three thousand pounds conditioned as the law directs certificate was granted her for obtaining Letters of administration on the said estate with the said Will annexed in due form.

Teste [signed] Will: Russell C.H.C.
A copy W. Russell C.C.

[The detailed account of the estate of George Reid listed as a part of his estate the following Negroes: Nelly and children, Dick, Edmund, Joe, Lewis, Betty, Lucy, Daphney, Lucy (younger), Amy, Rachel, Dinah, Winny, Sam, Frank and John. The total estate amounted to £1392/9/8½, with a balance of £419/3/2½ due James Wright. The account was returned and signed by James Davis, John Houston and Jn° Bryan and recorded in the Court of Hustings of the City of Williamsburg, with the date of 1st of September 1800. Notation on reverse side]: Wright & Wife's Pet° To Lets. Jus Ref[d] Dec. 16 1805. Decemb[r] 19, 1805 Reason rep[d.]   Transcribed by VLHD

York County Legislative Petitions, 16 Dec 1805, Archival and Information Services, Library of Virginia, Richmond, VA.

Henrico County Will Book 1, 1781-1787

Continued from Volume 6, Number 4, page 254.

The entries from the Henrico Will Book 1, 1781-1787, as abstracted by Dr. Benjamin B. Weisiger (1924-1995), ended with page 199. His abstractions of county records were both meticulous and prolific. Your editor has continued the abstraction of Will Book 1, hopefully, as accurately as Dr. Weisiger. These records, beginning with page 201, will be a continued feature of TIDEWATER VIRGINIA FAMILIES to the completion of Will Book 1.

Abstracts of the wills following give the page number in the will book on which the will is first entered. Names are entered in bold using the format of Dr. Weisiger.

p. 200 Note: the will of **Robin Povall** continued through page 200.

p.201 Appraisal of estate of **Thomas Williams** 15 Jan 1785 by **William C. Redford, Abraham Sharp, John Crawford.** Value £8/18/9. Returned 2 May 1785

p.201 Inventory and appraisal of estate of **William New**, dec'd. 30 Mar 1785. Negro men: Sepus, Sharper, Jack; boys: Mingo, Frank, George; women: Anitra, Cate, Lucy & small children; Tab & 1 child; Cate, Else. Stock and household items value £989/8/6.   Returned 2 May 1785.

p.203 Inventory of estate of **John Shackleton**, dec'd. household items, value £6/9 appraisal **Thos. Childrey, Wm. Gathright, Richard Sharp**. 2 May 1785.

p.204 Appraisal of estate of **John Logan**, dec'd. value £22/20/11. **Martin Burton, Saml Williamson, John Williamson**.   3 May 1785.

p.205 Inventory of estate of **John Gathright**, dec'd. Negro men: Pompey, Jacob; woman Jude; stock and tools, value £368/1. Returned by **Matthew Hobson, William Bethell, Anselm Gathright.**   6 May 1785.

p.206 Inventory & appraisal of estate of **Robert Brown**, dec'd. 574 volumes books, Doctor's traveling medicine chest, many household possessions, value £413/16/6, by **Gabriel Galt, Saml Scherer, Jacob Ege.**   6 June 1785.

p.209 Will of **Milner Redford**, parish and county of Henrico, "sick & weak, sound mind & memory".

To son **Milner Redford**, plantation I dwell on (repeated this).

To wife, Negro man Jemmy, 1/5 stock & household items.

To son **John Redford**, 1 Negro man Ben, 1/5 part of stock & household furniture.

To daughter **Elizabeth Sharpe**, 1 Negro man Joe, 1/5 stock & household items.

To grandson **Elijah Haskins**, 1/5 part.

Sons **John** & **Milner Redford** executors.   11 Mar 1785

signed **Milner X Redford**

Witnesses: **Wm C. Redford, Joseph Redford, Mary Redford**

Securities: **John James Woodfin, George Williamson**

Recorded 6 June 1785

p.211 Will of **Frederick Childers**, parish & county of Henrico, "sick & weak, sound mind & memory".

To dear & loving wife all whole estate as long as she lives my widow, after her death to be equally divided amongst all my children. Wife **Ann Childers** & son **Abraham Childers**, executors.   11 Dec 1784

signed **Frederick X Childers**

Witnesses: **Wm Cock Redford, Wm X Arrington**

Securities: **William C. Redford, Mark Woodcock**

Recorded 6 June 1785

p.212 Inventory & appraisal estate **Peyton Randolph, Esqr.** dec'd. at Bush River Plantation, 14 Dec 1784. Jean, Annaca, (Rice's Plantation) Harry, Launey, Abby, Charles, Mingo, George, Moll, Will, Harry, Suckey, Roger, Bob, Betty, Sye, Siller, Scotland, Aggy, Pompey, Mercury; stock & tools.

At Jacob's Quarter Jack, John, Oxford, Will, Abe, Sall, Amey, Jupiter, Antony, Fanny, Lucy, Gift, Lucy, Beck & stock. value £2980/0/6.

Plantation on Buffalo in Prince Edward Co. Redrough, Sambo, Jack, Chesterfield, Dublin, Nick, Bob, Kojak, Tero, Isaac, Moracco, Harry, Saviny(?), Billy, James, Chloe, Sigh, Anuka & child, Ambrose, Nancy & child, Watt, Isbell & child, Judy, Rachel, Grace, Nan, Hannah, Tabb, Lucy & child, George, Sally & child, Aggy, Jane & child, Milly, Patt & child, Alice, Jamima, Anthony, Anny, Jacob, Janey, Effy, Peg, Tom, Betty, Milly, Sukey, Laudrum, Bob, James, Patience, Charity, Giles, Sony, Sally, Kujak, James, Ange, Hannah, Sary, Frank, Boman, Lewis, Queene, Charles, Dragon, Joney, Phoebe, Betty & child, Isaac & stock. No value totaled.

Peter LeGrand, Will Bibb, Robert Elliott.   27 Nov 1784

40

Powhatan Co. Plantation, plantation on Fighting Creek, Mungo, Stephen, Isham, Aney, Brester, Betty, Sancho, Isaac, Ned, Amos, Jack, Molley, Barbara, Balinda & child, Pompey, Hackett, Roger, Dinah & child, Harry, Lucy, Tom, Juney, Kent, John, Bott, Hackett, Dick, Hannah & child, Ned Rachel, Dinah, Janey, Sukey & child, China, Hannah & child, Nan, Livia, Aggy, Rose, Rachel, Avey, Irus, Sukey, Juney, Harry, Michael, Madeira, Mingo, Avey, Kent, Marjoc, Betty, Briston, Lucy, Jacob, Isaac, Arthur, Cleab, John, Janey, Ben, Ceaser, Lawney, Stephen, Edmund, Easther, Easter, Edmund, Limon, Arthur, Peter, Molly, Henry, Susanna, Davy, Fanny, Will, Charity, John, Doll, Jacob, Mary, Peter, Sukey, Iris & child, Milley, Aggy, Dinah, Lucy, Doll, Phoebe, Lucy, Janey, Billah, Ned, Jamey, Aggy, Stephen, Nancy, Molly, Charles, Ben, Minner, Guy, Molley, Frank, Tom, Sam, Judy, Betty, Humphrey & stock & tools. No value totaled.
John Povall, Brett Randolph, Peter T Archer.   6 June 1785

p.218 Will of **John Kent,** county & parish of Henrico, "sound mind & memory".
To wife **Jemima Kent** 1/3 personal estate, 1/3 real estate during lifetime. At death same to 2 daughters, **Priscilla Kent** & **Polly Kent** equally divided.
To 2 daughters remaining 2/3 estate, to have interest until of age and marry. If both daughters die without issue, then to wife & brother-in-law, **William Vannerson,** equally divided.
Executors **Robert Pleasants, Sen., Thomas Pleasants, Junr,** brother-in-law **William Vannerson, James Ladd.**   13 Nov 1784
                    signed **John Kent**
Witnesses: **Wm Gathright, Geo. Wm:son, Wm Vannerson**
Recorded 6 June 1785

p.219 Will of **Littleberry Allen,** parish & county of Henrico, "sound mind & perfect senses".
To loving wife **Elizabeth Allen** during natural life or widowhood, land where I now live, 80 acres. Lend wife 7 Negroes: Edy, Sook, Joe, Cisty, Robin, Jenny & Absolom; mare and mare colt until son **Fleming Allen** reaches 21.
For use & maintenance & schooling of 4 youngest children, to wit: **Fleming Allen, Littleberry Allen, Sarah Allen, Jenny Allen.** When **Fleming** of age Negroes & mare equally divided between wife and all children. **Elizabeth** wife 1 part; **Richard Allen, Fleming Allen, Littleberry Allen, Anne Turner, Francis (Frances?) Wade, Sarah Allen, Jenny Allen;** 3 youngest, Littleberry, Sarah, **Jenny.**
To **Littleberry** land and plantation where I now live at death of wife.

41

To **Richard & Fleming** remaining land in Henrico.

To **Landrum Allen & Martha Allen**, children of son **Edmund** to have £20 for schooling.

Executors; **Elizabeth Allen, Richard Allen, James Turner, Julius Allen**.

20 Aug 1783   signed **Littleberry Allen**

Witnesses: **Jno. Allen, Mary X Allen, Sarah X Talley**

Securities: **James Allen, James Sharpe**

Recorded 6 June 1785

p.221 Appraisal of estate of **Littleberry Allen**, dec'd. slaves: Edy, Sook & child, Joe, Cisly, Robin, Jimmy, Absolom, tools & stock. value £375/9/5½.

John Spear, Jacob Carter, John Ferris.   4 July 1785

p.222 Will of **Joseph Pleasants**, County of Henrico "sick & weak, sound mind & memory".

Money due me by book, bond or otherwise to be collected.

To loving wife **Elizabeth** during natural life, tract of land with appurtenances where I live, with whole of personal estate for support & maintenance of children, overpayment put to interest for children when of age.

To son **Jordan Pleasants** tract of land on James River in Goochland County, items, if he dies then to be divided among daughters.

To son **Joseph Carlin Pleasants** after death of wife, land where I live, if he die to **Jordan**.

At death of wife, personal estate to be divided equally among daughters: **Dorothy, Sophia, Clementina, Mahale Pleasants**.

Executors: wife, **John Brooke, William Burton**.   8 May 1785

                                                              signed **J. Pleasants**

Witnesses: **Turner Southall, Jno. Russell, Isaac Sharpe, Tarlton Pleasants**

Securities: **John Pleasants, Samuel Coleman, Nathaniel Anderson**

Recorded 4 July 1785

p.225 Appraisal of estate of **Peyton Randolph, Esq.**, dec'd. Wilton Estate, 20 June 1785. Negroes: Moses, Dread, Betty, London, Lucy, James, Dick, Ceaser, Matt, Jimey, Lucy, Saveny, Sukey, Henry, Phil, Jamey, Toney, Dudder, Frank, Cupid, Will, David, Anthy, Cary Gray, Richard, Celesta, Absolem, Tamer, Peter, Dilcey, Philis, Milly, Phoebe, Dunge, Avery, Tom, Molly, Balinda, Bob, Jack, Nutty, Ange, Judy, Betty, Dilcey, Billey, Betty, Dolad, Johnny, Calesta, Betty, Phil, Nelly, Frank, Emanuel, Easter, Billy, Adam, Gloster, Charles, Ankey, Hannah, Dick, Roger, Sukey, Phoebe, Billy, Lary Gedy, Aggy, Sary, Janey, Ben, Vina, Katchina, Lucy, Dolly, Pattey, Nancy,

Dorcus, Johnny, Cato, Doctor, Johnny, Nat, Edson, Kutchina, Janey, Ceaser, Sue, Nick, Giles, Betty. value £4644/10; not at home and not appraised: Charles, Lewis, Isaac, Aaron, carpenters; Sam a wagoner; Franky an invalid; Rachel, Betty, Sally children, stock & chariot. total value £5453/7/6.

20 June 1785

Isaac Younghusband, Geo. Webb, T. Webb, Jr.
Returned 1 Aug 1785   **Adam Craig**, Clerk Court

p.227 Will of **William Gathright** parish & county of Henrico, "ill & weak, sound & composed mind & memory".
To wit: Estate to be kept together until it arise several legacies expressed in money.
To son **William Gathright** land beginning at middle of Great Fishing Pond to Bear Road & Trueman's path to **Richd. Spence's** line to Chickahominy Swamp 133 acres.
To son **John Gathright** land beginning at Trueman's path to **Miles Gathright** to Chickahominy Swamp adjacent **Wm Gathright** 133 acres. If he dies to son **Saml Gathright** including house & plantation I now live on.
To son **Miles Gathright** remaining land on north side of Boar Rivan (ravine?).
To **Mr. Isaac White** 1 acres land next & most convenient where his mill now stands.
To pay the valuation money to son **Joseph Gathright**.
To son **Joseph Gathright** ½ of land in fork of Boar Swamp 120 acres adjacent White's mill.
To son **Benj. Gathright** other ½ land Boar Swamp 120 acres. If either **Joseph** or **Benj.** die without heirs to **Saml Gathright.**
To daughter **Elizabeth Gathright** 1 Negro boy Guy & £30 current money, one side saddle of £4 value.
To daughter **Jane Anna Gathright** 1 Negro girl Patt & £30 and 1 side saddle value £4.
To daughter **Anne Gathright** 1 Negro girl Inch (sic) & £30 and 1 side saddle value £4.
To son **Saml** 2 Negroes Harry & Turner.
To loving wife 2 Negroes Fann & Major, for life then to children as she sees fit. Lend wife use & residue of estate during life or widowhood.
To payout of profits the several legacies to **Elizabeth, Jane Anna & Anne.**
To 5 sons **William, Miles, Joseph, Benja, John** all estate lent wife.
Wife **Ann** executrix with friend **Thos. Morton** and 3 sons, **William, Joseph & Miles**, executors.   18 Sep 1762
signed   **Wm Gathright**
copy of will original destroyed in fire by enemy
Witnesses: **Geo. Clopton, Ephraim Gathright, Mary Trueman**
Recorded 1 August 1783   **Adam Craig** Clerk Court

p.230 Will of **William Maddox** Henrico Co, "ill state of health but sound memory". Appoint **William Farrish** & wife **Mary Ann Maddox** to be executors. Desire 200 acres of land in Prince Edward Co on branch Sandy River to be sold and ½ money given to wife, ½ to daughter **Patsey Maddox**.

To wife mare, saddle & bridle, 1 bed & furniture, square pine table & chest.

To daughter **Patsey** 1 bed & furniture, black walnut table.

Remaining part of my property to be sold & money divided between wife and daughter.   no date

                                signed **William X Maddox**

Proved by: **Benjamin Bradley, Carter Farris**, security **Mathew Hobson**

Securities: **William Farris, Michael Maddox**

recorded no date   **Adam Craig** Clerk Court

p.232 Inventory of estate of **John Hutchings**, dec'd. July 29, 1785

(Negroes): Obediah, Doska, Nun, Judah, Isaac, Fan, Edmond, Betty, Bob.

Returned 1 August 1785   **Adam Craig** Clerk Court

p.233 Will of **Thomas Bentley** village of Kaskaskins in the Illinois Country, merchant being at the point of undertaking a dangerous & precarious journey; leave this last will & testament in case of accident to my life.

First, recommend executor pay debts.

Second, as **Margaret Beauvais** alias **Bentley** has by her infamous conduct during my absence in Canada forfeited all pretensions or claim to my estate by virtue of her marriage covenant; thereby cut her off with $1.00 (to be paid her) from all claim to my estate.

Empower executors to proceed against her as adulteress demanding satisfaction from her for my property which she has dissipated; goods amounting to $8000 but also the cargo sent from Canada at great expense.

Executor empowered to prosecute to utmost rigors of the law.

Thirdly, from confidence placed in the Rev. Mr. **Ichabod Camp** of this place & Mr. **John Baptist Laffort** merchant of St. Genivieve request they act as executors during absence of **Mr. Joseph Howard** merchant in Montreal, who is to be sole executor on spot, leaving **Camp** & **Laffort** 1000 Livers each for friendship & trouble.

Fourth, rest of estate, real & personal: lands, tenements, cattle, furniture, boats, merchandise, etc. to beloved **Joseph Howard** friend of Montreal (in commemoration of his kindness to me during my time in captivity in Canada). To dearly beloved sister **Susannah Blizard** of city of London to be divided equally.

Fifth, revoke & annul former wills.   28 Feb 1781

signed **T Bentley**
Presented by **Benjamin Harrison, Jr. Gent, William Elliott, William Haywood,**
Proved. **Joseph Howard,** executor.
Securities: **Benjamin Harrison, Jr., David M Randolph, John Harvie.**
recorded 3 May 1785   **Adam Craig** Clerk Court

p.235 Appraisal of estate of **Wm Robinson**, dec'd.   1 Sept 1785
Wm Cocke, Joshua Morris, James Patterson value £642/19/1.
returned 5 Sept 1785

p.239 Inventory of estate of **Seymon Francis Albertie**, dec'd.   12 Sept 1785
Matthew Wright, Frank Graves, Benj. Lewis value £24/13/5
returned 3 Oct 1785

p.241 Account of estate of **William Bullington** with **Joseph Bailey,**
administrator, examined by **John Pleasants, Sterling Thornton**
value £254/10/1   returned 3 Oct 1785

p.244 Will of **John Brackett,** Henrico County, "sick & weak, but of sound &
disposing mind".
To living (sic) wife bed & furniture "we lye on", mare, items during her life. To
son **Jonathan Brackett** ½ land where I live in Henrico Co.
To son **Amos Brackett** ½ land where I live in Henrico Co. Either die, other to
take whole.
To son **John Brackett** Negro woman Doll with increase.
To son **Thomas Brackett** land in Hanover Co over & above what sold to
William Bumpass.
To **William Bumpass** land in Hanover Co agreed with him 100 acres if he pay
money agreed upon.
To children & wife for maintenance, crop on plantation, that is children
remaining with her.
Rest of estate to be divided between wife **Elizabeth,** sons **John, William,
Thomas, Jonathan, Amos** and daughters **Ann, Elizabeth, Charity, Mary, Lucy,
Sarah, Phoebe Bracket.**
Executors son **John** and friend **William Binford.**   13 Nov 1784
                                                       signed **John Brackett**
Witnesses: **Geo. Clopton, William Binford, Thos. Binford, Mary X Brackett**
Proved: **George Clopton, William Binford** (who being a Quaker made
affirmation).
Securities: **William Bradley, Samuel Goode.**

p.246 Will of **George Cox** Henrico Co, "perfect & sound memory & judgment. To well beloved wife during life use of tract where I now live, land adjoining **Col. Thomas Mason Randolph, Thomas Jordan**, as also plantation of Cox and Dale purchased of **Edward Osborne, Thomas Howlett**, also slaves Toby, Charles, Arthur, Peg, Judy, Matt, Nat, Miles, Dan, Harry, Kate, Nanny, Amey, Joe, Tommy, Pat, John, Visly, Fanny, Lolly & Beck. 1/3 part of household furniture, 1/4 stock if "child with which she now goes" be female wife to receive £500. If male wife is to receive no further part of estate.
Executors to purchase tract of land for son. Negroes: Little, Will & Stepheroy to son. If female to receive slaves: Nat, Milo, Dan, Harry, Joe, Cate, Nanny, Amey. Peg, Judy & Matt being those given to wife.
To daughter **Elizabeth** slaves: Daniel, Jenny, Dick, Simon, Sylvia, Anthony, Phoebe, Tiller, Phillis, Little Jenny, Aggy & Sam.
To daughter **Martha** slaves: Greaser, Little Lal, Moll, Joan, Betty, Daphne, Iris, Sampson, Jack, Eda & Hampton.
To daughter **Judith** slaves: Gooselmond (sic), Jimmy, Tom, Nell, Stephney, Nancy, Peg, Tom, Alick, Lewis, Rosse, Roger & Langston. **Judith** under 18.
To son **Edward** rest & remainder of estate (he under 21). If **Edward** die then to son **George**, if all sons die before they come of age and without issue, then plantation I live on, 600 acres and 100 acres of land bought of **Sharps** estate to daughter **Elizabeth**. Plantation bought of **William Perkins** & that of **Branches** estate to daughter **Martha, Judith** all land in county of Chesterfield & unborn child if female land in Amelia.
Mary executrix, **Henry Batte, Thomas Osborne, Nathaniel Friend**, executors.
29 Jan 1779   signed   **George Cox**

Witnesses: **John Johnson, John Stratton, Richd. Renard, William Perkins**
Henrico County April Court 1780   **William White** Clerk Court
Record destroyed by enemy rerecorded 4 Oct 1785
                                            Adam Craig Clerk Court

p.252 Will of **Peter Clark** Henrico Co
Lend my beloved wife all my estate real & personal during natural life, at her death sold & divided among whole of children, provision that wife **Mary Anne** be maintained, children educated.
Mary Anne executrix, son **Wm Clark, Charles Cottrell** executors
20 July 1785   signed   **Peter Clark**
Witnesses: **Wm Gathright, John Miller, Mary Lankester**

Henrico Court at new house of **Mr. Graves** in City of Richmond near Shockoe
Warehouse. 8 Nov 1785
Proved: **William Gathright, John Miller, Mary Lankester.**
Executors: **William Clark, Charles Cottrell.**
Securities: **William Gathright, John Miller**, acknow. bond.
recorded 8 Nov 1785 **Adam Craig** Clerk Court

p.253 Will of **John Liggon** City of Richmond, Parish of Henrico "weak in body,
sound in mind".
Lot & improvements where I live known in place of City of Richmond by half
of G & half of I, reserving 50' in front & back, be sold, also Negro man
Christopher & Negro wench Nancy & her child.
To brother **Samuel Liggon** £20.
To nieces **Agatha Liggon, Bushabe** (sic) **Liggon**, nephews. **Andrew Caslen,
Elitia Liggon, Mrs Ann Newland, Elizabeth Povel, Sarah Povel,** my nieces and
John Sampson Povel, my nephew £25 each. (abstracted as read, for
clarification of relationships, see original record, ed.)
Lend nephew **Samuel Liggon, Jr** the 40' ground in front & breadth of lot where I
live for 5 years then to return to purchaser.
To nephew **John Liggon** 1 sh/3 pence.
To nephew **Sherwood Liggon** 1 sh/3 pence.
To friend **Richard Crouch**, blacksmith tools.
Remaining estate divided between **Samuel Liggon, Willis Liggon, Agatha Liggon,
Bushabe Liggon, Elitia Liggon, John Caslen, Ann Newland, Elizabeth Povel,
William Povel, Henry Povel, John Sampson Povel, Sarah Povel, John Cock**, son of
my niece **Sarah Cock.**
Executors: Friends **Richard Crouch, John Roper, John Clark, John Ellis**, son of
Thomas Ellis. 27 Aug 1785
signed **John Liggon**

Witnesses: **Robt. Gilbert, Robt Burns, Wm Henry Wilson**
Proved: **Robert Burns, William Henry Wilson**
Securities: **Richard Crouch, Smith Blakey**
recorded 8 Nov 1785 (house of **Mr. Graves**) **Adam Craig** Clerk Court

To be continued

Turner Family Bible, 1847-1875
King George County

Notes from the Bible of Susan A. Rose (Mrs. Carolinus Turner)

At the Thomas Turner Association reunion in King George County, Julie Hunter (Mrs. John Morris Hunter, King George, Virginia gave me this Bible to take to the Virginia State Library Archives. She says it is the Bible of her late husband's great-grandmother. It seems to contain the marriage record of Carolinus Turner and Susan Augusta Rose, and four of their children (the parents of the children are not given here), followed by the birth records of four grandchildren; two Robbs, one Hunter and one Matthews. The two Robb grandchildren are followed within a year or so by the death records as infants. There is no record for their child George or any of his seven children by Jane Murphey McGuire, or for children for their daughter Caroline who married W.A. Jett, if they had any children.

The entries are all very uniform in penmanship, ink and pen, suggesting they were written at the same time. There are four entries in 1875. The last entry is the birth of Alice T. Matthews in October 1875. Here follows my best effort at an accurate transcript.
Robert deT. Lawrence IV, 71 Winchester Street, Warrenton, Virginia, 31 October 1994.

[inscription]   *Susan A Turner/from her husband*
                        December 25th 1851

Bible Edition and Publisher:
            Butler's Edition, *THE HOLY BIBLE.*
        Philadelphia: Published by E.H. Butler & Co. 1851

At the end of the Apocrypha:

Family Record.   **Marriages**
Carolinus Turner and / Susan Augusta Rose / 22nd of Sept. 1847.
Robert L. Robb and / A. Augusta Turner / April 29th 1869.
Frederick C.S. Hunter / and Susan Rose Turner / April 7th 1874.
W.A. Jett and / Caroline M. Turner / Sept. 2nd 1874.
Wm B. Matthews and / Alice Pratt Turner / January 12th 1875.

On the reverse of that page:
Family Record.   **Births**
Susan Rose Robb / June 8th 1870.
Carolinus Turner Robb / August 4th 1873.
Thomas L. Hunter / March 6th 1875.
Alice T. Matthews / October 14th 1875.

On the next page:
Family Record.   **Deaths**
Susan Rose Robb / March 25th 1871.
Carolinus Turner Robb / July 21st 1875.

Note: / indicates a new line in entering the inscription.

Bible Records, Accession No. 34777. Archival and Information Services, Library of Virginia, Richmond, Virginia.

* * * * *

Richard Dunn of King and Queen County, 1816

Contributed by June Banks Evans

In abstracting the *Lunenburg County Deed Book 24, 1815-1819*, the following item was found. It will be of interest to those researching King and Queen County residents.

Page 179: 22 Oct 1816 — (King and Queen County) Peggy, wife of Richard Dunn, relinquishes dower rights in 92 acres Lunenburg County sold Horatio Winn 5 Feb 1813.
Rec. 14 Nov. 1816, Lunenburg Co

Signed Humphrey Walker, R B Hill j/p

49

York Rendezvous

TWENTY DOLLARS REWARD,

For apprehending and delivering to any recruiting officer,
or securing in jail,
TWO DESERTERS, *viz.*
HOLLAN MARSH & RODMAN WEBB

Who deserted from this place on the 14th instant; They both went off with their military clothing; were inlisted at Northumberland court house, to which place they were seen going. —— MARSH, a likely young man, five feet six and half inches high, black hair and eyes, a likely animated countenance, has lost a tow from his right foot. WEBB is five feet five inches high, fair complexion, a sickly and inanimate countenance, short black hair, black eyes, paces rather than walks. The above reward and all reasonable expenses, will be paid to any person, who will apprehend and deliver the said deserters as above required.

ROBERT KING
Capt. 17th U.S. Regiment

York Town, Nov. 25, 1799.

TEN DOLLARS REWARD

DESERTED, from this Rendezvous on the eight of this month, JOHN WILLIS MALLERY, who enlisted under the name of JOHN DIXON, I have been since informed he is a deserter from Capt. John Heth; the said Mallery was born in King William county, Virginia, 29 years of age, 5 feet 9 inches high, dark complexion, blue eyes, short black hair; he took away with him his uniform, and I have since been informed he has cut off the facings of his coat. Whoever will secure him or deliver him to me at the Rendezvous shall receive the above reward.

PHILIP ROOTES, Lieut.
7th United States Regiment

Petersburg Camp, Federal Hill, January 13th, 1800.

The Virginia Gazette & General Advertiser. Richmond, VA. Friday, February 7, 1800, p4 cols 3 & 4.

Robert Armistead and Anne Smith
Marriage Agreement, 1754

ARTICLES of agreement Indented, made, concluded and agreed upon on 23^d Day of Decr in the year of our Lord One Thousand Seven Hundred and Fifty-Four

BETWEEN Robert Armistead of the County of King George Gent of the one Part, and Anne Smith Spinster Thomas Booth Gent Guardian of the said Anne & Lucy Booth Wife of the said Thomas & Mother of the said Anne, all of the County of Hanover of the other Part.

Imprimis Whereas a marriage is Intended by Gods Permission shortly to be had and Solemnized between the said Robert Armistead and the said Anne Smith *and Whereas* the said Robert is now Possessed of Five Negro slaves called and named as Followeth to wit, Tarter, Peter, Ned, Beck & Frank and also of a considerable stock of Cattle Horses Hogs and Sheep, **to wit,** Forty Two head of Cattle four Horses thirty head of Hogs and twenty head of sheep and Likewise of sundry valuable Household goods and Furniture and Gregory Smith late of the County of King and Queen Gent deceased Father of the said Anne having by his last Will & Testament given and bequeathed to the said Anne one Negro Girl named Sarah and also Two Hundred Pounds Current Money which money is to be Paid to the said Anne when she shall attain the age of Twenty-one years or marry, and the said Anne being by the said will also Intitled as a further Part of her said Fathers Estate after the Death of her Mother the aforesaid Lucy Booth and having also a Legacy of Fifty Pounds given her by the Will of her later GrandMother Anne Smith of the County of Middlesex deceased Now the said Robert Armistead for and in consideration of the said Intended Marriage and of the use proffit & benefit right title interest and advantage that he is to have claim receive and make of in and to or use of the Estate of aforesaid of the said Anne by virtue of the Articles herein after stipulated and agreed upon. And the said Anne, Thomas and Lucy for and in consideration of the Estate right Title Interest benefit and advantage that the said Anne is to have by issue of the said Articles of agreement of in to or out of the several Estates herein before and after mentioned, do mutually and reciprocally covenant and agree and it is hereby for the consideration aforesaid covenanted consented and agreed by and between the parties to these Presents as followeth---

Viz first That the said Robert and Anne shall have hold use Occupy and enjoy their several Estates aforesaid to their Several Estates aforesaid to their own several use and behoof of their several Heirs and assigns as they might or would do so if these Presents had never been made, untill the marriage between them shall be had and solemnized,

Item that as soon as conveniently may be after the solemnization of the said marriage Two Hundred pounds given by the Last Will and Testament of the said Gregory Smith deceased to the said Anne Party of these presents shall be laid out in Negro slaves to be approved of by the said Thomas and Lucy, Item that the said slaves so to be Purchased together with the Division of the Females amongst them together with all the other Estate or Estates herein before mentioned shall be and this same is hereby given Granted, settled and confirmed in manner and form and to the several use Interests and purposes herein after mentioned, limited, expressed and declared/ that is to say To the use and Behoof of the said Anne and Anne during their Joint lives and if the said Anne shall survive the said Robert and the said Robert shall not leave Issue of his Body Lawfully begotten living at the time of his Death shall then and in such case from and Immediately after the death of the said Robert all the said estate or estates and every Part thereof Should be for the sole use and behoof of the said Anne her Heirs and assigns for ever/ but if Robert shall die before the said Anne and shall leave Issue of his body Lawfully begotten living at the Time of his Death that then and in such case the Legacy Given by the will of the said Anne Smith deceased to the said Anne Smith party to these Presents the Negro Girl Sarah and all such Estate or Estates as by the Will of the aforesaid Gregory Smith deceased shall fall and come to the said Anne Smith Party to these Presents upon the Death of her Mother the said Lucy Booth Party to these Presents shall be to and for the sole use and behoof of the said Anne Smith her Heirs and assigns for [next line illegible where paper was folded]...so and for the use and behoof of the said Anne for and during her natural life which said residue or remainder of the Estate or Estates aforesaid shall be likewise subject nevertheless to the maintenance and education of all such Child or Children of the said Robert Lawfully begotten, that he shall have living at the time of his Death until they respectively arrive to the age of Twenty-one years and is and shall be in lieu and a full satisfaction and compensation of all Dower and Thirds on which she the said Anne might otherwise have Claims of in to and out of the Estate as herein Granted and settled from and after the Death of the said Anne shall be to and for the use and Behoof of such Child or Children of the said Robert & his Heirs and assigns forever.

Item in case the said Robert shall survive the said Anne it shall and may be Lawfull to and for the said Anne by any Deed or by her Last Will and Testament to give settle and dispose of said Legacy given her by the Will aforesaid of the said Anne Smith deceased the Negro Girl Sarah and the Estate that shall fall to her upon the Death of her Mother aforesaid in such manner and Form and to such Person or persons as she thinks fit and the residue or remainder of the Estate or Estates herein granted settled shall be to the use and behoof of the said Robert Armistead for life and at Death to the use and behoof of such Child or Children of the said Robert lawfully begotten as he shall have living at the time of his Death equally to be Divided and if the said Robert shall not have Child or Children Lawfully begotten living at the time of his Death then the said remainder shall be to and for the use and behoof of any other Person or Persons that the said Robert by any Deed or by his Last Will and Testament, shall give and devise the same or in case the said Robert shall not make and disposition thereof as aforesaid then to the right Heirs the said Robert forever and it is also granted and covenanted and agreed by the said Robert that if he the said Robert shall die Possessed of any Lands thereon and shall leave the said Anne then living, that then and in such case the said Anne shall may continue to live on the Mannor Plantation during her natural live and shall also have liberty to work eight hands thereon and it is further Granted covenanted and agree by and between the parties to these Presents that in case Thomas Smith and Gregory Smith Brothers of the said Anne or either of them shall die without Issue and any Estate or Estates shall thereupon pass and descend to the said Anne or if any Estate shall hereafter be given to the said Anne by any Person or Persons whatsoever the same and every Part and Parcel thereof from and immediately [illeg] such decent or Gift shall/in Case the said marriage shall have [line illegible because of paper fold and tear]....and the life of that longest liver of them and after the Death of the said Robert and Anne to such Child or Children that the said Robert shall have living at the time of his Death lawfully begotten on the body of said Anne and if the said Robert shall not leave any such Child or Children then living then to such Person or Persons and in such manner and form as the said Anne by her Last will and Testament or by any Deed or writing shall give and dispose of the same whether the said Anna shall survive the said Robert or not, and if the said Anne shall not make any such gifts or disposition then the said Estate or Estates last mentioned shall descend and fall to John Cook Booth and Mary Booth Children of the said Lucy Booth and their heirs forEver, and lastly it is covenanted and agreed between the Parties aforesaid for themselves their Heirs Executors and assigns by these Presents that they or anyone or more of their Children Heirs or any of their Heirs Executors Administrators or assigns shall [one word torn] will at any Time or times hereafter upon the reasonable request of any other of the said Parties their Heirs Executors administrators or assigns named may acknowledge Execute & suffer or cause to be made done [word torn] acknowledged levied Executed and suffered all or to every such

53

further and other Lawful and reasonable act & acts Thing & Things devise and devises and conveyances, assurance & assurances in the Law whatsoever, for furthermore Perfect and better assuring sure making & conveying Estate and Estates here before Granted and settled to the said Robert and their Heirs and assigns, to the uses intents and purposes and under conditions, provisos and limitations herein before mentioned expressed and declared and to no other use Intent or Purpose whatsoever.

In Witness of all which the Parties to these Presents have here set their Hands and Seals the Day and Year first above Written ——
Rob: Armistead [Seal] Ann Smith [Seal] Thomas Booth [Seal]
Lucy Booth [Seal]

Signed Sealed & Delivered in the Presence of
Pat Henry, Jno. Bickerton, Thomas Booth Gent & Wm Brooks

At a Court held for Hanover County [rest of line illegible]
Patrick Henry, Clerk, Jno. Bickerton, Thomas Booth Gent & William Brooks made Oath that they did see Robert Armistead, Ann Smith, Thomas Booth and Lucy Booth sign seal and Deliver these their articles of agreement as their act and Deed and they were thereupon Admitted to Record
                    Test [signed] Henry Robinson CHC

A Copy
    William Pollard CHC

Transcribed by VLHD

Burned Record Counties, Loose Papers, Hanover County; Bedford County Determined Causes, 1765-1774, May 1772. Archives and Information Services, Library of Virginia, Richmond, VA.

BOOK REVIEWS:

Elizabeth Shown Mills, CG, CGL, FASG, FNGS, *Evidence! Citation & Analysis for the Family Historian*. 124 pp., indexed, hardcover. 1997. $16.95, plus ship. $3.50. This should be the first reference book purchased when one begins family research. With this one can record meticulously the references used in collecting family data. This book brings together the means of accessing information and the necessary criteria for the analysis of conclusions based on primary as well as circumstantial evidence. A comprehensive chart provides the format for citing each type of documentation and under each possible circumstance, eg. primary citation, subsequent citation and bibliographic entry. Mrs. Mills is to be commended (and thanked) for providing a comprehensive handbook for both genealogical and historical researchers. #3846. Genealogical Publishing Co, 1001 N Calvert St, Baltimore, MD 21202.

CDs Available: System requirements: must have a CD-ROM drive, and in order to read the CDs you must use either *Family Tree Maker* **version 3.02 or higher or the** *Family Archive Viewer***, version 3.02 or higher, which is free with the purchase of any of the CDs offered here.**

CD-ROM: *Immigrants to the New World, 1600s-1800s. Family Archive Viewer* **free upon request (see above).** An excellent way to own a number of significant reference books in one compact disk, with the benefits of a readily available index to all of the publications. The images of the pages from the following five books as originally published by the Genealogical Publishing Company are presented on this disk: *New World Immigrants, Volume I; New World Immigrants, Volume II; Emigrants to Pennsylvania, 1641-1819; Immigrants to the Middle Colonies;* and *Passengers to America*. Edited by Michael Tepper, each book contains articles on the ships' passenger lists which appeared in the most highly regarded genealogical publications. $29.99, plus $3.50 ship. CD #7170. Genealogical Publishing Co, 1001 N Calvert St, Baltimore, MD 21202.

CD-ROM: *Virginia Vital Records #1, 1600s-1800s. Family Archive Viewer* **free upon request (see above).** $39.99, plus $3.50 ship. Your reviewer owns each of these publications; would that CD-ROMs were available when these books were acquired. This compact disk provides images of the pages from the six well-known, and extensively cited books originally published by the Genealogical Publishing Company: *Virginia Vital Records, Virginia Marriage Records, Virginia Will Books, Virginia Land Records, Virginia Military Records* and *Virginia Tax Records*. These records have been assembled from the three most referenced Virginia periodicals: *The Virginia Magazine of History and Biography, William and Mary Quarterly* and *Tyler's Quarterly*. More than 130,000 individuals are cited, with an index provided for easy access. CD #7174.

Genealogical Publishing, add $1.25 each add. item.

David V. Heise, *Somerset County, Maryland, Orphans Court Proceedings, 1823-1838, Volume 2.* 246 pp., index, paper. 1997. $19.50, plus ship $2.50. #T1335. Vol. 1, 1777-1792, 1811-1823. $17.50. (#T1194) and Vol. 3, 1838-1852. $25.00. (#T1351) are also available. While only volume 2 is reviewed here, it is assumed that volumes 1 and 3 follow the same format. Volume 2 contains abstracts of two libers: Book 3, 1823-1829 and Book 4, 1829-1838. While actual testimony is seldom recorded, one can determine relationships and frequently ages; infer approximate death dates, estate settlements and heirs of the deceased. Indexes to the two court libers provide references to obtain complete court record book entries where desired. Family Line Publications, Rear 63 East Main St, Westminster, MD 21157.

Richard F. Oyler, *Ancestors (and some descendants) Grant Oyler and Susan Ferguson.* i-xxxvi, 678 pp., index, charts, illus., color photos, sketches, glossy paper, 8½ x 11, hardcover. 1997. $110.00, plus ship $5.00. This is a beautifully, and expansively executed family history, with many photographs of interest not only to Oyler descendants, but others also. The accounts of the families are well-written, and go far beyond the vital record presentation. While the documentation is not the conventional, it is well-researched. Beyond the Oyler family the following families are included (many with recognizable colonial Virginia origins): Bach, Barnett, Barrow, Billington, Bishop, Burchett, Chrisler, Christy, Clark, Clore, Clug, Covill, Davis, Dungan, Egbert, Ferguson, Foster, Gardner, Gerhard, Goble, Gorley, Haugwout, Hayward, Helfrich, Herling, Hermans, Hogge, Hovenden, Hunt, Iler, Jans, Johns, Jones, Jung, Kaifer, Lee, Leedom, Marsh, McNabb, Mercer, Nevitt, Newell, Osborn, Phelan, Pieterse, Railsback, Ringer, Stanley, Steer, Stewart, Tatum, Thomas, VanPelt, Walter, Warren, Wayman, West, White, Wickersham and Yager. Order from Richard F. Oyler, 265A Loberio, San Clemente, CA 92672.

Dorothy S. Samuel, *The Samuell/Samuel Families of Tidewater Virginia.* i-xii, 626 pp., illus., charts, index, maps, hardcover. 1997. $45.00, plus $2.24 postage. While this is an account of the Samuel family (Mrs. Samuel's husband is Taliaferro Leslie Samuel), many collateral family members are also included. It is a well-written family history, made especially interesting with anecdotal accounts, family letters and newspaper articles. It begins with Thomas Samuel, born in 1742 and Ann Brooking, his wife, born in 1743, both of Caroline County. Early Brooking family data is also included. Family connections are found in Caroline, Culpeper, Essex, Gloucester, King William, Lancaster, King and Queen, Richmond counties. Some of these families migrated south to areas including Alabama and Kentucky. While not documented in the usual sense, it is well researched and has been a welcome addition for those searching the Samuel family, relations and the burned record counties presented. Order from Mrs. Dorothy S. Samuel, PO Box 11688, Montgomery, AL 36111.

Brent H. Holcomb, *Petitions for Land From the South Carolina Council Journals, Volume II: 1748-1752.* 279 pp., index (both name and place), hardcover. $40.00, plus $3.00, ship (SC residents add sales tax). See review following Volume III.

Brent H. Holcomb, *Petitions for Land From the South Carolina Council Journals, Volume III, 1752-1753.* 316 pp., index (both name and place), hardcover. $40.00 ship, 2nd book, $1.00. Brent Holcomb is a meticulous researcher and transcriber. These are the second and third volumes of the series of petitions for land as transcribed from the Council Journals. They provide the best source for learning of the early immigration and migration to South Carolina and of the early land owners. Included is information about earlier places of residence, slave holdings, estates and heirs, as well as descriptions of the petitioned land. Through these petitions the locations of land owned can thus be definitively identified. It is known that there were many early Virginians who migrated to South Carolina and these volumes provide excellent identification and verification, not only for viewing the original journal entry, but for later land records. Order from Brent H. Holcomb, PO Box 21766, Columbia, SC 29221.

Brent H. Holcomb, *Petitions for Land From the South Carolina Council Journals, Volume I: 1734/5-1748.* While not reviewed here, this volume, with the same format, is also available and will complete the series. It is also $40.00 plus $3.00 ship, $1.00 each add. book in series ordered at same time. Order all of these from Brent H. Holcomb, PO Box 21766, Columbia, SC 29221.

Brent H. Holcomb, *Lower Fairforest Baptist Church, Union County, South Carolina, Minutes, 1809-1875.* 120 pp., index, hardcover. 1997. Includes church membership rolls through 1906. The Fairforest Meeting history goes back to the 1760s, and one may care to read of this Baptist history in the book, *South Carolina Baptists, 1670-1805*, by Leah Townsend (1935). Fairforest Church was established as an arm of Padgett's Creek Baptist Church. Mr. Holcomb's special interest in this church stems from the fact that his ancestor, Benjamin Holcomb gave two acres of land for the Fairforest Meeting. The minutes of the Lower Fairforest Baptist Church transcribed here extend this history, and the membership lists through 1906 extend the history even further. The names of slave members are interwoven in the records and provide valuable information for African-American historians and genealogists. Many early Virginia names appear in these minutes and membership rolls. Order from Brent H. Holcomb, PO Box 21766, Columbia, SC 29221.

J. Staunton Moore, *History of Henrico Parish and Old St. John's Church, Richmond, Virginia, 1611-1904.* 2 volumes, 762 pp., illus.,append., index, paper. (1904) rep. 1997. $32.00, plus $4.00 ship. Henrico Parish goes back to the settlement of the Citie of Henricus, and while this settlement did not survive after the massacre of 1622, the parish continued and settlement expanded. These two volumes bring together a continuing history of the parish, and Henrico county and an area that later became a part of the City of Richmond. A history of St. John's Church, the vestry book, vital records of the church, gravestone inscriptions and membership lists are included. There are two indexes, but not all names are indexed. The contents are varied and the book is a classic source for research. #559. Heritage Books, Inc, 1540-E Pointer Ridge Pl, #300, Bowie, MD 20716.

June Banks Evans, *The Blackwells of Blackwell's Neck.* 83 pp., index, illus., charts, maps, 8½ x 11, spiral bound, soft cover. 1997. $25.50, postpaid. Mrs. Evans states on the title page that this is an inferential genealogy based on material available. Anyone who has attempted to reconstruct a family in York County, (later James City, New Kent, then Hanover counties) will appreciate the expert and tenacious research required to assemble primary source references, then tease out the circumstantial evidence necessary to establish relationships. Robert Blackwell of the second generation lived in the lower end of Hanover County (earlier New Kent). The Blackwell sons are followed in Hanover and King William counties and their progeny as they moved south and west in Virginia. Whether one has a Blackwell ancestor or not, this is a valuable resource in understanding records that are available, and the nature of inferring relationships where the records are lost. Bryn Ffyliaid Publications, Lake Marina Tower, 16 B W, 300 Lake Marina Dr, New Orleans, LA 70124-1676.

Virginia Genealogical Society, *Marriage Notices from Richmond, Virginia Newspapers, 1841-1853.* 360 pp., index (full name & location), 8½ x 11, soft cover. 1997. $25.00, (VGS members receive 20% disc.), plus $3.00 ship. The Virginia Genealogical Society has published three previous volumes of marriage and death notices from Richmond newspapers. This volume continues with marriage notices from 1841-1853. There were at least six newspapers published during these years, and notices may have appeared in only one, or in several of the papers. Not all papers were published during all of the time period, nor are all issues extant. Many of the notices were of residents outside the Richmond area. While such sources are considered secondary, they provide either all of the available information of the time, or references for searching primary sources. Order from Virginia Genealogical Society, 5001 W Broad St, Richmond, VA 23230-3023.

Robert Haydon, *Thomas Haydon II, Colonial Virginia Planter.* i-viii, 263 pp., index, illus., charts, documents, maps, append., 8½ x 11, hardcover 1997. $59.00 inc. ship. Thomas Haydon II was probably born about 1698 in Northumberland County. A social history of Thomas and his times is written in an interesting manner, including reproductions of many court documents, charts and illustrations. Subsequent generations, the descendants of Thomas II, are presented in an extensive generational chart. End notes are presented, but not all statements of fact are so documented. The documents included provide some primary documentation. Haydon descendants should seek out this book, as it provides an interesting account of their progenitor. Order from Robert Haydon, 12 Fenchley Ct, Little Rock, AR 72212.

ANNOUNCEMENTS:

Leftwich Family Reunion will be held October 9-11, 1998 at the Holiday Inn Airport, 6629 Thirlane Rd, Roanoke, VA 24019. Make reservations directly with the hotel: 540-366-8861 or 1-800-HOLIDAY. Address questions to Mrs. C. Wayne Shell, 2909 Lansdowne Dr, Montgomery, AL 36111-1715 or phone 314-834-4231.

The Jones House Association has developed and is maintaining a data base of Matthew Jones genealogy. It welcomes additions to this data base. It is in the process of compiling and transcribing Warwick County court records. The American Studies Program of the College of William and Mary is sponsoring a fellowship to study the history (see *TVF* 4:254-255) of the area surrounding the Matthew Jones House (1625-1725), with the financial assistance of the Jones House Association. Contributions (with tax exempt status) are being received: The Jones House Association, 100 Oxford Circle, Williamsburg, VA 23185.

Available from Tidewater Genealogical Society: *Cemeteries of Lower Gloucester County, Virginia*. Hardcover, 292 pages, pictures, about 50 cemeteries listed. $33.00, inc. ship. send order to Barbara F. Senecal, TGS Publications Chairman, P O Box 7650, Hampton, VA 23666.

Golansville Cemetery Restoration Trust. Now that the survey has confirmed the presence of the cemetery a corporation can be formed and contributions received to restore the Friends Meeting House site. Those interested persons and those who are descendants of the early Caroline Quakers, many of whom are buried in this cemetery, will want to contribute to this memorial to a stalwart people. See *TVF* 5:159-163, 221-226) Contributions may be made to: Golansville Cemetery Restoration Trust, % Fay Parrish Wade, 8703 Ewes Ct, Richmond, VA 23235.

SEARCH

NEALE, Christopher, bap 1671, Northumberland Co, m Jane Presley, wid of Richard Rogers. Issue: Peter (d 1765), m (Elizabeth(?), ss: Edward, Presley (1699-1749); Ursula Neale; (p)John and (p)Rodham. Seek w of Presley; issue: Daniel, Elizabeth Spence, Ann Wisheart, Shapleigh, Richard, Jamima Gunnell. Was Presley's w Margaret Fauntleroy or Margaret Sanford? Seek descendants of Christopher and children. Janet Pease 10310 W 62nd Pl, Arvada, CO 80004.

BULLARD, WOOLFOLK. Ambrose Bullard, b c.1686, Gloucester Co, m Betty Woolfolk, b 1690, Gloucester Co, removed to Spotsylvania Co. Who were his parents, birth/death data? Did Ambrose have sister who m Joseph Woolfolk, Betty's brother? E W Wade, 8703 Ewes Ct, Richmond, VA 23236.

YOUNGER, Alexander and w Rebecca Mills: seek their lost daughters: Elizabeth, b c.1704, m John Dillard; Suzanna, b c.1706; Mary, b c.1712; Janett, b c. 1717. Born Essex Co, were wards of their brother, Thomas Younger, King & Queen Co in 1732. Sister Ann m John Price, 17 June 1737, Middlesex Co. Jan L. Richardson, 4929 Holt Ave, Las Vegas, NV 89115.

ROWLEY, John, w Catherine Williams, dau Hugh Williams, killed by Indians c.1699, Richmond Co. How is s William Rowley related to Joseph Thomas Smith who m Kitty Ann Anderson. Will of William Smith (Mar 1723) mentions Williams, what are relationships of these folks? Jim Burgess, 37 S Udall, Mesa, AZ 85204.

FOX, WEST. Seeking info proving Henry Fox, c.1674-1750, sheriff, King William Co was s of Henry Fox, c.1650-1714, vestryman St. John's Parish, King William Co, and Anne West, c.1655/7-1708. Richard E. Patton, 1301 Woodlawn Ct, Pittsburgh, PA 15241.

MACON, WOODWARD. Gideon Macon (b 1637, d 1702) & Martha Woodward, New Kent Co. Does his home, *Prospect Hill* on Pamunkey R remain? G'dau m William Massie. Seek info on Macon, Woodward & Massie families. Graham & Charlyn Connor, 37913 County Rd 144, Clarksburg, CA 95612.

HARRISON, Benjamin, d Brunswick Co 1789, s James. He and large family in Brunswick & Mecklenburg cos early 1700s. Need to identify his parents and ancestry. Gray W Harrison, 259 Eastbrooke II, Jackson, MS 39216.

HENDERSON, Charles, Scottish Jacobite prisoner, loser in "The 15th Rising"; transported to Yorktown 1718 on *Elizabeth & Anne*, indentured Warwick Co(?). Was Thomas his son? Seek info about these Hendersons. Kathleen W Crooks, 2564 Mockingbird Dr, Sierra Vista, AZ 85635.

ROSEWELL, WOOLFOLK. Seeking info re: wife of Richard Woolfolk, b c.1650(?) who m bef 1687 in Gloucester Co, and had 7 children bapt. in Abingdon Parish; was she Elizabeth Rosewell? Who were her parents; birth/death data? Fay P Wade 8703 Ewes Ct, Richmond, VA 23236.

INDEX

61

Burwell
  Francis 12
  Lewis 10-13
  Nathaniel29,31-32
Butler
  E.H. 48
  Thomas 31
Camp
  Ichabod 44
Carley
  William 3
Carter
  Jacob 42
Cary
  Miles 33
  Richard 34
  Thomas 34
Caslen
  Andrew 47
  John 47
Catlett
  John 31, 32
Chamberlayne
  Edward 31
Chanvoy
  William 34
Childers
  Abraham 40
  Ann 40
  Frederick 40
Childrey
  Thos. 39
Christy
  family 56
Claiborne
  William 29
Clark
  family 56
  John 47
  Mary 46
  Peter 46
  William 46, 47
Clopton
  Geo. 43
  George 45
Clore
  family 56
Clug
  family 56
Cock
  John 47
  Sarah 47
Cocke
  William 45

Cole
  Andrew 33
Coleman
  Samuel 42
  Wyatt 38
Collawn
  Charles 21
Coram
  Jurat 33
Cottrell
  Charles 46, 47
Covill
  family 56
Cox
  Edward 46
  Elizabeth 46
  George 46
  Judith 46
  Martha 46
  Mary 46
  William 13
Craig
  Adam 43-47
Crawford
  John 39
Croshaw
  Mr. 12
Crouch
  Richard 47
Crumpe
  William 11, 13
Dandridge
  Francis 31, 32
Daniall
  Symon 33
Davis
  family 56
  James 38
Dillard
  Elizabeth 60
  John 60
Dixon
  John 50
Doyle
  James 6, 10
Dudley
  John 20-25
  Martha 22
  Sarah 21-25
  Thomas 22
Dungan
  family 56
Dunn
  Peggy 49
  Richard 49

Dyer
  Richard 11
Edwards
  Conley 4
Egbert
  family 56
Ege
  Jacob 39
Elliott
  Robert 40
  Thomas 29, 31
  William 45
Ellis
  John 47
  Thomas 47
Evans
  June 49, 58
family
  Chrisler 56
Farris
  Carter 44
  William 44
Farrish
  William 44
Fauntleroy
  Margaret 59
Ferguson
  family 56
  Susan 56
Ferris
  John 42
Finn
  Thomas 34
Flood
  Francis 11
Fludd
  Francis 11
Foster
  family 56
Fox
  Anne 60
  Henry 60
  Joseph 28, 30, 31
  William 31
Freeman
  Philip 13
Friend
  Nathaniel 46
Gaines
  William 31
Galt
  Gabriel 39
Gardner
  family 56

Gathright
  Ann 43
  Anne 43
  Anselm 39
  Benj. 43
  Elizabeth 43
  Ephraim 43
  Jane 43
  John 39, 43
  Joseph 43
  Miles 43
  Saml 43
  William 41, 43,
    46-47
  Wm. 39
Gawen
  John 33
Gerhard
  family 56
Gibbs
  Henry 33
Gibson
  Nicholas 14
  Thomas 14
Gilbert
  Robt. 47
Gill
  George 10
Goble
  family 56
Goode
  Samuel 45
Gorley
  family 56
Gough
  R. 34
  Ralph 34
Grant
  Ulysess 22
Graves
  Frank 45
  Mr. 47
Gregory
  William 31, 32
Gunnell
  Jamima 59
Haley
  James 20, 24
  Sarah 20-24
Hammon
  Francis 12
Harris
  William 31, 32
Harrison
  Benjamin 45, 60

Harrison
  James 60
Harvie
  John 45
Harwood
  Margaret 23
Haskins
  Elijah 40
Haugwout
  family 56
Hayden
  Thomas 58
Haydon
  Robert 58
  Thomas 58
Hayward
  family 56
Haywood
  William 45
Headley
  Robert 4
Heise
  David 56
Helfrich
  family 56
Henderson
  Charles 60
  Thomas 60
Henry
  Patrick 54
Herling
  family 56
Hermans
  family 56
Heth
  John 50
Hickman
  John 29
Hill
  James 31, 32
  John 22
  R B 49
Hobson
  Mathew 44
  Matthew 39
Hogge
  family 56
Holcomb
  Brent 56, 57
Houston
  John 38
Hovenden
  family 56
Howard
  Joseph 44, 45

Howlett
  Thomas 46
Hubbard
  Cuthbert 34
Hudgins
  Dennis 35
Hunt
  family 56
Hunter
  Frederick 48
  John 48
  Julie 48
  Susan 48
  Thomas 49
Hutchings
  John 44
Iler
  family 56
Jans
  family 56
Jeffreys
  Croborn 36
Jett
  Caroline 48
  W.A. 48
Johns
  family 56
Johnson
  Benjamin 28, 30
  John 46
  Mary 21, 24
  Mr. 24
Jones
  Albritton 34
  Allen 34
  family 56
  Francis 33
  Matthew 33, 59
  Nath. 33
  Servant 34
  William 34
Jordan
  Thomas 46
Jung
  family 56
Kaifer
  family 56
Kent
  Jemima 41
  John 41
  Polly 41
  Priscilla 41
Kevan
  Alexander 38

64

Negro
Jacob 39
James 42
Jamey 42
Janey 42, 43
Jemmy 40
Jenny 41
Jimey 42
Joe 38, 40, 41, 46
John 38
Johnny 42, 43
Judah 44
Jude 39
Judy 42, 46
Katchina 42
Kutchina 43
Lewis 38, 42, 43
Little 46
London 42
Lucy 38, 39, 42
Major 43
Matt 42, 46
Milly 42
Milo 46
Mingo 39
Molly 42
Moses 42
Nancy 42, 47
Nanny 46
Nat 43, 46
Ned 51
Nelly 38, 42
Nick 43
Num 44
Nutty 42
Obediah 44
Patt 43
Pattey 42
Peg 46
Peter 42, 51
Phil 42
Philis 42
Phoebe 42
Pompey 39
Rachel 38, 42, 43
Richard 42
Robin 41
Roger 42
Sally 42, 43
Sam 38, 42, 43
Sarah 51, 52
Sary 42
Saveny 42
Sepus 39
Sharper 39

Negro
Sook 41
Stepheroy 46
Sue 43
Sukey 42
Tab 39
Tamer 42
Tarter 51
Tom 42
Toney 42
Turner 43
Vina 42
Will 42, 46
Winny 38
Nelson
Thomas 31
Nevitt
family 56
New
William 39
Newell
family 56
Newland
Ann 47
Nibblet
John 24
Mary 24
Osborn
family 56
Osborne
Edward 46
Thomas 46
Oyler
Grant 56
Richard 56
Susan 56
Page
Francis 33
Pannell
David 32
Patterson
James 45
Perkins
William 46
Phelan
family 56
Philips
Lucy 21
Richard 21
Phillips
Lucy 21, 24
Richard 24
Pieterse
family 56

Pleasants
Clementina 42
Dorothy 42
Elizabeth 42
John 42, 45
Jordan 42
Joseph 42
Mahale 42
Robert 41
Sophia 42
Tarlton 42
Thomas 41
Pollard
Robert 31
William 54
Pouncey
John 10
Povall
John 41
Povel
Elizabeth 47
Henry 47
John 47
Sarah 47
William 47
Powell
James 28
Presley
Jane 59
Price
Ann 60
John 60
Pulley
Robert 34
Quarles
Isaac 31
John 28-32
Ragsdale
Drury 29, 31
Railsback
family 56
Randolph
Beverley 30
Brett 41
David 45
Peyton 40, 42
Thomas 46
Redford
John 40
Joseph 40
Mary 40
Milner 40
William 39, 40
Reeves
George 33

Slave
  Kent 41
  Kojak 40
  Kujak 40
  Lal 46
  Langston 46
  Laudrum 40
  Launey 40
  Lawney 41
  Lewis 40, 46
  Limon 41
  Livia 41
  Lolly 46
  Lucy 40, 41
  Madeira 41
  Marjoc 41
  Mary 41
  Matt 46
  Mercury 40
  Michael 41
  Miles 46
  Milley 41
  Milly 40
  Mingo 40, 41
  Minner 41
  Moll 40, 46
  Molley 41
  Molly 41
  Morocco 40
  Mungo 41
  Nan 40, 41
  Nancy 40, 41, 46
  Nanny 46
  Nat 46
  Ned 41
  Nell 46
  Nick 40
  Oxford 40
  Pat 46
  Patience 40
  Patt 40
  Peg 40, 46
  Peter 41
  Phillis 46
  Phoebe 40, 41, 46
  Pompey 40, 41
  Queene 40
  Rachel 40, 41
  Redrough 40
  Robin 42
  Roger 40, 41, 46
  Rose 41
  Rosse 46
  Sall 40
  Sally 40

Slave
  Sam 41, 46
  Sambo 40
  Sampson 46
  Sancho 41
  Sary 40
  Saviny 40
  Scotland 40
  Sigh 40
  Siller 40
  Simon 46
  Sony 40
  Sook 42
  Stephen 41
  Stephney 46
  Suckey 40
  Sukey 40, 41
  Susanna 41
  Sye 40
  Sylvia 46
  Tabb 40
  Tero 40
  Tiller 46
  Toby 46
  Tom 40, 41, 46
  Tommy 46
  Visly 46
  Watt 40
  Will 40, 41
Smith
  Anne 51-54
  Gregory 51-53
  Joseph 60
  Kitty 60
  Lucy 51, 54
  Thomas 37, 53
  William 31, 60
Southall
  Ann 23, 24
  Elizabeth 23
  James 23, 24, 26
  John 20, 21, 24
  Margaret 23-24, 26
  Sarah 20-24, 26
  Tabitha 21, 23, 26
  Turner 42
  William 23
Spear
  John 42
Spence
  Elizabeth 59
  Richd. 43
Stanley
  family 56

Steer
  family 56
Stewart
  family 56
Stratton
  John 46
Talbot
  Elizabeth 21, 25
  Frances 21, 23-25
  Haley 21, 22, 25
  Jane 20, 21, 24
  Lucy 20-22, 24
  Mary 21, 24, 25
  Michael 20, 24-26
  Peter 20-22, 24-26
  Sarah 20-25
  Tabitha 23-26
  William   20-22,
      24-25
Talbott
  Carlos 20
  Elizabeth 21
  Sarah 20
  William 21
Talley
  Sarah 42
Tarrant
  Joseph 33
Tatum
  family 56
Temple
  Benjamin 31, 32
  Liston 28
Tepper
  Michael 55
Terrell
  Blackey 14
  family 14
  Richmond 14
  Robert 14
Thomas
  family 56
Thornton
  Sterling 45
Tomkies
  Francis 34
Tompkins
  Christopher 31
Trueman
  Mary 43
Turner
  Alice 48
  Anne 41
  Augusta 48
  Caroline 48

Turner
Carolinus 48
George 48
James 42
Jane 48
Reuben 30
Susan 48
Underwood
Elizabeth 36
John 36
Vand
Hump. 11, 12
Thomas 11
Vannerson
Jemima 41
John 41
William 41
VanPelt
family 56
Vaughan
William 24
Vaulx
Humphry 11, 13
Robert 12, 14
Thomas 12
Vaus
Eliz. 11, 12
Hump. 11, 12
Robert 12
Susan 12
Thomas 11
Vause
family 12
Thomas 10-13
Waad
Edward 12
Wade
Edward 12
Fay 2, 59
Frances 41
Walker
Humphrey 49
Walter
family 56

Warren
family 56
Washbourne
Daniel 24
Mary 24
Wayman
family 56
Webb
Geo. 43
Rodman 50
T. 43
Weisiger
Benjamin 39
Minor 28
Weldon
Daniel 37
Welson
Daniel 37
West
Anne 60
family 56
Mary 25
William 21, 25
White
family 56
Isaac 43
John 31
William 46
Wickersham
family 56
Wilchin
Richard 11
Williams
Catherine 60
Hugh 60
Thomas 39
Williamson
Geo. 41
George 40
John 39
Saml 39

Wilson
Elizabeth 23
John 23
William 47
Winn
Horatio 49
Wisheart
Ann 59
Wood
Bowery 21
Matthew 34
Woodcock
Mark 40
Woodfin
John 40
Woodington
John 14
Woodward
Martha 60
Woolfolk
Betty 59
Joseph 59
Richard 60
Worsham
Elizabeth 21

Peter 21, 25
Richard 21, 25
William 21, 25
Wright
Eve 35, 36
James 35, 36, 38
Matthew 45
Yager
family 56
Younger
Alexander 60
Ann 60
Elizabeth 60
Mary 60
Rebecca 60
Suzanna 60
Thomas 60
Younghusband
Isaac 43

TIDEWATER VIRGINIA FAMILIES:
A Magazine of History and Genealogy

TABLE OF CONTENTS

Volume 7 Number 2   August/September 1998

TIDEWATER BOOKS AVAILABLE IN AUGUST !

TIDEWATER VIRGINIA FAMILIES (1990 edition) **Back in Print!**

and........

Now
TIDEWATER VIRGINIA FAMILIES: GENERATIONS BEYOND **Available!**

Begun as an addendum to complement the original volume, *Tidewater Virginia Families*; *GENERATIONS BEYOND* became much more. It is also of value to all researchers interested in tidewater Virginia settlers and history. The supplement is made up of additional information: both brief, vital record entries and more lengthy accounts where new information has been found of the families related to the author.

Additional families, neighbors and family relationships are identified and extended as family lines, in the same format as those presented in the original publication. There are extensions of sibling lines and vignettes of family life, with letters and anecdotal accounts of times past. Included are links to an *Ancient Planter* and a *First Family of North Carolina.*

Homes and parish churches associated with these tidewater Virginia families, identified since the book was written are described, as well as locations of homesites, cemeteries and churches; county maps are included, and a place name index. There is extensive documentation, as well as an every name index.

Methods that are applicable to the analysis of data where primary source records have not survived, methods using circumstantial evidence and methods employing legal analysis are described in identifying relationships.

Corrections to the original publication have been made where necessary. Explanations of previous information, now confirmed and documented are also presented.

TIDEWATER VIRGINIA FAMILIES (1990 edition) and *TIDEWATER VIRGINIA FAMILIES: GENERATIONS BEYOND* **are both available from Genealogical Publishing. The price of the original** *TIDEWATER VIRGINIA FAMILIES* **is $75.00,** *GENERATIONS BEYOND* **is $45.00; shipping fees are extra for each book. For more information about these publications, and to place your order, call the Genealogical Publishing Co. at:**

1-800-296-6687

Researching and Writing Your Family History

Virginia Lee Hutcheson Davis

Joan Pettyjohn was one of two women accused of malicious gossip in Northampton County in 1652. She was ordered to stand at the door of the parish church with a gag in her mouth on two successive Sundays. Joan was the first Pettyjohn ancestor recorded in the county court records of this family in Virginia. Such an introduction was enough to spur one to learn more about Joan and about the customs of the times.

Two other persons, both of modern times had a lasting influence on this researcher. A genealogical archivist patiently explained how and where to conduct family research, and interpreted what had been found when it was found. He also felt this entitled him to goad one into writing. Over and over he stated, emphatically **"None of your research is of value unless you organize it in some meaningful manner and write it down! And do make your ancestors come alive."** The escape into research ended when it was realized that trips to the archives, retracing research already accomplished, meant that taking pen could easily be avoided indefinitely. The answer to the agonizing lament as to what to write was always answered with, **"Just sit down and start writing."** While a gag seemed a viable solution to these two voices, the realistic solution was to "start writing".

This introduction is made with levity, but has a far greater significance to those who engage in family research and conveys important advice. Thus this account of how the book, *Tidewater Virginia Families* came into being has been written. It provided insight about research in burned record counties, how to make these ancestors "come alive", and how to go about writing a family history.

Since most research in the burned record counties involves using unconventional county record sources, it is necessary to study the customs and laws that influenced the documents that were generated and have survived. Several examples of these records will show just how important it is to read all of the background history that one can find, study *Hening's Statutes at Large*[1], *Black's Law Dictionary*[2], the parish church records, learn about the activities of the people, and about their customs and their surroundings.

Where wills and deeds have not survived, persistence has one reading, first, the abstracted records of the county courts, and cross referencing the occurrences of the names of one's interest. Compulsion also requires one to copy every date and name associated with the person in whom one is interested, and those in whom one thinks he may become interested.

Abstracted court records should be used as a starting point...one then proceeding to the complete court record. Abstracted court orders should be compared with the original entries. Where the abstracted records stop, an entry-by-entry reading of the record should follow. In this way it has often been possible to determine that two generations of the same named person resided in a county... and the approximate death date of each can be established. Logic demands that one record mentally that the same name that appears fifty years later is likely to be a second person by the same name.

The given name of the wife at the time of death might also be divulged. However, this may not have been the only wife. Earlier, another woman might have relinquished her dower right in a deed; she would have been an earlier wife. A family account may name still earlier, another wife as the mother of the children.

As a gentle reminder, where a will has survived, one cannot assume that the children named in the will were the only children of that couple. An engaging family account can be based on the information in a will, only to learn when family Bible records are subsequently made available, that instead of one wife and nine children; the gentleman in question had two wives and twenty children.

Once again it is imperative that one understand the history of the area, the date of the county's formation, and the area from which it was formed. Study the evolution of the parishes of the Church of England to identify places of residence. One needs to know whether the family has moved or the county and parish have been newly formed.

Learn the names of the people and the area from which they came. In counties where few early records have survived one may still follow the residents through the processioning returns in the parish vestry book. An account of the residents and their neighbors and even where and when they moved, for they frequently moved as neighbors. People came and went, widows owned land, and land was inherited by children, all recorded in these detailed reports every four years of the land processioned.

A second history lesson must take the form of learning about the ways of the people. The account books of merchants that have survived often establish relationships. Many of these stores were a beehive of activity for people, not only in their county but from surrounding counties. These stores served as the early banks; giving credit, charging and even paying customers for customers.

The third necessary component is an understanding of the legal requirements of the time. It was English common law that prevailed in colonial Virginia and records cannot be interpreted in terms of our present-day laws. One must know the laws of inheritance of the period researched; the inheritance of land by the eldest son, the term "heir-at-law", and "heretrix" all have meaning in interpreting records.

It cannot be stressed enough that original records must be consulted. No given name appeared in the abstracted parish records for a long-sought ancestor. A photocopy of the original register gave enough of the name to be certain it was the person sought.

It is also both interesting and necessary to learn the custom concerning the use of diminutive names of women during the eighteenth and nineteenth centuries. One ancestor was thought to have been married more than once; it was finally believed he had one wife with four names: Sarah, Sally, Nancy, and Sarah Ann, all used interchangeably, and in legal documents (but never her maiden name). Nancy was not generally a given name then, but was the diminutive for Ann; Polly the diminutive for Mary.

Many times families used the same names over and over and it is such as the surviving Surveyors' Lists (which give the names of neighbors ordered to help maintain the roads), and Land and Personal Property Tax Records that allow one to differentiate among them. This can be accomplished through these records by determining where they lived and with whom they associated.

In learning about the ways of the people it has been found that the associations of the freeholders in many counties were almost entirely limited to their immediate neighbors. They seldom left their own communities, even to transact business. Even though many records have been lost, it has been possible to identify some of the people by this very characteristic.

The identity of two individuals of the same name is essential to the determination of the correct ancestor and it requires tedious research. Not to do this would be irresponsible, for this is the way inaccurate information is transmitted and perpetuated. Enough mistakes are made because of a lack of information.

Some of these same records may be employed to determine when people died. The Land Tax Records and Personal Property Tax Lists may confirm the transition of land and possessions. Land listed in an individual's name one year may be listed as his Estate the following year and his widow may be named the head of the household in the Personal Property Tax Lists.

It is difficult to say to oneself, "conclusions cannot be drawn; there isn't enough information"; especially after one has searched diligently and pondered greatly, but sometimes this is the case and one must be willing to make this qualification.

As early Virginia records were discovered, in their original form, it became a mission to present, and thus preserve these records. Many of these records are from counties in which the records have been burned, and the preservation of these old records themselves is significant. Copies of original deeds and wills that may date back as far as the seventeenth century should be included in a family history. It is exciting to discover original documents with original signatures of ancestors. These should be included in one's book to add a personal sense of these people. One signature was discovered that dates to 1670. To many readers this is mind boggling.

Learn about the laws and customs relating to church attendance and who went to court and what they did there. Some of these churches can still be visited, and a number of the courthouses are of considerable age. Paint your written picture of these places and gatherings. Read about the militia musters, why they were compulsory, who attended, and the further significance of these occasions.

Without listing specific references that one can use to make one's ancestors come alive in their own time and place, it is enough to say, "Read all you can of the times". There are many listings of books of the early settlers, the colonial period, and of the nineteenth century that tell of the ways of the people in a readable manner. Use those that provide accurate and authoritative accounts and incorporate these accounts in your writings.

Tidewater Virginia Families was first written before the Internet became widely used for searching for ones' relations. Many of the libraries with original archival holdings can now be searched through their web sites, and many online catalogues of holdings of libraries are available. These facilitate research immeasurably. Genealogical web sites and home pages have proliferated. Those offering original or documented material are a great help. Unless one is using primary source records, one must be aware that everything one finds on the Internet is not necessarily so. Family lines may be constructed and disseminated without a shred of documented evidence. One must chose wisely and be sure that one's own work is well-documented and accurate. Simply "surfing the net" for family connections is not enough.

Another caveat that should be considered relates to the use of the Family History Center Libraries. Primary source records such as court, tax and parish records available on microfilm through the Latter Day Saints (LDS) Library services are a major contribution to genealogical research. The Ancestral Files which are computerized family group sheets and pedigree charts compiled by individuals may or may not be accurate and should be used with caution.

* * * * *

Now you have the tools to present your research in some "meaningful form and to make your ancestors come alive". **Just sit down and start writing.** One must spend enough time to decide upon a workable organizational plan. And one's plan should not be the churning out of family sheets and pedigree charts as formatted by the various genealogical software programs. One must **compose** a family history. It must be an accurate account of the people and their time, they must be presented as "people," and not simply statistics.

There has been great emphasis on using the accepted numbering system in presenting a family. When one begins with a family surname and proceeds from the earliest generation to the most recent, enumerating all of the descendants that one can identify, this is appropriate. If one begins with ones' own life and goes back in time to all of the earlier ancestors that can be identified, a different means of identifying the generations may be in order. If one has seen this researcher's book, *Tidewater Virginia Families*, one understands the issues. The most important aspect of the problem is that the organization of the book must be easily understood and followed to be enjoyable reading.

Perhaps in analyzing the success of *Tidewater Virginia Families* several characteristics come to mind. It was, first of all, purely a fun adventure; not only in searching for the identity of the inter-related families, but in how these people lived and why they acted as they did. A number of readers have commented that they relived their childhood in these writings, or the lives of their grandparents as they might have been.

The larger interest has come about because of the identification and description of so many inter-related families. This has broadened the scope and nature of the book and therefore has been of interest to a larger population of readers.

The inclusion of the history of the times from the earliest colonial period forward, and by making the families seem real through the presentation of the various aspects of their lives, has increased interest in the book. Not only were copies of original records included, but also sketches and photographs from the past.

For those persons living away from tidewater Virginia, an identification of where the people lived, and a description of the physical characteristics of the areas have given the book broader appeal. A number of readers have expressed appreciation for the definitive locations of homes and cemeteries. They have also appreciated the accounts of the old churches, their locations, and descriptions. The juxtaposition of the historic and modern also has appeal: Temperance Harris's gravestone, dated 1716, stands today next to the elephant lot at Kings Dominion.

The book is a subtle sociological study of the changing times, depicting such as the changing roles of women, and of social customs. Also comparisons are included: among others, a trip by horseback through the Cumberland Gap, a camping trip with a Model-T Ford, and a modern trip across country with a Dodge van-conversion, a veritable land cruiser. Such statistics make for interesting comparisons.

Because the records are written this way, and because it seemed an appropriate style, the book is written in the central-tidewater Virginia vernacular. It is felt by a number of writer-critics that this will be an enduring quality of the book.

While many of these attributes have contributed to the acceptance of *Tidewater Virginia Families* by the public, they are also characteristics that one will want to consider in writing any family history. These are the characteristics that make for one's individuality and give the present generations the opportunity of seeing themselves in earlier generations. It provides the heritage and continuity that we all need and seek, and assurance of the preservation of this heritage.

* * * * *

It is at this point one should decide exactly how to proceed to "write". It will ultimately have to be type-set in a computer so this is an important consideration, but the manner in which one proceeds must be well organized. In the case of *Tidewater Virginia Families*, one family at a time was organized beginning with the earliest generation and working to the most recent. Each generation was sorted by that ancestor's name, and information that applied to more than one generation was advanced to the next for reference as one was completed. There were many notes and reference books with each family and it was necessary to organize them in a convenient, accessible manner. Each reference should be included and recorded as an endnote (preferably) at the time a statement is made. One must diligently let the reader know from what authority a statement is derived. Documentation must become an obsession.

77

Flowery descriptions and flights of imagination do not an accurate family history make. Present emotions as one would normally assume them to be, not as one would view them by modern mores. Activities should be based on documented records for that particular person, or appropriate and normal for that period and socio-economic level. A description of a widow of the late 1600s was simply a listing of her inventory at her death. She owned one gown, one frock, one waistcoat, two blue aprons, a cloak, and thimble and scissors.

It is important to make one's work credible by virtue of its documentation and its scholarly presentation. This is imperative, if the work is to endure and be taken seriously. Assume that you are writing for posterity. A few words of advice:

● Acquire a good manual of style early and consistently follow it. This relates not only to the grammar and punctuation, but also to the forms the endnotes, footnotes and bibliography take. The *Chicago Manual of Style* is the accepted authority. The *MLA Handbook for Writers of Research Papers*[3], latest edition by Joseph Gibaldi and Walter Achtert, is easier to navigate. Also see *Evidence! Citation and Analysis for the Family Historian*[4] by Elizabeth Shown Mills.

● Find someone, preferably a good English teacher, to read and critique your writing. Be sure that you are saying what you mean to say. There are far too many mis-modified clauses forever committed to print. Remember once it is in print it is there forever, to honor you or to haunt you!

● Enlist the aid of a good archivist/genealogist to read your manuscript and be sure you have not made some glaring false assumptions and drawn some embarrassing conclusions. Use the words "it appears", "it seems", or "it is believed", when there is no documented evidence, then state WHY.

• When you get ready to index your work, read the article on the correct procedures and format for indexing by Patricia Hatcher and John Wylie in the *National Genealogical Society Quarterly*[5]. You will be proud that you have done it correctly, and it will be a major contribution to your work.

Why this article on writing your family history? Every subscriber and researcher of family history has a collection of notes, perhaps notebooks, shoe boxes of notes, or a hodgepodge of papers. It should be a commitment to organize these notes and set this research down in print. With desk-top publishing as readily available as it is now, one has no excuse for not making family research available not only to family members, but to a larger audience. It is one's contribution in preserving a part of the heritage of this country.

Time must be taken to explore the possibilities of having the work privately printed, published by a subsidy press, or having a publisher accept your work for publication. There are great differences in the three options, and it behooves one to explore each.

If contracting with a printer is the way to go, take time to learn what is necessary to make the right choices in providing a camera-ready copy, an acceptable layout, and in choosing appropriate paper and binding. Go to the printer with a list of questions, listen to what he says, go home and mull over it. Go back with a refined list of questions until you know exactly what you want and what will present well.

The way your book looks is forever. There are always things one would have done differently, and some of these haunt the writer forever. Learn as much as you can before it becomes forever! May this inspire you to search and to write, and convey your family history and the feeling of emotional connection with your past and your heritage for the future.

Ed. note: May this inspire you to write your own family history. May it also inspire you to learn from the mistakes your editor made in *Tidewater Virginia Families*. They do rise up to haunt. This article has not been written with the wisdom of the learned, but with the wisdom of hindsight. May you benefit from that later wisdom![6]

Notes

1. William Waller Hening, *The Statutes at Large, Being a Collection of the Laws of Virginia, from the First Session of the Legislature in the Year 1619.* vols 1(1619)-13(1792). 1823 (Charlottesville: Jamestown Foundation, rep 1969). *passim.*
2. Henry Campbell Black, *Black's Law Dictionary.* 4th ed. (St. Paul, MN: West Publishing, 1951).
3. Joseph Gibaldi and Walter S. Achtert, *MLA Handbook for Writers of Research Papers.* (New York: Modern Language Association, 1988). *passim.*
4. Elizabeth Shown Mills, *Evidence! Citation & Analysis for the Family Historian.* Baltimore: Genealogical Publishing, 1997).
5. Patricia Law Hatcher and John V. Wylie, "*Indexing Family Histories*", *National Genealogical Society Quarterly.* 81(1993): 85-98.

From Virginia.............

Thanks to all of you who have asked about "the book"! And thanks to all of you who have been in touch since the publication of "the book". Many of the family records that you have sent me about the families of *Tidewater Virginia Families* appear in the *Tidewater Virginia Families: Generations Beyond*, with credit given to each contributor. Both "old" and "new" cousins will be appreciative!

Speaking of appreciation, readers, as well as your editor have welcomed the family histories that have been submitted by subscribers to *Tidewater Virginia Families: A Magazine of History and Genealogy.* They have provided a diversity to the magazine that would not have been not possible to achieve by your editor alone.

Please continue to submit these family histories. They should encompass well-documented research and relate to families that originated in the geographic area covered by the magazine. If you are in doubt about the format of the article and documentation, refer to articles that have appeared in the magazine, notably those by LtCol. James W. Doyle, Jr. as an example (there are also many others). A printout of guidelines will be sent upon request.

Please submit a hard copy of your article, as well as your article committed to computer disk. To be transferred to my WordPerfect 5.1 program the disk should be in DOS or ASCII file. Write or call for instructions if you have a question.

Be in touch, and tell me about your research and projected articles, I will be pleased to hear from you.

Land Patents in St. Stephen's Parish

LtCol James W. Doyle, Jr., USAF, Ret.[1]

In a previous article entitled *Saint Stephen's Parish, King and Queen County, James Madison, and the Bill of Rights* (*TVF* 5:9), a map was presented to show where the ancestor of James Madison lived and how he might have been influenced by the experiences of his neighbors. That map was certainly sufficient to support the points made in that article. With further work, it has become possible to refine the map, and give a further discussion of the less famous people who lived in the area.

Keep in mind that family, business, politics and religion were powerful bonds which kept these people united for generations, even as they moved across the ocean and into the wilderness. In this article, some examples of these bonds are mentioned, and the suggestion made that genealogies might be derived from a study of land tract maps and the land patent data. In counties such as King and Queen, where virtually all other records for the first 250 years have been destroyed, there is no other data base to build on.

On the map, land tracts are identified by a number and a patentee's last name. In most cases, the named owner is not the first to own the tract, but his patent provided the best data for drawing accurate bounds. Early patents were usually very vague in description, and later patents tended to be made up of confusing divisions and mergers of earlier tracts. A few of the plots show how some of the boundaries evolved and how a view of the superimposed plots can be used to establish reference points.

There are also several names on the map that have no reference numbers. Those which appear to be owners of well-defined tracts to the west will be discussed in an upcoming issue. Those appearing in unbounded areas have been mentioned as sharing a bound with nearby tracts, but can't be plotted from data collected by the author.

When relating old patent and deed data to modern maps, one must always keep in mind that many place names, especially names of streams, have changed over time. Several of these can be inferred from a trial-and-error fitting of the patent data into a mosaic of tracts and relating the overall tract map to known landmarks. The stream just up the Mattaponi River from Courthouse Creek has no name printed on the USGS map, but was apparently called Aquicke Swamp before 1700. Courthouse Creek was called Aquintanock, and the western branch of this creek, which goes to the land of George Morris, was called the Woolf Pit Branch. Mitchell Hill Creek was called Apostique, and Grass Creek/Carlton Hill Swamp was called Mosticoque Swamp. To the north, the small stream bounding the east end of the Gresham tract was called Helican Swamp, but is not named on the modern USGS map. Other names: Axoll (Exol) Swamp, Holmes and Timber swamps have survived without change.

With that, we shall launch right into a discussion of the numbered tracts. References given with each patent are keyed to *Cavaliers and Pioneers*[2], and Virginia Land Patent Books. **1. John Pigge, 300 ac, 10 Jul 1658, (C&P I:368/PB4:182).** John Pigge held a number of patents, sometimes going into partnership with others, especially George Morris and Robert Abrahall.

2. John Axoll and Anthony Heynes [Haines], 600 ac, 10 Jul 1658, (C&P I:369, PB4:183). Axoll apparently bought out Haines, as later neighboring patents mention only Axoll. Axoll probably sold to Rogers before 16 Apr 1683, as a patent to George Morris on that date names successive neighbors (Ralph) Leftwich, Pigg, and Rogers along his north bound. Axoll gave his name to a major stream through his land.

3. Edward Gresham Sr., 641 ac, 23 Oct 1690, (C&P II:353/PB8:98). This patent included 500 acres from a previous patent dated 18 Mar 1662. It appears that the original marked bounds enclosed more than his patent called for, as shown by a subsequent survey. It is not known whether this was due to poor measurement technique or deliberate "chiseling," but it is common to find more land marked out than the patent specified. As usually was the case, Gresham had to pay for the 141 acres "overplus," as it was customarily called, with three more headrights.

4. George Morris, 1100 ac, 16 Aug 1683, (C&P II:260/PB7:275). This patent is apparently a clarification of two earlier patents by Morris, one for 1350 acres in 1663, and another for 860 acres in 1668. By the naming of John Broach as a neighbor in 1683, when he was not mentioned in 1668, we may conclude that Broach arrived at some time between these dates. George Morris was the most active entrepreneur. He not only held large tracts as sole owner, but entered into numerous partnerships and surveyed land for others as well as himself. It is interesting that after a century had passed, another George Morris sold 160 acres of land to John Brooks in Northampton County, North Carolina, on 21 Nov 1764. (*TVF* 1:143) This Northampton Brooks would almost certainly be the same John Brooks who once lived in Charles City County, Virginia, and who bought 100 acres of land from John Brooks of Orange (now Chatham) County, North Carolina, on 2 Nov 1767. That deed was witnessed by two Hockaday brothers. (*TVF* 5:155) There is no well-known kinship among the Morris, Hockaday and Broach/Brooks families, but this researcher suspects that there may well be a kinship. See also the Hill-Cole-Brooks-Hockaday affiliation in the discussion of Gabriell Hill's patents below.

5. Elizabeth Smith, 400 ac, 16 Apr 1683, (C&P II:263/PB7:288). Names John Broach as neighbor on two sides.

6. John Broach, about 750 ac. There is no patent for land to John Broach in this location, so one must conclude that he acquired it from an earlier owner, as yet not identified. The tract is quite well defined by four neighboring patents which establish five boundary lines. The earliest of these was in 1678 (Hill), with others in 1680 (Style & Story),1683 (Smith) and 1683 (Morris). Broach was not mentioned in the Morris patents of 1663 or 1668. These dates are in good agreement with the sale of land in (Old) Rappahannock County by John and Mary (Jones) Broche/Brocke *of New Kent* (now K & Q) *County* on 4 Jan 1670.[3] On the map, those bounds of neighboring tracts which are said to join Broach are highlighted by heavy lines.

7. John Style & Joshua Story   200 ac, 20 Oct 1680, (C&P II:215/PB7:65). This is an interesting patent in that it says the land was *surveyed by Michaell Robinson & by him never pattented.* In fact, a patent was issued to Mich. Robinson on 24 Feb 1674/5, (C&P II:171/PB6:593). Then, a third patent for this land was issued to Robert Bird on 21 Oct 1684, (C&P II:284/PB7:417). This last patent states that the land was owned by Michaell Robinson when he died, and that it was found to escheat. We may never know whether or not Robinson actually had legal title for any period of time. Land ownership seemed to be subject to legal rulings we might think capricious in our time.

In the original Robinson patent, the neighbor to the west is named Mr. Br--ks. This could be Brucks or Brooks. It is clearly not Black, as extracted by Mrs. Nugent in *Cavaliers and Pioneers*. The handwriting in the second patent to Style & Story is even less readable, and looks like Bruq in one place and Bruches in another. The French name was apparently still giving the clerks trouble.

8. Henry Lawrence, 90 ac, 20 May 1682, (C&P II:229/PB7:127).

9. Gabriell Hill, 514 ac, 25 May 1678, (C&P II:187/PB6:652). This patent states that the land was previously patented by Ja. Cole on 6 Mar 1660. The earlier patent is one which was recorded in a section of Patent Book 4 which has been lost. The description of bounds names John Broach as neighbor. It is interesting that the names Hill, Cole, Hockaday and Brookes all appear as neighbors in Charles City County a half century later (*TVF* 6:5). Hill, Brooks and Cole families may also be found in Chatham County, NC after 1770.

10. Gabriell Hill, 661 ac, 29 Nov 1665, (C&P I:541/PB5:456). This tract purchased from James Cole, who patented it on 15 Mar 1660. (C&P I:408/PB4:(469)). Though extracted by Nugent, this is one of some fifty pages not included in the microfilm of the patent books.

11. Robert Bird, 250 ac, 29 Apr 1693, (C&P II:383/PB8:277). Of this, 200 acres overlays a part of the above 661 acres of Hill, and 50 acres may have been part of an earlier patent by Bird or Holmes, though no mention is made of this. The surveyed lines of Bird and Hill deviate slightly, but there is no doubt as to the location.

12. Robert Bird, 330 ac, 16 Apr 1683, (C&P II:262/PB7:282). Part of this land overlays the above Hill patent, and the remainder may be part of an earlier patent by Bird or Holmes. Positioning this tract accurately is a key to the location of the Ramsey tract, below.

13. Christo. Charelton (Carlton), 836 ac, undated [21 Sep 1684], (C&P II:151/PB6:522). Among neighbors named is a Mr. Dunston. No doubt this should be Tunstall, who is named as a neighbor in the adjoining patent to John & Richard Wyatt. Mr. Carlton, or one of his descendants probably gave his name to Carlton Corner, which is about a half mile to the east.

14. William Watts, 270 ac, 18 Feb 1674, (C&P II:143/PB6:503).

15. Timothy Carter, 700 ac, 29 May 1683, (C&P II:264/PB7:293).

16. John and Richard Wyatt, 650 ac, 20 Sep 1683, (C&P II:267/PB7:321). Of this land, 640 ac was previously patented by Robert Abrahall and sold to the Wyatts on 19 Mar 1660. This tract probably includes the 120 acres in St. Stephen's Parish sold by Richard Wyatt to John Broach/Broche on (blank) June 1706, as documented by a security bond filed at King & Queen Court 12 Jun 1706. It is interesting that this original document shows that the clerk has consistently used the Broach spelling, while the signature is clearly *John Broche* in his own hand.[4]

17. William Blake, 550 ac, 16 Mar 1683, (C&P II:257/PB7:253). This patent clearly states that it is on the *Tymber Branch*, but fits perfectly into a mosaic of tracts a mile to the north of that stream. Such a confusion in names of streams is not unique, and greatly adds to the work required to construct an accurate map of patents.

18. Bartholomew Ramsey, 1300 ac, 6 Jun 1699, (C&P III:27, PB9:196). Of this, 1000 ac was sold by George Morris to John Roberts 12 Oct 1661 (for which no patent can be found), and 300 acres was new land. Resurveyed and a new patent granted to Ramsey, who married the relict of Roberts.

19. Lt.Col. William Hockaday, 1000 ac, 31 Mar 1664, (C&P I:563/PB5:526). This is the immigrant Hockaday, who first had large tracts of land in the Broach Neck/Eltham area of New Kent County.

20. Mr. John Broach, 342 ac, 20 Oct 1689, (C&P II:338/PB8:16). As with the Blake patent, above, it is almost certain that the surveyor named the wrong stream when he placed this tract on *Mantipike Swamp*. Not only does the tract fit with other tracts at a location about a mile farther down the Mattaponi River, but all of the land bordering on the Mantapike Swamp was patented by William Banks just six months later. In a recurring pattern of settlement, Broach always seems to have Robert Abrahall as a neighbor.

21. Col. Robt Abrall, 500 ac, 26 Apr 1664, (C&P I:502/PB5:333).

22. Lt.Col. Robert Abrall, 950 ac, 8 Jun 1657, (C&P I:346/PB4:98).

23. Mr. Richard Barnhouse, Jr., 200 ac, 17 Mar 1665, (C&P I:276/PB3:193). This patent was renewed 17 Mar 1665, and sold to John Stark, who included the 200 acres in a larger patent, below. This Richard Barnhouse may be the man of that name who was baptized at Northam, Devon, on 4 Apr 1605.[5] Readers may recall that Northam was home to members of the Hockaday family, and had other strong ties to the colonization of Virginia. (*TVF* 2:136)

24. Mr. John Stark, 484 ac, 30 Oct 1686, (C&P II:301/PB7:525).

25. Mary Broche, 400 ac, 1 Apr 1717, (C&P III:189/PB10:313). This land is almost certainly the same tract referred to as 420 acres in King & Queen County, surveyed for John Broche by Harry Beverly on 13 Sep 1706.[6] Mary Broche is probably the widow of John Broche, son of the immigrant. John and Mary were married before 1670, which would imply that she was above 70 years old at the time this patent was granted. One might also speculate that Mary was an unmarried daughter or a widowed daughter-in-law. This appears to be the last official record of the Broche spelling of the name in King & Queen County.

26. William Wyatt, Junr., 500 ac, 20 Jun 1670, (C&P II:83/PB6:322). This land was patented by Peter Foard (640 ac ny Foard & Edward Racle in 1653 and again in 1664) and later by William Leigh (370 ac in 1682). The actual chain of title and changing bounds are not easy to recreate from the scant records.

27. Major William Wyatt, 1900 ac, 21 Oct 1670, (C&P II:95/PB6:364).

Notes

1. 2923 Tara Trail, Beavercreek, OH 45434. JWDoyleJr@aol.com

2. Nell Marion Nugent, *Cavaliers and Pioneers* vol I. (Baltimore: Genealogical Publishing, 1983); vol II & III, (Richmond: VSL, 1977, 1979). passim.

3. Records of Old Rappahannock County.

4. MSS1, K5823, FA: Wyatt #3.(Copy). Virginia Historical Society, Richmond, VA. Original thought to be in manuscript collection, Alderman Library, University of VA, Charlottesville, VA.

5. *Northam Parish Register*.

6. Louis des Cognets, Jr. *English Duplicates of Lost Virginia Records.*(Baltimore: Genealogical Publishing, 1990). 88.

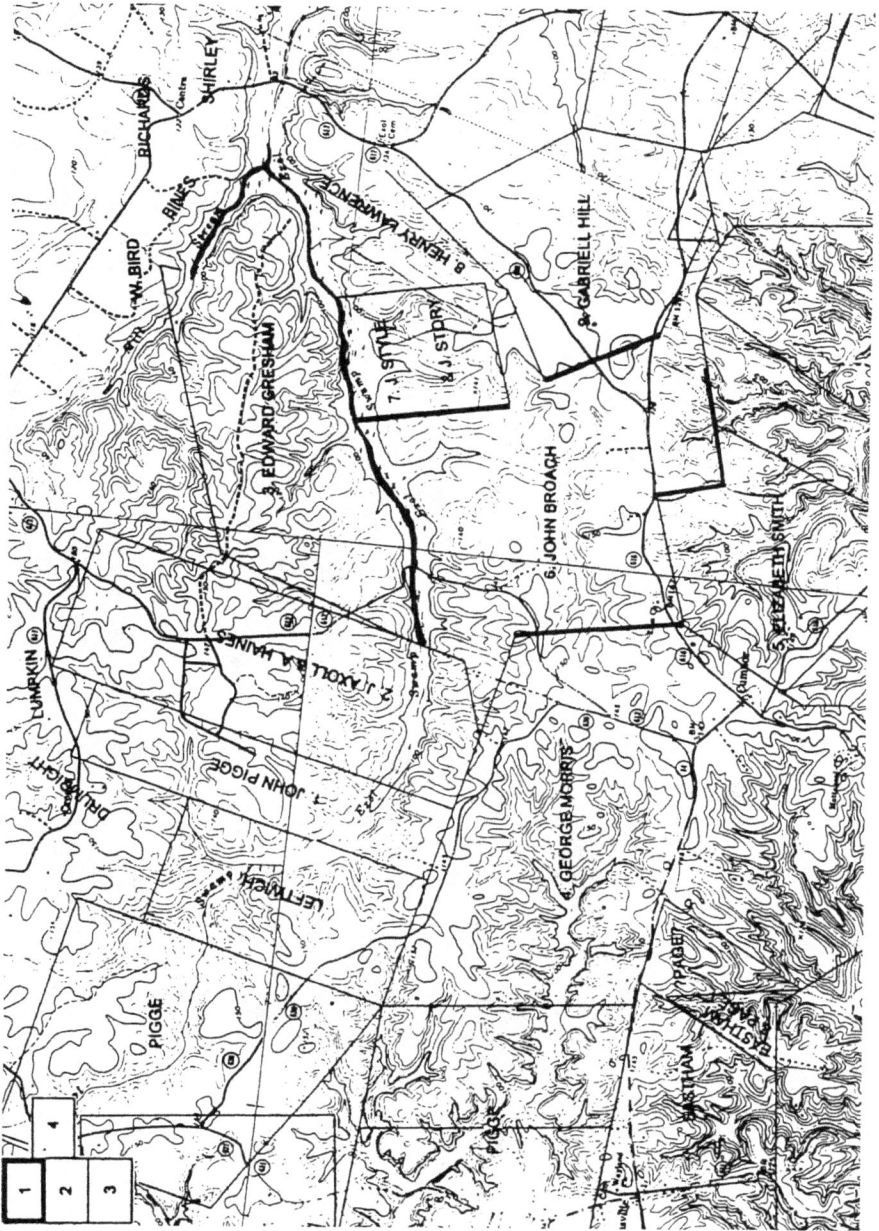

22. ROBT. ABRALL

26. WILLIAM WYATT

23. RICHARD BARROWHOUSE

24. JOHN STARK

25. MARY BROCHE

27. WILLIAM WYATT

KING AND QUEEN CO
KING WILLIAM CO

MATTAPONI
KING AND QUEEN CO
KING WILLIAM CO

and QUEEN COUNTY
:phen's Parish

h = 242 poles
e = 1.32 inches

Rubble With a Cause,
The Story of Menokin, Richmond County

Authored by Marvin Kirwan King, et al.
Contributed by W. Gregory Burkett,

Menokin was the plantation and home of patriot Francis Lightfoot Lee and his wife, Rebecca Tayloe. Rebecca's father, John Tayloe II of nearby Mt. Airy, made a wedding gift of the Georgian mansion and 1,000 acres of land to the couple in 1769. The estate now consists of 500 acres situated on Cat Point Creek in Richmond County in Virginia's Northern Neck. Many of Virginia's most famous plantations are nearby: *Mt. Airy, Sabine Hall, Stratford Hall, Wakefield* and *Nomini Hall*. The property is home to many species of wild life including: beaver, otter, pileated woodpecker, osprey and bald eagle. The Lees died without children in 1797, and the property was left to the heirs of Francis Lee.

In 1800 the land reverted to the Tayloes. In the early nineteenth century it was the home of John Tayloe Lomax, first professor of law at the University of Virginia. The property was sold in 1823 and, eventually, it was passed down to Thomas Edgar Omohundro and his sister, Dora Omohundro Ricciardi. Upon Dora's death, she willed her share to Thomas and, on July 4, 1995, he gave the entire property to the Menokin Foundation.

Francis Lightfoot Lee was born in 1734 and raised at *Stratford Hall Plantation* in Westmoreland County. Frank Lee, as he was called, devoted his life to public service. Frank Lee lived in Loudoun County where he was chief of the local militia and a member of the Virginia House of Burgesses. He was concerned about the rights of the colonies and in 1766 signed the Westmoreland Association resolution against the Stamp Act.

While Francis Lee was in the legislature in Williamsburg he met Rebecca Tayloe and courted her at the Tayloe home in Williamsburg. They were married in 1769 and moved to Richmond County, where he was also elected as a Burgess. He served as a member of the Virginia Conventions of 1774 and 1775 and as a member of the Continental Congress. He and Richard Henry Lee were the only brothers to sign the Declaration of Independence.

As a wedding gift, John Tayloe gave the couple *Menokin*, the one thousand acres probably adjacent to his own land of *Mt. Airy*. The plantation consisted of many outbuildings dominated by the sandstone mansion which was flanked by the office and kitchen dependencies. The mansion is a three-bay, double-pile with central entrance edifice. It had two stories over a full storage basement, a hip-on-hip roof and two large brick chimneys. The north, front entrance had heavy pilasters, topped by a delicate fanlight and an unusual keystone with floral design. Double doors led into the paneled stair hall. To the left is the surviving study and to the right was a small bed chamber.

The stylishly large dining room and master bed chamber dominate the rear or south side of the floor plan. Both rooms had outstanding Georgian woodwork. The paneled over mantles in these two rooms were richly carved. The four second-floor bed chambers had much simpler woodwork, as is shown by the surviving mantles and molding. The double doors from the dining room stepped down to the terraced garden levels that can still be found on the southern slope toward Menokin Bay.

Frank and Rebecca Lee lived at *Menokin* during the years when this nation was born. They led an active social life with many visits to and from *Nomini Hall* and many other neighbors. They were deeply attached to one another but unfortunately did not have any children. They both died in the year 1797 and are buried at *Mt. Airy*.

Although *Menokin* is now in ruin, it is a remarkable encyclopedia of colonial knowledge. Original drawings and later descriptions, photographs and measured drawings document the original buildings. Most of the eighteenth-century woodwork has been removed and saved. The plantation consists of many outbuildings, dominated by the mansion that is flanked by the office and kitchen dependencies.

It is extremely fortuitous that the original architectural drawings have survived at *Mt. Airy* and were given to the Virginia Historical Society by Mrs. H. Gwynne Tayloe, Jr., the present owner of *Mt. Airy*. The plans show the builder's intentions in great detail, even down to the names of the various rooms and storage spaces. A part of the house remains. One corner with two rooms is largely intact, and shows the water table, the two belt courses on the north facade and one on the east, and much window detail. There are even remnants of plaster still in place.

The architectural importance of *Menokin* was recognized early in this century and the Historic American Building Survey of 1940 produced detailed photography and comprehensive drawings. The surprisingly intact interior woodwork was removed in 1968 and has been held in storage by the Association for the Preservation of Virginia Antiquities (APVA). This wealth of information and original building fabric provides a special opportunity for study, preservation and eventual restoration. It will be a classroom for historic preservation practitioners and students.

An equally important mission is to use the opportunity to train students. Field schools will cover eighteenth-century construction, below and above ground archaeology, documented and oral history, historic landscapes, and all of the skills needed to preserve, study and restore a colonial plantation. Students will excavate American Indian sites, slave and tenant houses and study the lives and cultures of all of the people associated with Menokin. The Menokin Foundation is also dedicated to the conservation of *Menokin's* natural resources through careful management of the woodland, fields, marshes and shoreline, and a study of past and present flora and fauna.

Photo of Menokin c. 1940   Menokin Floor Plan c. 1769

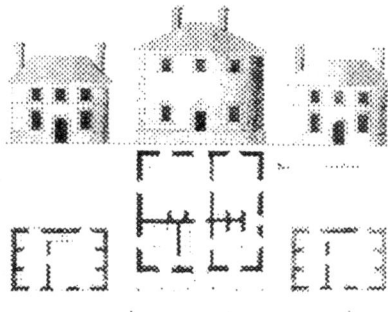

Those interested in preserving the history and culture of Virginia's tidewater are invited to help open this encyclopedia that is *Menokin.* The Menokin Foundation is a tax-exempt private organization, established to preserve this National Historic Landmark and eventually restore it to its eighteenth-century splendor.

Ed. note: It is unusual for such an article to appear in *TIDEWATER VIRGINIA FAMILIES: A Magazine of History and Genealogy*; however, it is felt that this endeavor is of such a significant nature that it will be of special interest to subscribers. Those who would like to become a part of this history may write to the Menokin Foundation at the address below.

This article is a synthesis of several articles describing the history, acquisition, organization and plans for the home *Menokin* in Richmond County. It is located on CR 690, which turns north west from SR 3 on the north side of the town of Warsaw. Brochure of The Menokin Foundation, 1997. Marvin Kirwan King, President, The Menokin Foundation Board of Trustees, The Menokin Foundation, P O Box 1221, Warsaw, VA 22572; Arnold Berke, *"Rubble With a Cause,"* *Historic Preservation*, May/June 1996, n.p.; Mark St. John Erickson, *Inform, Architectural Design*, 1996, n.p.

Civil Appointments, 1788-1792
James City County

Contributed By Minor Tompkins Weisiger

These Civil Appointments from the Executive Department are transcribed from the original notes and letters that have survived. They provide information of the lives and business of the residents of James City County. They are especially important where the county court records are not extant. Civil apointments for James City County were first published in Tidewater Virginia Families, Volume 4, Number 3, pages 156-162. These are a continuation, transcribed by VLHD.

List of Acts respecting the appointment of Sheriffs

1748 Chapt 6th page 183, Sheriff not compelled to serve more than one year but may by consent be continued two.
============
1763 Chapt 2d page 409, Sheriffs may be continued longer than two years.
Laws passed under the present constitution
1782 Chapt 134 page 26, Sheriffs to qualify in Nov.

At a Court held for James City County the 14th day of July 1788.
This Court doth recommend to his Excellency the Governor and Honorable Council Samuel Griffin and Dudley Digges Gent: for one of them to be appointed to execute the Office of Sheriff of this County for the coming year.   Copy Teste
                                                    Geo: Dunlevy D.C.C.

James City County Court the 14th day of May 1792
            present: William Norvell
                                          Nathaniel Burwell
                                          Champion Travis
                                          John Walker
                                          John Browne
                                          William Walker and
                                          William Wilkinson junior
                                          Gentlemen Justices

Ordered that James Sheilds, John Bracken Clerk, William Coleman, Littleton Tazwell, William Lightfoot, and John Kerby be recommended to his Excellency the Governor and Honourable Council as proper persons to be added to the Commission of the Peace and Oyer and Terminer of this County

Copy teste

[Robert Waller, Clerk]   Ro: H. Waller Cl: Curi:

James City County Court June the 11th 1792

This Court doth recommend to his Excellency the Governor and Honorable Council Samuel Beall, John Walker and John Browne Gent; as proper persons for one of them to be by him appointed Sherif of this County for the ensuing year.

A true Copy teste

Ro: H. Waller Cl: curi:

James City County Court July the 9th 1792

Ordered that it be certified to his Excellency the Governor and Honorable Council that Samuel Beall Gent: who was commissioned as Sherif of this County by Letters patent bearing date the twenty second day of June last is not at this time within the State of Virginia and that his return thereto is uncertain and that it be further certified that William Lee Gent: the present Sherif of this County Qualified to that Office the fourteenth day of June 1790.

A true Copy teste

Ro: H. Waller Cl: curi:

James City County Court August the thirteenth 1792

This court doth recommend to his Excellency the Governor and Honorable Council James Sheilds Gent: as a proper person to be by him appointed Coroner of this County in the room of John Walker Gent: who is nominated Sherif of the same.

A Copy Teste

Ro: H. Waller Cl: curi:

James City County Court October 8th 1792

The Court took into consideration a Letter from the Clerk of the Council communicating to them the Governor's objections against commissioning

James Sheilds, John Bracken Clerk, William Coleman, Littleton Tazwell, William Lightfoot and John Kerby who were recommended by this Court on the fourteenth day of May last, whereupon It is Ordered that the Clerk of this Court do transmit to his Excellency the Governor a List of the Magistrates named in the Commission of the Peace and Oyer and Terminer of this county dated the fourteenth day of January 1786 that he particularly state in the said List the deaths, resignations, and removals of Magistrates that have occurred since that period, and that he do also further certify the number and names of the Magistrates present at the Court day in May last, and that the said number was at that time a Majority of the acting Magistrates of this County

Copy Teste

Ro: H. Waller Cl: curi:

Justices Named in the Commission of the Peace and Oyer and Terminer dated the fourteenth day of January 1786.

William Norvell		Dudley Diggs	dead
Richard Taliaferro	dead	William Lee	seldom attends
Nathaniel Burwell		Samuel Beall	never attends
Champion Travis		Charles Barham	dead
William Barrett	dead	John Walker	Sherif
John Pierce		John Browne	
Robert Andrews	disqualified	John Ambler	seldom attends
Samuel Griffin	seldom attends	William Walker	
	William Wilkinson, the younger		

Copy Teste   Ro: H Waller &c ad

From the records of the Executive Department, Commonwealth of Virginia. Civil Appointments. Research and Information Services Division, The Library of Virginia, Richmond, Virginia.

Will of Thomas Edwards, 1857
Mathews County

I Thomas Edwards of the County of Mathews and State of Virginia being of sound and disposing mind and memory, do make and publish this my last will and testament; hereby revoking all former wills or testaments heretofore made in form and manner following:

Item 1st I give and bequeath to my dear wife, Mary T Edwards the whole of the estate both land and negroes and money which I got by her, when I intermarried with her as the widow of Walter G Hudgins, decd. Also my carriage and horses, one choice bed and furniture, my wardrobe, one yoke of good oxen, two choice cows, one half of my parlor furniture, my piano excepted, and $1500 in fee simple, to be paid her out of the sales of my lands by my Executor hereafter named, which amount is to be paid to her, so soon as my Executor can reasonably do so. The interest on said amount ($1500) to be paid her within nine months after the sales of sale of said lands and annual thereafter until the principal is paid.

Item 2nd I desire my son Charles H Edwards to have one equal share of my estate with the rest of my children, but at the same time I wish and direct that portion allotted to him so secured in the hands of a competent trustee, hereafter provided for that he, his wife and children may enjoy the use and benefit of said interest without its being in his or their power to make way with or spend it, which interest shall not be liable for any debts he may have contracted, or which he may hereafter contract. In taking his portion of my estate I charge and require him to account to my estate for the negroes which I have advanced to him and his children by a deed of trust of record in the Clerk's Office in this county at their valuation at the time he received them, and also to account for a negro girl named Courtney, which I loaned his wife on the eve of starting for the West, which girl he sold and has never account to me for, and a negro boy named Andrew, conveyed in said deed of trust which he also sold and not accounted for. I do not charge him or wish him held responsible for the money which I have advanced him at various times. If any time hereafter my son Charles H Edwards or his children should attempt to hold my estate responsible for this negro boy Andrew, whom he sold and not accounted for —then I direct and require that he or they shall have no further interest in or claim upon my estate whatever.

Item 3rd I desire that my daughter Sarah F Armistead wife of Francis Armistead have an equal share of my estate with my other children, but I require her to account to my estate for the negroes which I have advanced her, at their valuation at the time she received them.

Item 4th *I desire and direct that my children Robert E, Ann Elizabeth, Martha Louisa and Mary Catherine Edwards children of my intermarriage with Louisa Garnett, and my youngest daughter Ella Edwards child by my intermarriage with Mary T Hudgins, to have an equal share of my estate with my son Charles H Edwards and my daughter Sarah F Armistead. I wish and direct that the portion or portions of my estate allotted to my children by my marriage with Louisa Garnett be kept together and managed for their mutual use and benefit until the oldest of them arrives at legal age or marry. In this event I wish his or her portion to be set apart to him or her and the remaining portion kept together for their mutual use and benefit as before directed, and so on until the youngest child arrives to legal age or marry. In the event of the death of either of my children by my marriage with Louisa Garnett, or the death of my youngest daughter Ella Edwards, child by my marriage with Mary T Hudgins before they attain their majority or marry, I desire and direct that his or her portion shall be equally divided among the surviving child or children of my last two marriages. I direct and devise that the portion of my estate allotted to my daughter Ella to be placed in the hands of her mother Mary T Edwards and of her half brother Robert E Hudgins to be by them managed to the best advantage for her use and benefit. I desire & request that my executor or Guardian of my children shall see that they all have a good education, such as is in his opinion, their capacities and their income will justify. If the interest arising from their portion of my estate shall not be sufficient for this desirable and important object, then I direct him to use so much of the principal of their estate as may be necessary.*

Item 5. I desire and direct my executor hereafter named to sell the whole of my landed estate, of which I may die seized & possessed, to the best advantage at such times & or such terms as is in his opinion or judgment may be most conducive to the interest of my family, and after paying to my wife Mary F Edwards the $1500 as before directed the balance of this fund to be equally divided among all of my children as heretofore desired, and I authorize him to make a good and sufficient deed or deeds for the same.

Item 6. I have heretofore directed that the portion of my estate allotted to my son Charles H Edwards, for the benefit of himself and family, to be placed in the hands of a competent Trustee, to be managed for their benefit. In case a competent trustee cannot be obtained, I desire and direct my Executor hereafter named to act as such, and in the event of his refusal I desire and request the County Court of Mathews to appoint a suitable trustee, or have the funds so fixed or invested that my son Charles H Edwards and his family shall have the use and benefit of this fund but not have it in his or their power to waste or spend it.

Item 7. I wish and request my Executor or the Guardian of my children, that in hiring out my servants especially my women who have young children, not unless absolutely necessary, to hire them from the public stand but privately procure for them good and comfortable homes and that they be well cared for.

Lastly I constitute and appoint my friend and son in law Francis Armistead my Executor to this my last will and testament and request that he will act, and I also constitute and appoint him Guardian to my children by my marriage with Louisa Garnett and as I have the utmost confidence in his integrity and fidelity, I desire and request the County Court of Mathews to permit him to qualify as such without requiring security, and I moreover enjoin upon him and particularly request him to manage my estate to the best advantage and in such a manner most conducive to the interest of my children.

In testimony whereof I have hereunto subscribed my name and affixed my seal this 29 day of May 1857.

[signed] Thos Edwards {seal}

Signed sealed & published in our presence,
and we in the presence of the testator and in
the presence of each other have attested this will
Wm S Thurston
John I. Benke
Wm W Lewis

In Mathews County Court Nov. 9 1857

This last will and testament of Thos Edwards decd. was this day proved in open court by the oaths of Wm S Thurston, John I Benke & Wm W Lewis the subscribing witnesses hereto and ordered to be recorded.

| *Teste* | *[signed] Shepard G Miller C C* |
| *A Copy Teste* | *[signed] Shepard G Miller C C* |

This copy not made by the Clk of the Court of Mathews or any Deputy of the sd Clk. [signed] S G Miller Clk

Transcribed by VLHD

County and Superior Court Papers, 1860s, Loose Papers, Wills from Burned Recored Counties, 1729-1830. The Library of Virginia, Richmond, VA.

Westmoreland County Land Taxes, 1782

A Copy of Account of Assessment of all the Land in the County of Westmoreland taken by Christoper Butler and George Garner, Gent. Commissioners of the Land Tax for the year 1782 and Copied by Richard Bernard Clk of the said County Court according to Law, for the Auditor of Public Accounts.

Proprietors' Names	No. Acres	Proprietors' Names	No. Acres
page 1		Briscoe, Daniel	31
Ashton, John	203	Butler, Laurence	171
Anton, Alexander	69	Bayne, Matthew	414
Ashton, David	60	Bayne, John	73
Attwell, Mary	240	Beane, William	61
Attwell, Richard	195	Brewer, William	1
Amos, Philip	15	Blundell, Thomas	160
Bowcock, Thomas	187	Blundell, Thomas junr	144
Butler, Elenore Est	200	Brown, William	450
Bowcock, John	125	Brown, John	272
Bowcock, John jun	125	Brickey, Peter sen	20
Butler, John	72	Bailey, James	100
Berryman, William	383	Bailey, Daniel	40
Bankhead, James	530	Bailey, Vincent	100
Ball, Margaret	327	Bailey, John	100
Brown, William	305	Bailey, Samuel	60
Brown, John Est	67	Brinnon, John	185
Bayne, Elizabeth	60	Buckner, Richard	400
Butler, Dorcas	40	Butler, William	100
Bankhead, William	1475	Butler, Nathaniel	33
Butler, Christopher	200	Beale, Thomas	500
Burges, James	75	page 2	
Burges, Joseph	100	Ballentine, John	471
Brokenbrough, Austin	1200	Bailey Jno: Garland	675
Barker, John	100	Beale, Thomas	52
Bulger, Jane	200	Beale, Thomas, jun	56
Brewer, James	100	Bennett, Thomas	220
Backus, John	125	Bennett, Solomon	40
Bassett, William	100	Bailey, William	80

Butler, Thomas	147	Drake, William	150
Boyer, Hannah	80	Deane, Charles jun	125
Corbin, Gawin	400	Davenport, Birkett	50
Chancellor,Thomas	100	Drake, Anne	Lots 2
Campbell, Archibald	217	Dickie, John	Lots 2
Carpenter, John	100	Drake, Thomas Est	100
Cooke, Mordicai	600	Dodd, William	50
Cannady, James	186	Davis, Elias	100
Chrison, Catherine	15	Dozier, William Robinson	210
Crawford, Andrew	Lots 5½	Dozier, William Senr	150
Claytor, Anne	50	page 3	
Claytor, William	100	Dozier, Joseph	137
Carter, Robert Esq	7333	Dozier, Richard sen	133
Carter, Robᵗ Wormely	740	Dozier, Richard jun	163
Crabb, Benedict	287	Davis, William	100
Chilton, Thomas Esq	1313	Epington, Christopher	285
Cowles, Thomas	100	Edwards, George	300
Cox, Fleet	2080	Edwards, William	550
Carter, Charles Esq	500	Fitzhugh, Daniel	120
(Corotoman)		Fitzhugh, William	1738
Collins, Christopher	436	Fendal, Philip Richard	651
Crabb, John Est	120	Fisher, Thomas Est	250
Coward, William	70	Fox, Joseph	320
Collinsworth, Thomas	50	Green, Jonathan	105
Collinsworth, John Est	63	Gray, William	100
Collinsworth, Willoughby	43	Green, William	140
Crenshaw, David	50	Gutridge, Anne	100
Claughton, Pemberton	176	Gauter's	Lots 5
Critcher, John	157	Garner, Lettice	108
Corbin, Hannah	179	Gordon, James (North'land)	127
Cisel (Cissell), William	80	Gordon, George	188
Coventon, John	75	Gregory, James sen	148
Crump, James	509	Gilbert, William	200
Crabb, John	150	G[ill?], Edward	127
Campbell, Gilbert	40	Garlick, Lewis Bennett	50
Dishman, William	242	Gill, George	130
Dodd, Quisenberry	100	Garner, James	73
Deane, Thomas	116	Garner, Rose	37
Dishman, John	100	Griffin, Leory's Estate	510
Drake, Rowe	153	Hilton, Mary	100

Hales, George	150	Lee, Richard Henry	500
Hungerford, Anne	200	Lawson, John	243
Hill, Thomas	360	Lane, Joseph	923
Hipkins, Richard	1250	Lamkin, Peter	250
Hodge, Molly	1261	Lewis, George	60
Hackney, Benjamin	430	Lee, George Fairfax	2743
Hutt, William	1022	Lee, Richard Esq	4043
Hutt, John	200	Long, Robert	70
Hazlingg, William	75	Lowe, Rich^d sen	150
Hutt, Caty	490	Laycock, Thomas	40
Hutt, Gerr^d Robinson	200	Muse, Nicholas	250
Harrison, William	138	Martin, Jacob	400
Harrison, Samuel	62	Monroe, Elliot	350
Harrison, Elenor	62	McCarty, Daniel	3510
Hobson, Elizabeth	32	Monroe, Jemima	250
Harrison, Jeremiah	55	Monroe, John	666
Hillard, Josiah[?] Estate	204	Massey, Martha	130
Hull, George	10	Massey, Elizabeth	50
[illeg.]tt, Thomas Esqr	1454	Monroe, William	108
[torn]kson, Francis	129	Monroe, Benjamin	250
[torn]kson, Samuel	60	Morris, Charles	400
[torn]tt, William	100	Monroe, David	134
Jett, Birkett Est	125	Muse, James	250
Jett, Jesse	100	Muse, Thomas	250
Jett, Catherine	150	Muse, Jane	60
James, Walter	67	Muse, Samuel	96
James, Elizabeth	33	Mazaret, John	220
Jackson, Richard	500	Moore, James	50
page 4		Muse, John	130
Jeffries, William	275	Moxley, John	100
Jeffries, Robert	160	Muse, James	107
Jones, Catesby	654	Muse, Edward	100
King, Thomas	260	Moxley, Rodham	100
King, Smith	184	Mothershead, George	175
King, William	50	Mothershead, Alvin	125
Kirk, Randal	95	Moore, Thomas	200
Lee, Phil: Lud: Estate	3454	Moxley, Augustine	171
Love, Samuel	190	Moxley, Atkins Est	250
Lee, Richard, Senr (Mary P.)	654	Moxley, Daniel	303
Lee, Richard jun	505	McClanaham, John	177

Mothershead, John	100	Oliff, James	120
Mitchell, George	100	Owens, Anne	33
Marmaduke, Vincent	100	OMoohundro, Thomas	260
McKenny, Garrard	140	OMoohundro, James	100
Mullins, Wm Est	99	Payton, William	160
Marmaduke, William	240	Price, John junr	200
Mullins, John	159	Peed, Thomas	100
Moxley, Griffin	50	Peed, Philip	100
McKenny, Presly	50	Payton, Anthony	664
McKenny, Daniel	140	Payne, William	337
page 5		Price, John senr	150
McKenny, John	50	Peirce, Wm decd	100
McKenny, Watlington	27	Price, Meredith	50
McKenny, George	130	Pope, Laurence	469
Middleton, William	890	Payne, George	716
Middleton, Benedict	500	Porter, Edward	200
McClananham, Margaret	150	Porter, William	200
McFarlane, Elizabeth	345	Peirce, Wm Est	655
Middleton, John (Pepham)	235	Pugh, David Est	110
Moore, Thomas	30	Peirce, Joseph	756
Middleton, Jemima	94	Porter, William senr	100
Moore, William	30	Pratt, Elizabeth	60
Middleton, Benjamin	30	Porter, Demsey	115
Moore, Robert	32	Quisenberry, James	263
Middleton, Robert's Estate	140	Quisenberry, Nicholas	283
Moore, Mary	100	Robinson, William	2702
Mullins, Peter	50	Roe, Jemima	174
Moles, Samuel	75	Roe, William	150
Morgan, Daniel	70	Richardson, Jno (Essex)	Lot 1
Minor, John	100	Rudolph, George	Lots 2
Nelson, William	274	Robinson, George	130
Nelson, Mary	106	Rigg, Thomas	100
Nash, George	50	Redmon, Solomon	900
Neale, Presly	310	page 6	
Newton, Milly	100	Rundal, Thomas	144
Neale, Dan¹ Est	300	Rowles, William	50
Newberry, Robert	53	Read, Andrew	525
Norwood, John	39	Robinson, Thos Redman	27
Newton, John Est	190	Redman, Jemima	99
Newton, Willoughby	453	Rochester, John	334

Redman, Stewart	100	Sanford, Margaret	155
Redman, Anne	100	Sanford, William	100
Rouand, Thomas	2625	Sutton, Richard	82
Robinson, John	77	Sutton, James	54
Rice, John	180	page 7	
Rice, William senr	300	Sanford, William	130
Rust, Peter Est	445	Sandy, Urich	150
Rust, Benjamin	200	Sanford, Thomas	200
Rust, Samuel	400	Sutton, William	100
Rust, George	180	Sutton, Jacob	83
Rust, James	140	Steward, Benjamin	89
Rust, Elizabeth	180	Sanford, Reuben	75
Rust, Vincent	551	Self, Stephen junr	86
Rust, John	279	Self, Stephen senr	70
Reux, Daniel	4	Smith, Sarah	30
Strother, Tabitha	67	Smith, Elizabeth	150
Smith, William	230	Sorrell, James	311
Sthreshly, Thomas	400	Scutt, Tho: Est	100
Strother, Benjamin	200	Sowell, Thomas	300
Stone, Francis	100	Smith, Mary	1186
Stocke, William	550	Steptoe, George	1007
Simons, Franklin	150	Smith, Elenor	40
Spark, Alexander	1400	Self, Moses	50
Sanders, William	Lots 2	Self, Polly	50
Strouds, John	Lots 4	Smith, Elizabeth Est	120
Stone, George Est	Lot 1	Settles, Mary	270
Simpson, John	366	Short, John Est	84
Saunders, Cealy	Lots 2	Self, John	100
Smith, Philip Est	1700	Talloferro Jno	859
Smith, Lewis	200	(for Garnett Est)	
Sturman, Hannah	270	Thompson, Margaret	66
Spence, Thomas	350	Thompson, William	200
Sanford, Charles	139	Turner, Thomas	2400
Sanford, Youel	150	Triplett, William	1800
Sanford, Robt Est	130	Triplett, James	200
Stone, Thomas	121	Tully, Matthew	Lot 1
Sanford, Patrick	100	Taylor, John Est	Lot 1
Sanford, Augustine	165	Taite, James	210
Shadrock, Thomas	100	Tharp, Elizabeth	100
Sanford, Edward	670	Thomson, Thomas	900

Templeman, Thomas	154	Washington, William	500
Turberville, John	2198	page 8	
Tidwell, William Carr	330	Whealrol, John	150
Tebbs, William	373	Washington, John	480
Tebbs, Elizabeth	440	Wood, Samuel	240
Turberville, George	599	White, William	100
Washington, A. William	2295	Walker, John	75
Williams, Rachel	120	Wright, Thomas	248
Weedon, George	200	Washington, Thomas	100
Weedon, Mildred	100	Washington, Katy	100
Weedon, John	100	Washington, John	280
Washington, Nathaniel Es	350	Wright, Presly	120
Ward, John	60	Walker, Samuel	340
Washington, Lawrence Jn	500	Washington, Jno Augustine	1200
Weeks, Benjamin	613	Yeatman, John	250

The foregoing is a true Copy of the List of the Lands in the said County as returned by Mess^r Butler and Garner Gent. Commissioners.
July 30, 1782

[Note: It is thought that the lots listed were in Leedstown.]

Transcribed by VLHD

Westmoreland Land Tax Records, 1782, Reel 340, The Library of Virginia, Richmond, VA 23219.

Armistead Family Bible, 1766-1849
Elizabeth City and York Counties

Robert Armistead was Married to Elizabeth Smith January 8th 1789, being in the 23rd year of his age & his wife in the 22nd he was born Augt 9th, 1766 & she was Born Augt 22nd 1767. and died 30 January 1849 aged 81 years and 5 mos & 8 days.
Their Issue, as follows. —

Westwood Smith Armistead was Born June 17th, 1790 on Thursday at about 7 O'Clock in the afternoon (at Back Creek, York Cty).
and departed this life January 25, 1845. [note: deaths recorded at a much later time are in a different handwriting]

Maria Smith Armistead was Born August 18th, 1792 on Saturday about 7 O'Clock in the morning (in Norfolk).

Eliza [space] Armistead was born May 26th 1794 on Monday, about 9 O'Clock in the morning (in Norfolk).

Louisa Young Armistead was born in Hampton, Monday March 20th 1796 about 7 O'Clock Sunday morning and died in July 1832.

Thomas Smith Armistead was born in Hampton March 30th 1799 Saturday evening (at the Mill) in the County of Elizabeth City.

Helen Smith Armistead and Emilly Smith Armistead (Twins) were born at Hampton on Thursday January 22nd 1802 in the Morning and died 20th March 1838.

Susan Smith Armistead was born at Hampton on Sunday July 22nd 1804, at night, and died at Back Creek in York County on Friday the 6th day of September 1805: about 4 O'C afternoon aged 13 months and 15 days/ her death was supposed to be in consequence of the croup. and appeared on the Wednesday before her death.

Harriet [space] Armistead was born at Hampton Tuesday August 26 about 1 O'Clock in the morning in the Year 1806 and died the 2d October 1834.

Robert Augustus Armistead was Born at Hampton on Saturday the 7th day of May in the year 1808 in the morning.

Robert Armistead departed this life about ten o'Clock P.M. on Sunday the 31st of August 1817 aged fifty one years and twenty two days.

Emily S Keeling died on this 1st day of March 1842 in Hampton in the 40th year of her age.

Westwood Smith Armistead and Louisa Moore Todd were married the first day of May 1813. She was born the 8 of November 1794.

Westwood Todd Armistead was born the 26th day January 1814 at about 7 O'Clock P.M. at Smithfield.

[illeg.] Smith Armistead was born at Smithfield [illeg.] 1815. Departed this life [illeg.] same year.

Maria Smith Armistead and Thomas Crawford were married Sunday 28th August 1814 at the Mill. She in the 23rd year and he the 25th year of age.

William Armistead born 18th May 1816 at Hampton about 7 O'Clock P.M.

Nancy Todd Armistead daughter of Westwood and Louisa Armistead was born at Hampton on the 10th day of February 1817 between 11 & 12 O'Clock P.M.

Elizabeth Smith Armistead daughter of Westwood & Louisa Armistead was born at Hampton on the 25 day of July 1818 at about 7 O'Clock P.M.

Emily S. Armistead & John W. Keeling were married on the 30th day of Janry 1825.

Elizabeth Armistead departed this life January 30th 1849 at 6 O'Clock P.M. in Hampton aged 81 years five months and eight days. Transcribed by VLHD.

Ed. note: Westwood Armistead was the clerk of the court for Elizabeth City County for the years from 1810-1840. Rosemary Neal, *Elizabeth City County, Virginia, Deeds, Wills, Court Orders, Etc.* (Bowie, MD: Heritage, 1986) 298.
Armistead Family Bible, Acc. No. 33823, Library of Virginia, Richmond, Virginia.

A List of Free Negroes and Mulattoes, 1833
King and Queen County

A List of Free Negroes and mulattoes in the County of King and Queen this year 1833, their names, ages, place of abode, particular trades, occupations, etc.

The list was found in the Commissioner of Accounts records for King and Queen County and is transcribed here by VLH Davis. While presented in the record in columnar form, each name will be followed with the identifying information conforming to the catagories previously listed. The double underline approximates the underlining that seems to designate family groupings, or individuals not a part of a family group. While the writing is uniform and precise, it is very difficult to read. Interested researchers should consult the original for verification.

Edmund Nelson; male; Chaning G. Hinshaw's (mill tract); Carpenter
Fanny Nelson; female; wife of said Edmund and with him; Spinner
Joshua, Nat;   males
Lucy, Sally,   children of the said Edmund and Fanny & with them
Frances; females
Milly Gown; female; Edmund Nelson's; Spinner
Carter Nelson; male; Henry G. Segar's Land; Carpenter
Sally Nelson; female; wife of said Carter and with him; Spinner
Elizabeth, Mary;   females; children of said
Thos., Wm., Robert; male; Carter and Sally and with them
Betsy Norman; female; Henry G. Segar's land
Peny Norman; male; son of said Betsy, living with Richd H Garnett
John Norman; male; son of said Betsy, living with Henry G. Segar
Geo., Servis, Wm.; males;
Fanny, Sally,   other children of said Betsy and with her
Martha, Mary;   females;
Sarah Roberts; female; Catharine Pendleton's land; Spinner
James Roberts; male; son of said Sarah and living with Saml Gresham
Meredith, Henry; male; sons of said Sarah and living with Wm. Segar
Robert;   male,
Betty;   female; other children of said Sarah and with her
Milly Christian; female; Reuben M. Garnetts (mill tract); Spinner
Arthur, John;   male,
Edmund, Major;   male; children of said Milly and with her
Peggy Christian; female; Reuben M. Garnetts (mill tract); Spinner

William Davis; male;　　Newtown; Blacksmith

Martha Davis; female; wife of William and with him; Spinner

<u>Liston</u>; male; child of Wm and Martha and with them

<u>Pleasant Davis</u>; male with William Davis

Taliaferro Fortune; male; Sudy Cauthorns Mill (Beuleahville)K.W.　　[this added in different handwriting] Miller

Mary Ann Fortune; female; wife of said Taliaferro and with him;　Spinner

Peggy, Jweantha [sic], [female]

Polly;　　female;　children of said Taliaferro & Mary Ann and with them

<u>Walker, Franklin</u>; male

Peter Tuning; male; Smithfield ~~Befriend~~ enfront Corbin's store [sic]

Betsy Tuning; female; wife of said Peter and with him　Paupers

Austin;　　male

<u>Sally, Maria, Eliza</u>;　　　female; children of Peter & Betsy and with them

Lucy Hill; female; Milly Carltons; Spinner

Susie;　　　　female

<u>Tom</u>;　　　　male; children of said Lucy and with her

<u>Caty</u>; female; William Shepherds; House worker

<u>Nancy Cooper</u>; female; Own land; Farming

Wm. Brockenburg; male; Own land; Farming

Judy Brockenburg; female; wife of said William and with him;　　Spinner

Mary, Rebecca;　　female

<u>Albert, Arthur</u>;　　　　male children of William & Judy and with them

Betsy Brockenburg; female; with William Brockenburg; Spinner

<u>John</u>; male; child of said Betsy and with her

<u>Emanuel Hill</u>; male; About Walkerton; Carpenter

Judy Twopence; female; Solomon S. Rilies; Spinner

Missouri, Ellen, Mary;　female

<u>John, Henry</u>;　male;　children of said Judy and with her

Baylor; male; son of said Judy and bound to William Tucks

<u>John Gilmore</u>; male; Own Land; Blacksmith

<u>Ben Gilmore</u>; male; Own Land; Farmer

<u>Richard Gilmore</u>; male; Own Land; Blacksmith

<u>Geo: Gilmore</u>; male; Own Land; Farmer

<u>Richard Gilmore, Jr</u>; male; Own Land; Farmer

Juliet, Betty, Delphia;　　female;

<u>John, Elliott</u>;　male; children of Nancy Gilmore
　　　　　and living with Ben Gilmore

<u>Baylor Oaks</u>; male; Own Land; Farmer

<u>Caly Oaks</u>; female; with Baylor Oaks; Spinner

James Bond; male; John Birds land; Farmer

Beverley, Phil, Uriah, Alfred; male;

Hannah, Mary, Safronia; female; children of James and with him

John Bond; male; son of James Bond and with Geo. K. Carlton

William Delwor; male; Henry Greshams Land; Farmer

Hannah Delwor; female; wife of side William and with him; Spinner

Geo. Kauffman; male; James Mitchells Estate; Farmer

Polly Kauffman; female; wife of said George and with him; Spinner

Isbosta, Mary; female;

James, John; male; children of said George and Polly and with them

Salana Day; male; about the Courthouse; Farming & Ditching

Betty Hill; female; William Garnetts Estate; Spinner

Sally; female; daughter of said Betty and with Kitt Lockley

John; male; son of said Betty and with her

Sally Lockley; female; with Baylor Oaks; Spinner

Fanny, Betty; female;

John; male; children of Sally and with her

Eliza Roberts; female; William C. Courtney; Spinner

Emaly; female; child of Eliza and with her

Jenny; female; William C. Courtney; Spinner

John; male; child of said Jenny and with her

Polly; female; children of Free Barbara

Tom, Frank; male; and bound to William C. Courtney

William; male; another son of Free Barbara and bound to
　　　　　Thos. M. Jeffries

John Davis; male; William Temples land; Blacksmith

Maria Davis; female; wife of said John and with him; Spinner

Mary Davis; female;

Andrew, Norman; male; children of said John & Maria and with them

Thornton Bower; male; living with John Davis

Otway Samson; male; living with John Davis

Jack Barley; male; on William Temples land with John Davis; Farming

Jinny Barley; female; wife of said Jack and with him; Spinner

Sarah; female;

Jos., Thomas; male; children of said Jack and Jinny and with them

Betty Lockley; female; Richard Gilmores land; Spinner

Tom; male;

Lucy; female; children of said Betty and with her

Oney Forton; male; bound to John W. Robinson

Albert Forton; male; bound to William Garnett

110

Martha Forton; female; bound to John Redd
Mary Forton; female; about the Courthouse
Betty Twopence; female; Geo. B. Poindexter; Spinner
Mary;   female;
John, Geo., Tom;   male; children of said Betty and with her
Servis Hill; male; James Mitchells Estate; Carpenter
Charles Hill; male; Thomas Edwards; Farming, etc.
Ransome Harris; male; about Hartquake; Farming, etc.
Fanny Gilmore; female; Own land; Farming, etc.
Hannah, Elizabeth;   female;
James;   male; children of Fanny and with her
Aliza Gilmore; female; on Fanny Gilmores land; Farming, etc.
Patty Ham; female; Tho. Richesons land; Spinner
Henry Ham; male; with Patty Ham; Farming, etc.
Penelope Ham; female; with William Brockenburg; Spinner
Agnes Ham; female; with Shadrack Ham; Spinner
Roberta Ham; female; living with Catherine Eubank
Randal Ham; male; Itinerant
Dandridge Ham; male; Itinerant
Shadrack Ham; male; Tho. Richesons land ; Carpenter
Davy Ham; male; bound to Carlton Pollard & Co at the Courthouse
James Lockley; male; bound to Daniel Watts; Farming, etc.
Major Lockley; male; bound to John W. Hillgard
Lucy Collins; female; Thomas Simpsons land; Spinner
Eliza Collins; female; with Lucy Collins; Spinner
Elizabeth; female; child of said Eliza and with her
Nancy Campbell; female; with Lucy Collins
Susan, Betty; female; children of Nancy and with her
Polly Lockley, Jr; female; living with Shadrack Ham
Polly Bluefoot; female; John Southgates land; Spinner
Betty; female;
James, Phil;   male; children of said Betty
William; male; another son of said Betty and bound to James Southgate
Harriott Bluefoot; male; living with Franky Johnson
Bitey Bluefoot; male; bound to John Southgate
Ransom Harris, Jr; male; Own Land; Farmer
Betty Harris; female; wife of said Ranson and with him; Spinner
Mary, Lucy, Ethaline;   female; children of said Betty before her marriage
Walker, Cornelius, Otway;   male;   with Ransom and with them

Bob Mitchell; male; Daniel Watts land; Farmer
Kitt Lockley; male; John Carlton (miller); Farmer
Polly Lockley; female; wife of said Kitt and with him; Spinner
Grace Mitchell; female; Own land; Farming
John R. Robinson; male; Ditcher
Lorenzo, Dew; male; sons of Grace Mitchell and with her; Farming
Geo. Robinson; male; ditto
Peggy Robinson;   female; daughters of Grace Mitchell
Rose Robinson;   female;   and with her
Sam Kauffman; male; George Cardwells land; Farmer
Lucy Kauffman; female; wife of said Sam and with him; Spinner
George Kauffman; male; son of said Sam & Lucy and with Kitt Lockley
Euclid, James, John;   male; children of said Sam and Lucy
Parks & Polly;   female;   and with them
Jenny Sea; female; Beverly Waltons Estate; Spinner
Margaret, Ann;   female; children of said Jenny and with her
John, Walker, Is.;   male; ditto
William; male; son of Jenny and living with Ransom Harris, Jr
Jemy Day; male; Beverly Waltons Estate; Ditcher
Betty Day; female; wife of said Jemy and with him; Spinner
Caty Carter; female; Isaac Waltons; Spinner
Polly, Grace, Hetty;   female; children of said Caty and with her
John, Nat, William;   male; ditto
Patty Freeman; female; with Ann Fleet; Spinner
Jinand; male; son of said Patty and living with Wm B. Fleet
Daniel, Telemaishus & Lornzo;   male;   children of said Patty
Polly;   female;   and living with her
Sally Kidd; female; New Church; Farming
John Kidd; male; son of Sally and with her; Farming
William Kidd; male; ditto
Polly Kidd; female; Paul Phillips land; Wood cutting
Maria, Sarah, Polly, Elizabeth;   female; children of Polly
James;   male;   and living with her
Elizabeth Kidd; female; on Henry Wares Land (Very old)
Humphrey Kidd; male; George Morris Land; Farming
Peter Meggs; male; about Centerville; Ditcher, etc.
Mariah Hickman; female; Vincent Harts Estate; Spinner
Mary;   female; children of said Maria
Tom, James; male;   and with her
Hannah Williams; female; Frank Kidds

Betty Davenport; female; William Newcombs Estate; Spinner
George, Tom;   male;   children of said Betty
John, Emanuel;   male;   and with her
Emanuel Chapman; male; Rachel Brisbanes Land; Shoemaker
Caty; female; daughter of said Emanuel and with him
Willis Gouldman; male; Owns land; Farmer
Milly Gouldman; female; Owns land; Spinner
Martin Gouldman; male; Milly Gouldman; Farmer
Rachael Gouldman; female; wife of said Martin and with him; Spinner
Polly, Lavinia, Nancy;   female; children of said Martin & Rachael
Ralph, Jim;   male;   and with them
George Gouldman; male; Elizabeth Crittendens; Farmer
Nancy Gouldman; female; wife of said George and with him; Spinner
Betsy, Sally, Pinkie; female; children of said George and Nancy, with them
Keziah Lockley; female; Willis Gouldmans land; Spinner
Polly Duval; female; Henry Cookes; Spinner
Henry Wickons; female; on the land formerly Mary Roanes; Spinner
Wm, Ben, James, John, Richd;   male;   children of Henny
Mary;   female; and with her
Wm Bluefoot; male; Edward Garretts Land; Farming, etc.
Betty Bluefoot; female; wife of William and with him; Spinner
Lucy, Sally;   female;   children of William and Betty
Julia, Elizabeth;   female;   and with them
John, James;   male;   ditto
George Keys; male; Geo: D. Turmans Land; Ditcher
Jane Keys; female; wife of said Geo: and with him; Spinner
Betty Keys; female; living with Geo: Keys
Henry Bluefoot; male; bound to William Brown Do
Tom Hill; male; Tho. Simpkins land; Farming
Matilda Hill; female; wife of said Tom and with him; Spinner
Grace Harris; female; Thomas Simpkins land; Farming, etc.
Fanny, Mary, Grace, Judy;   female;
Ben, Armistead, Zachery;   male; children of Grace and with her
Caan, William, Tom; male
Sally Kauffman; female; with Grace Harris
Moses Kidd; male; about Centerville; Carpenter
Frank Kidd; male; Owns Land; Farming
Sam Kidd; male; Owns Land; Farming
Kitty Kidd; female; wife of said Sam and with him; Spinner
Polly, Lucy, Nancy, Frances;   female;

Lavinia, Esperella, Pinkey, Elmira; female; children of Sam and Kitty
George, John; male; and with them
Daniel Lockley; male; Major Wallers Land; Farmer
Rachel Lockley; female; wife of Daniel and with him; Spinner
Mary; female; children of Daniel and Rachel
Jim, Billy, Henry; male; and with them
Ralph Gouldman; male; Peter Albright; Shoemaker
Ben Gouldman; male; Peter Albright; Farmer
Jim Chever; male; Peter Albright; Mill Wright
Daphney Douglass; female; Richard Taliaferros (Mt. Landing); Spinner
Rachel; female; children of Daphney
Henry; male; and with her
William Douglass; male; Thomas Edwards Do; Farmer
Ephriam Hundley; male; John Atkins Land; Blacksmith
Milly Hundley; female; wife of said Ephriam and with him; Spinner
George, John; male; children of said Ephriam and Milly and with them
Scipio; male; Richard Taliaferros land; Oysterman
Betty Williams; female; William W. Spencers land; Spinner
Eliza, Elizabeth; female; children of said Betty
George, Edmund; male; and with her
Becky Williams; female; John P. Tuckers land; Spinner
Jane, Mary; female; children of said Becky and with her
Servis Chapman; male; Richard Crittendens land; Farmer
Nancy Bluefoot; female; with Servis Chapman; Spinner
Mary, Louisa, Betty; female; children of said Nancy
Thomas; male; and with her
William Samson; male; Servis Smiths
Betsy Lockley; female; William B. Boyds land; Spinner
Julia, Kitty; female; children of said Betsy
Walker; male; and with her
Fanny Lockley; female; with Betty Lockley; Spinner
Milly Jackson; female; Own Land; Spinner
Betty; female; daughter of said Milly and with her; Spinner
Nelson Jackson; male; son of said Milly and with her; Farming
James Jackson; male; son of said Milly and with her; Ditching
Nancy Jackson; female; with Milly Jackson; Spinner
Frances, Mary; female; children of said Nancy
Geo Ranson; male; and with her
Cedar Jackson; male; Geo. Cardwells; Ditcher
Milly Jackson; female; wife of said Cedar and with him; Spinner

Polly Dungon; female; Thomas Edwards land; Farming
Nancy;   female;   children of said Polly
George;   male;   and with her
Thomas Collins; male; Thomas F. Spencers land; Sawyer
Nancy Collins; female; wife of said Thomas and with him; Spinner
Fitshura, Cordelia;   female; children of said Thomas and Nancy
John;   male;   and with them
Riley Collins; male; Thomas Spencers land; Sawyer
Lucy Collins; female; wife of said Riley and with him; Spinner
Ann, Lucy;   female;   children of said Riley and Lucy
Wm., Rs., Riley;   male;   and with them
Nancy Lockley; female; William Hughes land; Spinner
Mary, Ann, Jane;   female; children of said Nancy
Willis;   male;   and with her
Frank Meggs; male; Mason Collins land; Ditcher
Polly Meggs; female; wife of said Frank and with him; Spinner
Robert, James; male; children of said Frank and Polly and with them

[signed] John Pollard Comr.
May 1st 1833

A Copy from the original John Pollard

Taken from the Commissioner of Accounts, Virginia State Records, The Library of Virginia, Richmond, VA.

Henrico County Will Book 1, 1781-1787

Transcribed by Dr. Benjamin B. Weisiger, III
Contributed by Minor T. Weisiger

Continued from Volume 7, Number 1, page 47.

The entries from the Henrico Will Book 1, 1781-1787, as abstracted by Dr. Benjamin B. Weisiger (1924-1995), ended with page 199. His abstractions of county records were both meticulous and prolific. Your editor has continued the abstraction of this will book, hopefully, as accurately as Dr. Weisiger. These records, continuing, will be a feature of Tidewater Virginia Families: A Magazine of History and Genealogy to the completion of Will Book 1.

Abstracts of the wills following give the page number in the will book on which the will is first entered. Names are entered in bold using the format of Dr. Weisiger. (VLHD)

p.255 Will of **Samuel Ford, Senr.** co of Henrico, "sick in body, sound & perfect memory".
To son **Culbert (Cuthbert) Ford** plantation next to **Mr. James Brittains** with 50 acres land.
To dear & loving wife **Susannah Ford** plantation where I live during life then to son **William Ford.**
To daughter **Lucy Ford** items.
Horse Dick & mare Dimond for use of both plantations.
Wife rest of estate during life then divided equally among children.
Executors: 3 sons **Culbert, Samuel, & John Ford.**   6 Sept 1785
                                                                                        signed **Saml X Ford**
Witnesses: **Francis Cornett, Thos. Thorp, Nancy Lucas**
Proved: **Francis Cornett, Nancy Lucas;** motion **Cuthbert Ford, Samuel Ford.**
Securities: **Thomas Prosser, George Melton.**
8 Nov 1785 (**Mr. Graves** house)   **Adam Craig** Clerk Court

p.256 Inventory of estate of **Samuel Ford** the Elder, dec'd.
Magistrate **Thomas Prosser, Gent.**
Appraisers **Lamuel(?) Ford, Samuel Britton, Francis Cornett.** value £71/4/9.
Returned 5 Dec 1785

p.257 Inventory of estate of **Wm Farris** dec'd. 14 Negroes.
Submitted by **William Farris**, executor, no value given.
Returned 5 Dec 1785

p.258 Inventory of estate of **Robert Baine**, 25 Apr 1785,
62 books, value £721/12.
Appraisers **Alex Rosse, Samuel Williamson, Jesse Smith.**
Returned 5 Dec 1785

p.263 Inventory of estate of **Robin Povall** dec'd. £2111/8/6
Negroes: Sam, Dilce, Sal, Judy & child, Emanuel, Abram, Charles, Watt,
Simon, Moses, Lucy, Chever, Fanny, Frank, Betty, Nancy, Milly, Isham, Will,
Sally, Ned, Isaac, Scott, Dick, Betsey, Samuel, Charles, Jacob & Letty.
Appraisers **John Stagg, Richard Sharp, Wm Gathright.**
Recorded 5 Dec 1785

p.265 Inventory of estate of **Peter Clarke** dec'd. appraised 2 Dec 1785
Negro man Porter; items; no value on estate
Appraisers **Ben Johnson, Michael Johnson, David Bowler**
Returned 5 Dec 1785

p.267 Estate of **Joseph Bailey** dec'd. with **Joseph Bailey, Jr.** executor.
value £1503/1/10. Returned **John Pleasants, Bowler Cocke**
returned 5 Dec 1785   **Adam Craig** Clerk Court

p.269 Inventory effects of **Thomas Bentley** dec'd. 12 May 1785
value £107/16/4 Appraisers **Wm Hay, Stephen Hollingsworth**
Recorded 5 Jan 1786

p.272 Will of **John Carter** parish & co of Henrico "perfect senses & sound
memory".
To son **Theoderick Carter** 20 sh.
To son **John Carter** that part of land in Henrico Co he now lives on, on White
Oak Swamp adj. **Anselm Gathright** 200 acres, Negro James.
To daughter **Francis (Frances) Walton** 20 sh.
To son **William Carter** remaining part of land adj. **William Carter** & son **Jacob
Carter's** land 100 acres, Negro Davy.
To son **Sherwood Carter** Negro Moll
To granddaughter **Betsy Gannaway Carter** (daughter of **Jacob & Mary Carter**)
3 Negroes: Sall & her 2 children, Mary Ann and Effie.

117

To **Betsy Carter** daughter of **John & Ann Carter** Negro boy John.

Two Negroes Rachel & Alsam & residue of estate to be sold & divided between four sons: **John Carter, William Carter, Sherwood Carter, Jacob Carter.** Four sons executors. 1 Dec 1785

signed **John Carter**

Witnesses: **Matthew Hobson, Julius Allen, Anselm Gathright**
Proved: **Matthew Hobson, Anselm Gathright,** motion **William Carter**
Securities: **Matthew Hobson, Anselm Gathright**
Recorded 2 Jan 1786 Henrico Courthouse

p.274 Will of **John Lockley** City of Richmond "good health, sound mind & memory".

To sister **Deborah Lowder** of City of London, except as mentioned to her son **Robert Lowder** of Southampton in Great Britian, both real & personal property.

To brother **Richard Lockley** of Norfolk in Virginia £20.

Executors **Mr. Francis Graves, Mr. Gabriel Galt** 16 Aug 1785

signed **J Lockley**

Witnesses: **A McRobert, John V Kuntzman, John Roper**
Proved: **Alexander McRobert,** motion **Francis Graves, Gabriel Galt**
Securities: **Dabney Miller, John Roper** Recorded 6 Feb 1786

p.275 Estate appraised **Fredk. Childress,** dec'd. To brother **Richard Lockley** of Norfolk in Virginia no value given

Appraisers **John Redford, Henry Jordan, Jackson Frazer**
Recorded 6 Feb 1786

p.276 Estate of **Francis Albertie,** dec'd. in acct with **John Pryor,** adm. Value £29/15. Account examined by **W. Barnet, F. Webb, Jr., A. Daviscomb.**
6 Feb 1786.

p.277 **Joseph Brown,** parish & Co of Henrico, "sick but in perfect sense & memory".

To beloved wife, **Jane Brown,** land and plantation where I live.

Items and Negro girl Judah, wife's death land to go to son, **Daniel Brown.** to **Daniel** items, if he die then to son **William; William,** items. Son, **Lewis** Items. Negro girl, Judah's increase to sons to **William, John & Daniel. William & John** £2, **Daniel,** £1. **William & Daniel** Executors. 20 Oct 1785.

signed **Joseph Brown**

Witnesses: **William Alley**

Elizabeth X Kelley
Susaner X Bridgewater
Recorded Henrico Courthouse 6 Feb 1786. Proved by **Elizabeth Kelley,**
Susanner Bridgewater.

p.278 **Julius Allen,** Henrico, "sick & weak, perfect sense & memory"
Item to loving wife, 3 Negroes, man named little Tom, woman Dinah &
Hanner's child Nan.
To wife in lieu of dower, items and stock, and she to pay **Joseph, Sarah &**
Martha Watson cattle, etc. To wife labor of Negro Cuff, then to son, **John**
Allen. To her land at Allen's Creek in right of her former dower. £2 to wife.
Items to son **Julius,** tract he lives on 292½ acres from Powhite tract, adj. to
Anthony Matthews, John Raglin & Thomas Bethel; five Negroes Will, Joe,
Nan, Doll & Little Janey.
Items to son, **David & John Allen,** parcel land Chickahominy Swamp, between
Swamp and new road 1000 acres. **David** to have 2 lower plantations and mill.
John to have plantation and house where I now live, divided by crossing place
to Millers Island.
Items to **Charles Allen** remainder of land I live on 600 acres also house and lot
in town of Richmond, No. 52. Also remainder of Powhite land, Negroes Sam,
Frank, Watt, Cochenor & Delphia.
Items to brother **Littleberry Allen** land 75 acres, part of larger tract from father
Edmund Allen.
Items to **David Allen,** Negroes Bob, Little Will, Dennis, Phillis & Dilce.
To son **John Allen,** Negroes Old Tom, Rachel, Violet, Little Phillis and Sall.
To daughter, **Elizabeth M Allen,** Negroes Little Sam, Phillis's daughter Dorcas,
Janey, Patience and Sue.
Items to son **Julius,** £25 per annum during life of **Henry Winfrey.**
Rest of estate divided among all children.
Executors **Samuel Price, Miles Selden, Jr.** and son, **Julius Allen.**
4 Apr 1777.   signed **Julius Allen**
Witnesses: **James Sharpe, Gideon Howle, Benjamin Morris**
Recorded June Henrico Court 1777.
Presented by **Julius Allen, Samuel Price** and **Miles Seldon, Jr.**
Proved by **James Sharpe, Benj. Morris**, security.
A Copy by **William White** D C County. Will Recorded 5 Mar 1786, original
destroyed by the enemy.   **Adam Craig**

p.282 **John Hales,** Parish & co of Henrico, "perfect senses and sound memory".

Imprimis, lend to wife **Elizabeth Hales** part of land I live on, White Oak Swamp to **Benjamin Harrison**'s line; ½ personal property lent to go to four children, **John Hales, Jr., Samuel Hales, Elizabeth Clopton, Nancy Hales.**
Item to **John Hales, Jr.** ½ land I live on, also other half at mother's death.
Item to **Samuel Hales** 600 acres, Negroes to be divided between four children.
Executors: **Richard Sharp, John Pleasants, George Woodson** and **William Carter.**
18 Oct 1785   **John Hales**
Witnesses: **Julius Allen, James Binford, William Binford**
Recorded Henrico 6 Mar 1786.
Proved by **Julius Allen, James Binford**
Securities: **Richard Sharpe, Pleasant Younghusband** and **Reuben Coutts.**

p.284 Appraisal of estate **John Carter**, dec'd. **Anselm Gathright, William Gathright** and **Matthew Hobson.** 6 Mar 1786.

p.286 Estate of **Robert Duval**, dec'd. in account with **Turner Southall.**
Value £537/15/9. Returned by **Thos. Prosser, Dan L. Hylton** and **William Hay.**
6 Mar 1786.

p.290 Inventory of estate of **Isaac Woodcock**, dec'd. Appraised by **John Hague, Francis Ratcliff** and **A.M. Robert.** Value £63/4/6.
Returned 26 Feb 1786. 6 Mar 1786.

p.291 Will of **Joshua Storrs** of Henrico Co merchant, "sound sense and memory".
Imprimis, land and plantation where I live to be possessed jointly by wife **Susanna** and son **Gervas Storrs**, then whole to son.
Item to son **Gervas** tenement on north side of Main Street in town of Richmond, profits to his maintenance.
Item to two daughters, **Hannah** and **Susanna Storrs** tenement on south side, street opposite that to **Gervas.**
Item personal property ½ to wife, ½ to be equally divided among children.
Item free Negroes Dick, Jiles and Syms. To provide their livelihood, give them to **Robert Pleasants, John Crew, James Ladd** and **Gerrard Ellyson** for purpose above mentioned. Henrico Monthly Meeting to provide persons for this purpose.
Item son **Gervas** to be sent to **Gervas** and **Mary Storrs** in Leedstown, England to be educated.

Executors: **James Pleasants, Edmund Stabler, Peter Lyons** and **Joseph Pleasants.**

18 day 10 mo. 1779.   signed **Joshua Storrs**

Witnesses: **Martin Burton, Samuel Bridgewater, Moore Bell, Pat Spencer, John Pleasants, Samuel Parsons.** Recorded Dec 1779.

Proved by **Martin Burton, Samuel Bridgewater** and **Moore Bell.**

Security: **Joseph Pleasants.**   **William White** Clerk

Re-Recorded 8 Mar 1786. Original Recorded destroyed by the enemy.

Adam Craig Clerk.

Thomas Prosser administrator with the will annexed.

p.293 **John Kent**, dec'd. Appraisal of estate. Negroes Nan, Sall. Value £343/18. Appraisers: **Bowler Cocke, William Gathright, George Williams, Jr.** Returned 3 Apr 1786.

p.296 Inventory of estate **John Wales**, dec'd. Negroes Neptune, Charles, Frank, Rachel and child, Amey, Clarkey, Grace, Dinah, Bess and child, Frances, Rachel, Harry and Jack. Value £1196/14/11½. Appraisers: **George Baker, William Gathright, Anselm Gathright.** 6 June 1786.

p.299 Will of **William Gathright**, Henrico Co, "perfect sense and memory".

Item to loving wife ½ estate.

Item to **John Spear** Negro Abram.

Item to **Robert Spear** Negro Ned.

Item to **William Gathright,** son of brother **Samuel Gathright**, Negro Sook.

Item to **Thomas Gathright,** son of brother **Samuel Gathright**, Negro Tom.

Item to sister **Ann Gathright** during lifetime, Negro Amey and sister not be depossessed of place she lives on.

Item to son **Samuel Gathright** ½ estate and then part left to wife at her death. If he dies, then to children of brother, **Samuel.**

Executors: **Samuel Goode, John Spear, William Gathright,** son of **Samuel.**

26 Mar 1786   signed **William Gathright**

Witnesses: **John Ferris, Robert Allen, Micajah X Bottoms.**

Recorded 5 June 1786. Proved by **Robert Allen, Micajah Bottoms, Samuel Goode, William Gathright.**

Securities: **Reuben George, Jr., John Pleasants, Matthew Hobson.**

Adam Craig, Clerk.

p.301 Will of **Richard Randolph** of Curles in Henrico Co, "sick and weak but sound mind".

Imprimis to loving wife **Anne** for life, use of land and plantation calles *Curles* with Negroes: Moses, Ned, Lewis, Ned Hawk, Will, Peny, Ben:, Wilden:, Billy Cooper, Ampey, Blenham, Neptune, Minge, Gardner Tom, Waggener Tom, House Peter, Milan, Jesse, Morocco, Sabina, Isbell, Nanny, Penny, Sukey, Betty, Lucinda, Sally the Cook, Sally and her husband Ben, boy Ben, boy George, boy Joe, boy Syphax, boy Arthur, boy My Tiller(?), boy Jimmy, Betty Moracco and Aggy.

To wife chariot and horse and items. Maintenance of younger children until they arrive at age.

Item to son **Richard Randolph** what was left to wife at her death.

Item to son **Brett Randolph** land and plantation called *Sandy Ford* in counties of Cumberland and Prince Edward, except mill and 50 acres, 40 Negroes including Peter and Monroe.

Item son **Ryland Randolph** tract of land *Clover Forest*, Cumberland Co, also land and plantation in Chesterfield Co opposite *Curles*, 40 Negroes and Milan and Jenny. Mill at *Sandy Ford* in Prince Edward Co with 50 acres.

Item to sons **Richard** and **David** Negro blacksmith Lewis and Ned Hawk.

Item to daughter **Anne Randolph** Negroes, Judy, Nelly and two children of Judy, Dick, Calie and her children Edmund Corsey, Dick, Sukey and Betty, boy Peter. £20.

Item to daughters **Elizabeth, Sarah** and **Mary** twelve Negroes each £20 each when they arrive of age.

Item Negroes Sylvia and Philip Alexander, children of Aggy and Billy Davis son of Lucinda be set free with express condition they do not claim legacy from estate of my brother **Edmund Randolph**. Debt of £6000 due me from estate of dec'd. brother **Ryland Randolph** securing payment I have right to tract called *Turkey Island* by way of mortgage, this to son **Brett Randolph** (for further provisos in disposition of above, see original will).

(further requirements concerning debt of brother **Ryland Randolph**).

Item to son **David Randolph** tract called *Elams* in Chesterfield 130 acres.

Item to worthy kinsman Miss **Jane Eldridge** £100.

Item to kinsman Mr. **John Eldridge** £100.

Recorded 3 July 1786   signed **Richard Randolph**
Witnesses: **Jerman Baker, James Currie, Henry Randolph, Th. Blodget**
Proved by **James Currie, Henry Randolph.**   **Adam Craig** clerk

To be concluded

BOOK REVIEWS:

Elizabeth R. Varon, *We Mean to Be Counted, White Women and Politics in Antebellum Virginia.* x, 234 pp., index, notes, paper. 1998. $16.95, cloth $45.00, plus $3.50 ship. The impression has prevailed that Southern women were pampered, submissive and genteel homemakers. While women did not have the prerogatives of voting, office holding and public speaking, they were informed and intelligent participants in making their political views known and in forming public opinion. They formed benevolent societies and were able to influence even legislation in this manner. They wrote books, pamphlets and made their views known. As the north and south became more divergent in their views, the women assumed even more influence through their participation in writing and even in assemblage, with the men. The author has copiously documented her work, and has drawn upon a wide range of materials in drawing her conclusions. Extant letters, diaries, articles, books and newspaper accounts were examined and a comprehensive account of the recognition of women as a viable force emerges. The author follows the emergence of women as political persons, though disenfranchised, through the period of session and the subsequent War and into the Reconstruction. Well-written and a real contribution for understanding the role of women in the culture of Virginia. The names of many of these women will also be of interest to tidewater researchers. University of North Carolina Press, P O Box 2288, Chapel Hill, NC 27515-2288.

Henry C. Peden, Jr., *Revolutionary Patriots of Charles County, Maryland, 1775-1783.* 332 pp., alphabetical, paper. 1997. $29.50, inc ship. This is an excellent research tool for locating the men and women of Charles County, Maryland who served in the miliary, rendered material aid to the army or navy, took the Oath of Allegiance and Fidelity, served as an officer or on a committee at the town, county, or state level; or in some way made a contribution and supported the fight for freedom for the American colonies during the Revolutionary War, 1775-1783. Each entry in the book has been documented and a key provided to that documentation, as indicated by each name. #T1379. Family Line Publications, Rear 63 E Main St, Westminster, MD 21157.

John H. Gwathmey, *Twelve Virginia Counties, Where the Western Migration Began.* 469 pp., illus., index, cloth. (1937) rep 1997. $30.00, plus $3.50 ship. Presents the counties of Albemarle, Augusta, Caroline, Essex, Gloucester, Goochland, Hanover, King William, King and Queen, Louisa, New Kent and Orange. While this book was written in 1937 and in some cases additional information has come to light about the places and persons described, it is well-written and provides a good anecdotal account of pioneers, early settlers, homes, land and landowners, statesmen and other citizens of note, that may not be found together elsewhere, especially in those counties where records have been lost. Very readable, with genealogical information, and with detailed accounts of people and events beginning in the colonial period of these counties. #2435. Genealogical Publishing Co, 1001 N Calvert St, Baltimore, MD 21202.

Cyndi Howells, *Netting Your Ancestors, Genealogical Research on the Internet*. 182 pp., index, glossary, illus., paperback. 1997. $19.95, plus $3.50. Cyndi Howells is the creator of the web site *Cyndi's List of Genealogy Sites*, the first place genealogical and family researchers are advised to search. It is the most powerful research tool available for family history researchers, with world wide sources made available. Cyndi is a computer whiz, an award winner and provider of excellent resource information, not only with her web site, but with her how-to book. She answers fundamental questions about getting started and goes on to help the researcher best utilize online time. Her book focuses on the three most useful components of the Internet: E-mail, Mailing Lists and Newsgroups, and the World Wide Web. Her research strategies are helpful to the novice and computer sophisticate alike. The ability to explore information and new databases on a global scale is astounding. There is no wonder that her book has become the most-sought after and the genealogical "Best Seller" for many months. #2931. Genealogical Publishing Co, 1001 N Calvert St, Baltimore, MD 21202.

CDs AVAILABLE: System requirements: must have a CD-ROM drive, and in order to read the CDs you must use either *Family Tree Maker* **version 3.02 or higher or the** *Family Archive Viewer*, **version 3.02 or higher, which is free with the purchase of any of the CDs offered here.**

CD-ROM: *Family History; Virginia Genealogies #1, pre-1600 to 1900s. Family Archive Viewer* **free upon request** (see above). Presenting the genealogies of Virginia families from the *Virginia Magazine of History and Biography*, originally published in 5 volumes by the Genealogical Publishing Co. This is the modern age, and this is the way to search for and retrieve information quickly about these families. The images are digitally reproduced, so that the pages from the 5 volumes are as originally published, they just take up considerably less library space and are readily available. Although additional information has been found in recent years, these articles from the *VMHB* have become the starting point of research in many family lines. $39.95, plus $3.50 ship. #7162. Genealogical Publishing Co, 1001 N Calvert St, Baltimore, MD 21202.

CD-ROM: *The Compendium of American Genealogy, 1600s-1800s. Family Archive Viewer* **free upon request** (see above). (this CD not recommended for viewing with *Family Tree Maker for Macintosh* Version 3.02). The 2 CDs are comprised of the *Genealogical Encyclopedia of the First Families of America* by Frederick A. Virkus with images of the pages of all 7 volumes of the Compendium. The work of Mr. Virkus has been considered the most famous work in the field of genealogy in his compilation of the lineages of the first families of America. He extended his lines from their arrival in this country to the time of his compilation, the early 1940s. While one must confirm the information with recently discovered and researched records (the genealogies were not compiled by professionals), it is a valuable resource and convenient to use. $49.95, plus $3.50 ship. #7200. Genealogical Publishing Co, 1001 N Calvert St, Baltimore, MD 21202.

Genealogical Publishing Co, add $1.25 each add. item.

T.L.C. Genealogy, *Middlesex County, Virginia, Court Orders, 1711-1713.* 152 pp., index, soundex, 8½ x 11, spiral bound, soft cover. 1997. $15.00, postpaid. This book offers detailed abstracts of all of the entries in the first 117 pages of the Middlesex County Court Order Book No 5. Many of the entries are more detailed than generally found in court order books. It provides not only information about wills probated, administrations of estates, but who served on juries and the legal cases involved. It also serves as a directory of the residents of the county. Because of the variant spelling of surnames the soundex is a welcome addition in identifying individuals. T.L.C. Genealogy, PO Box 403369, Miami Beach, FL 33140-1369.

Wesley E. Pippenger, *District of Columbia Ancestors, A Guide to Records in the District of Columbia.* 125 pp., index, maps, 8½ x 11, paper. 1997. $17.50, plus $2.50 ship. The history of the District of Columbia began in the 1790s, and represented a large geographic and cultural area as they established the nation's capitol. In this guide various sources of records and repositories are presented and described for the researcher. The usual census records, city directories, land records, church records, cemetery records and vital records are included. Court records consist of: wills, guardianship, estate administrations, district court records and land records, real and personal property tax records. #1334. Family Line Publications, Rear 63 East Main St, Westminster, MD 21157.

John Otto Yurechko, *Virginians Along and Near the Lower Rappahannock River, 1607-1799,* vol 1. 336 pp., index, 4,200 names, gazetteer, glossary, sources, paper. 1997. $30.50, inc ship. Presenting the families of Blake, Brooks (Brook), Churchill, Cook (Cock), Daniel, Dixon, Gore, Kidd, Lewis, Martin, Montague, Taylor and Wood; and the counties of Caroline, Essex, including Old Rappahannock, Gloucester, Middlesex, James City, King and Queen, Mathews, York and the Northern Neck. This is a sequential compilation of entries (by type of record) of deeds, wills, marriages, deaths, etc. from both primary and secondary sources that pertain to each of the families listed about. The book can be used as a handy reference for further research. #T1433. Family Line Publications, Rear 63 E Main St, Westminster, MD 21157.

Marsha Martin, *Abstracts of Alleghany County, Virginia Deeds, 1822-1829.* vol. 1, xi, 98 pp., index, maps, paper. 1997. $10.50, inc ship. These abstracts are from Alleghany County Deed Book 1 and provide information about locations of property as well as family relationships. Names of children, given names of wives, guardians and other relationships discovered, as well as the names of slaves entered in the record in the same manner as deeds. #T1383. Family Line Publications, Rear 63 E Main St, Westminster, MD 21157.

Carolyn L. Barkley, *Princess Anne County, Virginia Marriage Bonds, 1822-1850.* 227 pp., index, paper. 1997. This book in abstracting the marriage bonds of Princess Anne County begins where the careful work of Elizabeth Wingo (*Marriages of Princess Anne County, 1749-1821, vol. 1 and 1799-1821, vol. 2*) ends. The names of the grooms are presented alphabetically, with names of brides, parents, guardians and securities indexed. Ministers' returns are not included but can be found in the Circuit Court Clerk's Office, in what is now the city of Virginia Beach. $19.00, plus $3.00 ship. Willow Bend Books, 39475 Tollhouse Rd, Lovettsville, VA 20180-1817.

Margie G. Brown, *Genealogical Abstracts Revolutionary War Veterans Scrip Act 1852.* xxv, 463, index, paper. (1990) rep 1997. $32.00, plus $4.00 ship. Abstracted from the Bureau of Land Management, Record Group 49, National Archives and Records Administration. By Legislative Act, Virginia yielded all of her lands northwest of the Ohio River under the condition that if this was not sufficient to honor previously granted bounties then land between the Scioto and Miami rivers would also be used to honor these bounty awards. This book is an abstraction of the genealogical information from each of these bounty applications under this act. County of origin and other pertinent information of the veteran is included, and many times several generations of descendants who were considered heirs to the bounty land are identified. New name index and county level place name index have been compiled. Willow Bend Books, 39475 Tollhouse Rd, Lovettsville, VA 20180-1817.

June Banks Evans, *Hanover County, Virginia, Will Book 1, Circuit Court, 1862-1895; Will Book 1, 1862-1868.* 107 pp., index, paper. 1997. $18.00. Since the earlier records of Hanover County were destroyed by fire, these records provide the best account of the wills and estates of the county residents. Some copies of wills were brought in and re-recorded, some were deposed, hence the range of dates from this will book. In many cases this is the only link in the records to an earlier generation. Estates are listed and estate values recorded; the names of purchasers at estate sales are listed, but items offered are not. Mrs. Banks is familiar with the names of the inhabitants and is an accurate abstracter and transcriber, but has said that working with microfilm makes reading initials difficult. The researcher may want to consult census records to confirm these. #HWB1. Bryn Ffyliaid Publications, Lake Marina Tower, 16BW, 300 Lake Marina Dr, New Orleans, LA 70124-1676.

Dr. Stephen E. Bradley, Jr., *The 1860 Federal Census Mathews County, Virginia (All Schedules).* 150 pp., indexes, 8½ x 11, paper. 1998. Transcribed meticulously in original order with all schedules and columns: population, slave and agriculture schedules. This transcription is especially valuable in that all of the schedules are included in Dr. Bradley's book, not always so with others, and each of these schedules provides special and significant information to the researcher. The population schedule gives names of persons living in home, age, sex, color, profession, value of real estate and personal property, place of birth, married, attend school/illiterate, and state of disability if applicable. $25.00 postpaid. Order from Dr. Bradley, 114 Sixth Ave, Lawrenceville, VA 23868.

ANNOUNCEMENTS:

Henricus Foundation, The Citie of Henricus Publick Days to be held this year on Saturday and Sunday, September 19 and 20 at Henricus Park from 10-5 each day. It is the most exciting event of the Henricus Park year. See period reenactments, enjoy entertainment and food and purchase crafts and wares from traditional craftspeople. Fee. Contact the Henricus Foundation P O Box 523, Chesterfield, VA 23832 (804-796-2671) for further information and directions (also see *TVF* 6:71-75).

Farrar Family Reunion — Farrar Island Rendezvous, the weekend of Sept 20-22. Plans are to visit The Citie of Henricus (also known as Farrar Island) on Publick Days, Sunday, Sept 20th. Rendezvous point and headquarters: The Fairfield Inn, 12400 Redwater Creek Road, Chester, Virginia 23831. 804-778-7500. Contact Joseph Farrar, P O Box 402, Aguanga, CA 92536. 909-767-9130.

SEARCH:

BONNER, Thomas, d 1765, Beaufort Co, NC, m Abigail (—?—) may have been Daws or Bryant. Seek help with Bonner and possible Daws/Bryant connection. A Thomas Bonner said to have been in Dinwiddie Co 1680. Shirley Wagstaff, PO Box 1559, Bandon, OR 97411.

NANCE, SHERMAN, BINGLEY. Susannah Duke Sherman, b in VA, d 1780 Charles City Co, m (1) 1757 Zachariah Nance, he d 1772 in VA. Who were her parents & siblings? Zachariah Nance 2nd, b Charles City Co, m 1802, Elizabeth Morris Bingley, b 1771 James City Co, wid of Lewis Bingley. Who were her parents and siblings? Margaret L Rhodes, 707 S Mahaffie St, Olathe, KS 66061.

BARNETT, ADAMS. Hugh Barnett, in Orange, now Person Co, NC in 1751. Where did he come from? Seek ancestors of Priscilla and Gabriel Adams. He d 1750, Fairfax Co. Was Pricilla a Pierson? Catherine Bass 12 Wactor St, Sumter, SC 29150.

FREEMAN, John, w Mary; got land in 1701, Surry Co, which was thought to be in Charles City Co at the time of grant. Seek info on John and w Mary Freeman. Wilma C Kirkland, 145 Rutledge Rd, Greenwood, SC 29649.

ROLFE, BARNETT/BERNARD(?). Seek correct dates for m Thomas Rolfe & wives (gen 2); Anne Rolfe b & d, gen 3); info missing (gen 4); Wm Barnett m Anne Rolfe date ? (gen 5); Henry Barnett m ? (gen 6); John Perry Barnett dates? (gen 7). Wilma Phelan, 615 Dan St, Akron, OH 44310.

HOCKADAY, Edmund Warwick m Indian named Mary/Molly Tashiciapathical(?). Seek info about him and Hockaday family. Camille McCray, PO Box 1231, Sun Valley, ID 83353.

NEALE, Christopher, bapt 1671, St Stephen's Par, Northumberland Co, (s Christopher & Hannah Rodham Neale); m Jane Presley, wid Richard Rogers & had 4 known children: Peter, had son John; Edward; Presley; and Ursula. Seek descendants. Janet Pease 10310 W 62nd Pl #202, Arvada, C0 80004.

HEADEN/HAYDEN. William, d by 1808, b Loudon Co, m Jane (—?—), may have been a Morris or Beavers. Seek assistance w/ Hayden and Beavers families! Shirley Wagstaff, PO Box 1559, Bandon, OR 97411.

NOEL, DILLARD, TAYLOR, HOUSTON. Will exchange info on Richard Noel, b c.1823, m cos Catherine Noel, 1844, Essex Co. Lucy Dillard, b 1828, m John C Taylor (b 1816), 1846, Caroline Co. Margaret (Peggy) Houston, m Thomas B Taylor (b c.1795), 1815, Caroline Co. Polly Bertschuk, 1106 Picadilly Cir, Slidell, LA 70461.

SANDEFUR/SANDIFER. Interested in sharing information with anyone connecting to this family. Cathi Stice, 130 Newberry Dr, Tampa, FL 33615.

WYATT, BALLARD. Rev Haute Wyatt and s John, also Elizabeth Ballard of Bacon's Rebellion period, all of early Williamsburg. Seek info about these and descendants. Barbara Schulz, PO Box 1502, Oneco, FL 34264.

INDEX

NFN No first name given; NLN No last name given

129

Bower
  Thornton 110
Bowler
  David 117
Boyd
  William 114
Bracken
  John 95, 96
Bradley
  Stephen 126
Bridgewater
  Samuel 121
  Susaner 119
Brisbane
  Rachel 113
Brittain
  James 116
Britton
  Samuel 116
Broach
  John 82-85
Broche
  John 83, 85, 86
  Mary 83, 86
Brocke
  John 83
  Mary 83
Brockenburg
  Albert 109
  Arthur 109
  Betsy 109
  John 109
  Judy 109
  Mary 109
  Rebecca 109
  William 109, 111
  Wm. 109
Brook
  family 125
Brookes
  family 84
Brooks
  family 125
  James 83
  John 83
  Mr. 84
Brown
  Daniel 118
  Jane 118
  John 118
  Joseph 118
  Lewis 118
  Margie 126
  William 113, 118

Browne
  John 94-96
Brucks
  Mr. 84
Bryant
  Abigail 127
Burkett
  Gregory 91
Burton
  Martin 121
Burwell
  Nathaniel 94, 96
Campbell
  Betty 111
  Nancy 111
  Susan 111
Cardwell
  Geo. 114
  George 112
Carlton
  Geo. 110
  John 112
  Milly 109
Carter
  Betsy 117
  Caty 112
  Grace 112
  Hetty 112
  Jacob 117, 118
  John 112, 117,
    118, 120
  Mary 117
  Nat 112
  Polly 112
  Sherwood 117, 118
  Theoderick 117
  Timothy 84
  William 112, 117,
    118, 120
Cauthorn
  Sudy 109
Chapman
  Caty 113
  Emanuel 113
  Servis 114
Charelton
  Christo. 84
Chever
  Jim 114
Childress
  Fredk. 118
Christian
  Arthur 108
  Edmund 108

Christian
  John 108
  Major 108
  Milly 108
  Peggy 108
Churchill
  family 125
Clarke
  Peter 117
Clopton
  Elizabeth 120
Cock
  family 125
Cocke
  Bowler 117, 121
Cole
  family 84
  James 83, 84
Coleman
  William 95, 96
Collins
  Ann 115
  Cordelia 115
  Eliza 111
  Elizabeth 111
  Fitshura 115
  John 115
  Lucy 111, 115
  Mason 115
  Nancy 115
  Riley 115
  Rs. 115
  Thomas 115
  Wm. 115
Cook
  family 125
Cooke
  Henry 113
Cooper
  Billy 122
  Nancy 109
Corbin
  NFN 109
Cornett
  Francis 116
Courtney
  William 110
Coutts
  Reuben 120
Craig
  Adam 116, 117,
    119, 121, 122
Crawford
  Maria 107
  Thomas 107

130

Crew
 John 120
Crittenden
 Elizabeth 113
 Richard 114
Currie
 James 122
Daniel
 family 125
Davenport
 Betty 113
 Emanuel 113
 George 113
 John 113
 Tom 113
Davis
 Aggy 122
 Andrew 110
 Billy 122
 John 110
 Liston 109
 Maria 110
 Martha 109
 Mary 110
 Norman 110
 Pleasant 109
 VLH 71
 William 109
Daviscomb
 A. 118
Daws
 Abigail 127
Day
 Betty 112
 Jemy 112
 Salana 110
Delwor
 Hannah 110
 William 110
Digges
 Dudley 94
Diggs
 Dudley 96
Dillard
 Lucy 128
Dixon
 family 125
Douglass
 Daphney 114
 Henry 114
 Rachel 114
 William 114
Doyle
 James 79, 81

Dungon
 George 115
 Nancy 115
 Polly 115
Dunlevy
 George 94
Dunston
 Mr. 84
Duval
 Polly 113
 Robert 120
Edwards
 Ann 98
 Charles 97, 98
 Ella 98
 Louisa 98, 99
 Martha 98
 Mary 97, 98
 Robert 98
 Sarah 97, 98
 Thomas 97, 99,
  111, 114, 115
Eldridge
 Jane 122
 John 122
Ellyson
 Gerrard 120
Erickson
 Mark 93
Eubank
 Catherine 111
Evans
 June 126
Farrar
 family 127
Farris
 William 117
Ferris
 John 121
Fleet
 Ann 112
 William 112
Foard
 Peter 86
Ford
 Culbert 116
 Cuthbert 116
 John 116
 Lamuel 116
 Lucy 116
 Samuel 116
 Susannah 116
 William 116
Forton
 Albert 110

Forton
 Martha 111
 Mary 111
 Oney 110
Fortune
 Franklin 109
 Jweantha 109
 Mary 109
 Peggy 109
 Polly 109
 Taliaferro 109
 Walker 109
Frazer
 Jackson 118
Freeman
 Daniel 112
 Jinand 112
 John 127
 Lornzo 112
 Mary 127
 Patty 112
 Telemaishus 112
Freemna
 Polly 112
Galt
 Gabriel 118
Garnett
 Louisa 98, 99
 Reuben 108
 Richard 108
 William 110
Garrett
 Edward 113
Gathright
 Ann 121
 Anselm 117, 118,
  120, 121
 Samuel 121
 Thomas 121
 William 117, 120,
  121
George
 Reuben 121
Gibaldi
 Joseph 78
Gilmore
 Aliza 111
 Ben 109
 Betty 109
 Delphia 109
 Elizabeth 111
 Elliott 109
 Fanny 111
 Geo: 109
 Hannah 111

Gilmore
  James 111
  John 109
  Juliet 109
  Nancy 109
  Richard 109, 110
Goode
  Samuel 121
Gore
  family 125
Gouldman
  Ben 114
  Betsy 113
  George 113
  Jim 113
  Lavinia 113
  Martin 113
  Milly 113
  Nancy 113
  Pinkie 113
  Polly 113
  Rachael 113
  Ralph 113, 114
  Sally 113
  Willis 113
Gown
  Milly 108
Graves
  Francis 118
  Mr. 116
Gresham
  Edward 82
  Henry 110
  Saml 108
Griffin
  Samuel 94, 96
Gwathmey
  John 123
Hague
  John 120
Haines
  Anthony 82
Hales
  Elizabeth 120
  John 119, 120
  Nancy 120
  Samuel 120
Ham
  Agnes 111
  Dandridge 111
  Davy 111
  Henry 111
  Patty 111
  Penelope 111
  Randal 111

Ham
  Roberta 111
  Shadrack 111
Harris
  Armistead 113
  Ben 113
  Betty 111
  Caan 113
  Cornelius 111
  Ethaline 111
  Fanny 113
  Grace 113
  Judy 113
  Lucy 111
  Mary 111, 113
  Otway 111
  Ransome 111
  Temperance 77
  Tom 113
  Walker 111
  William 113
  Zachery 113
Harrison
  Benjamim 120
Hart
  Vincent 112
Hatcher
  Patricia 79
Hay
  William 117, 120
Hayden
  Jane 128
  William 128
Headen
  William 128
Hening
  William 71
Heynes
  Anthony 82
Hickman
  James 112
  Mariah 112
  Mary 112
  Tom 112
Hill
  Betty 110
  Caty 109
  Charles 111
  Emanuel 109
  family 84
  Gabriell 83, 84
  James 83
  John 110
  Lucy 109
  Matilda 113

Hill
  Sally 110
  Servis 111
  Susie 109
  Tom 109, 113
Hillgard
  John 111
Hinshaw
  Chaning 108
Hobson
  Matthew   118,
    120-121
Hockaday
  Edmund 127
  family 84, 86
  James 83
  Mary 127
  Warwick 83
  William 85
Hollingsworth
  Stephen 117
Howells
  Cyndi 124
Howle
  Gideon 119
Hudgins
  Mary 97, 98
  Robert 98
  Walter 97
Hughes
  William 115
Hundley
  Ephriam 114
  George 114
  John 114
  Milly 114
Hylton
  Dan 120
Jackson
  Betty 114
  Cedar 114
  Frances 114
  Geo 114
  James 114
  Mary 114
  Milly 114
  Nancy 114
  Nelson 114
Johnson
  Ben 117
  Franky 111
  Michael 117
Jones
  Mary 83

Jordan
  Henry 118
Kauffman
  Euclid 112
  Geo. 110
  George 112
  Isbosta 110
  James 110, 112
  John 110, 112
  Lucy 112
  Mary 110
  Parks 112
  Polly 110, 112
  Sally 113
  Sam 112
Keeling
  Emily 107
  John 107
Kelley
  Elizabeth 119
Kent
  John 121
Kerby
  John 95, 96
Keys
  Betty 113
  George 113
  Jane 113
Kidd
  Elizabeth 112
  Elmira 114
  Esperella 114
  family 125
  Frances 113
  Frank 112, 113
  George 114
  Humphrey 112
  James 112
  John 112, 114
  Kitty 113, 114
  Lavinia 114
  Lucy 113
  Maria 112
  Moses 113
  Nancy 113
  Pinkey 114
  Polly 112, 113
  Sally 112
  Sam 113, 114
  Sarah 112
  William 112
King
  Marvin 91, 93
Kuntzman
  John 118

Ladd
  James 120
Lawrence
  Henry 84
Lee
  Francis 91
  Frank 91, 92
  Rebecca 91, 92
  Richard 91
  William 95, 96
Leftwich
  Ralph 82
Leigh
  William 86
Lewis
  family 125
  William 99
Lightfoot
  William 95, 96
Lockley
  Ann 115
  Betsy 114
  Betty 110, 114
  Billy 114
  Daniel 114
  Fanny 110, 114
  Henry 114
  James 111
  Jane 115
  Jim 114
  John 110, 118
  Julia 114
  Keziah 113
  Kitt 110, 112
  Kitty 114
  Lucy 110
  Major 111
  Mary 114, 115
  Nancy 115
  Polly 111, 112
  Rachel 114
  Richard 118
  Sally 110
  Tom 110
  Walker 114
  Willis 115
Lomax
  John 91
Lowder
  Deborah 118
  Robert 118
Lucas
  Nancy 116
Lyons
  Peter 121

Madison
  James 81
Martin
  family 125
  Marsha 125
Matthews
  Anthony 119
McRobert
  A 118
  Alexander 118
Meggs
  Frank 115
  James 115
  Peter 112
  Polly 115
  Robert 115
Melton
  George 116
Miller
  Dabney 118
  Shepard 99
Mills
  Elizabeth 78
Mitchell
  Bob 112
  Dew 112
  Grace 112
  James 110, 111
  Lorenzo 112
Montague
  family 125
Morris
  Benj. 119
  Benjamin 119
  George 82, 83, 85,
    112
  Jane 128
Nance
  Elizabeth 127
  Susannah 127
  Zachariah 127
Neal
  Rosemary 107
Neale
  Christopher 128
  Edward 128
  Hannah 128
  Jane 128
  John 128
  Peter 128
  Presley 128
  Ursula 128
Negro
  Abram 117, 121
  Aggy 122

133

Negro
Alexander 122
Alsam 118
Amey 121
Ampey 122
Andrew 97
Arthur 122
Ben 122
Bess 121
Betsey 117
Betty 117, 122
Billy 122
Blenham 122
Bob 119
Calie 122
Charles 117, 121
Chever 117
Clarkey 121
Cochenor 119
Corsey 122
Courtney 97
Cuff 119
Davy 117
Delphia 119
Dennis 119
Dick 117, 120, 122
Dilce 117, 119
Dinah 119, 121
Doll 119
Dorcas 119
Edmund 122
Effie 117
Emanuel 117
Fanny 117
Frances 121
Frank 117, 119, 121
Gardner 122
George 122
Grace 121
Hanner 119
Harry 121
Hawk 122
Isaac 117
Isbell 122
Isham 117
Jack 121
Jacob 117
James 117
Janey 119
Jenny 122
Jesse 122
Jiles 120
Jimmy 122
Joe 119, 122
Judah 118

Negro
Judy 117, 122
Letty 117
Lewis 122
Lucinda 122
Lucy 117
Mary 117
Milan 122
Milly 117
Minge 122
Moll 117
Monroe 122
Morocco 122
Moses 117, 122
Nan 119, 121
Nancy 117
Nanny 122
Ned 117, 121, 122
Nelly 122
Neptune 121, 122
Patience 119
Penny 122
Peny 122
Peter 122
Philip 122
Phillis 119
Porter 117
Rachel 118, 119,
    121
Sabina 122
Sal 117
Sall 117, 119, 121
Sally 117, 122
Sam 117, 119
Samuel 117
Scott 117
Simon 117
Sook 121
Sue 119
Sukey 122
Sylvia 122
Syms 120
Syphax 122
Tiller 122
Tom 119, 121, 122
Violet 119
Waggener 122
Watt 117, 119
Wilden 122
Will 117, 119, 122
Negro Free
Barbara 110
Ben 113
Frank 110
James 113

Negro Free
Jenny 110
John 110, 113
Mary 113
Polly 110
Richd 113
Tom 110
William 110
Wm 113
Nelson
Carter 108
Edmund 108
Elizabeth 108
Fanny 108
Frances 108
Joshua 108
Lucy 108
Mary 108
Nat 108
Robert 108
Sally 108
Thos 108
Wm. 108
Newcomb
William 113
Noel
Catherine 128
Richard 128
Norman
Betsy 108
Fanny 108
Geo. 108
John 108
Martha 108
Mary 108
Peny 108
Sally 108
Servis 108
Wm. 108
Norvell
William 94, 96
Nugent
Nell 84
Oaks
Baylor 109, 110
Caly 109
Omohundro
Dora 91
Thomas 91
Parsons
Samuel 121
Peden
Henry 123
Pendleton
Catharine 108

134

TIDEWATER VIRGINIA FAMILIES:
A Magazine of History and Genealogy

TABLE OF CONTENTS

Volume 7 Number 3   November/December 1998

From Virginia...............

This issue is a departure from the usual policy to balance the content of material presented in the magazine. There are many readers who have expressed an interest in and a concern about the Golansville Meeting House site and cemetery. It seems appropriate to publish the findings of the two archaeological surveys that have been conducted. Not only does this give an update on the progress made to preserve the site but also provides a bit of insight into the field of archaeology. It further provides some guidance for others in how to proceed to save historically significant artifacts and sites in other locations.

The assistance of Robert Hicks, Law Enforcement Specialist, Law Enforcement Section of the Commonwealth of Virginia's Department of Criminal Justice Services was sought because of his expertise in assessing historic sites and artifacts and his involvement in seeing that proper channels are followed for such preservation. Through him an archaeological assessment was made through contact with the Virginia Department of Historic Resources and the Virginia Department of Transportation. With the background information provided in *TIDEWATER VIRGINIA FAMILIES: A Magazine of History and Genealogy*, 5(1996): 159-163; (1997): 221-226 it was possible to have the site declared a "Threatened Site Project" with the designation VDHR 44CE322. David K. Hazzard, Archaeologist, Director of Threatened Sites Program was assigned to conduct the initial survey to determine the existence of the cemetery. This was his sole mission: the identification of a threatened historic site. Excerpts from his report follow.

The Golansville Cemetery Restoration Trust then engaged an independent archaeological research group (Cultural Resources, Inc.) to survey the adjoining meeting house foundation site to confirm its identity and verify the period of its construction. James G. Harrison III conducted this archaeological assessment of the foundation of what has been accepted as the site of the Golansville Society of Friends Meeting House. With these two reports in hand, the Trust plans to proceed to engage an archaeological team to determine the full bounds of the Golansville cemetery and then proceed with its restoration.

With the emphasis on proper form and indexing, an explanation of the format used in *TIDEWATER VIRGINIA FAMILIES: A Magazine of History and Genealogy* is in order. It was decided originally to index each issue of the magazine so readers would have ready access to all entries at the time of publication. Because of the large number of names in each issue, it was also decided, for the sake of brevity, to use only the given name and surname in indexing. For the same reason place names are not included, as they generally appear in the article title or are evident from the subject matter.

The total number of pages of content remains constant, giving the subscriber a wide variety of articles, and this seems more important in such a publication than including several more pages of indexing. This format continues; recognizing that it is functional, if not perfect.   VLHD

An Archaeological Survey of a Golansville Cemetery Site 44CE322, Caroline County, Virginia

David K. Hazzard, Archaeologist

Editor's Notes: It is not possible to publish the complete report by David Hazzard, due to space constraints; however it will be excerpted and presented *verbatim* with any clarifications made by your editor so identified — excerpts from *Early Caroline County Quakers, and Their Meeting House*[1] are presented here as an introduction to Mr. Hazzard's report: *The first signs of Quakers in Caroline County date from the years immediately following the establishment of the county in 1727. These earliest Caroline Friends were probably associated with the young Cedar Creek Friends Meeting in western Hanover County, but in the 1730s began meeting for worship in their own homes, notably the home of John Cheadle....This small number, gradually growing with the continuing influx of settlers, was nurtured by traveling Friends....*[2]

By [1739] the Caroline Quakers were sufficiently strong to be approved as a Meeting by the Virginia Yearly Meeting. They built their own meeting house in the hamlet of Golansville at the present-day intersection of Jefferson Davis Highway (US Route 1) and Cedar Fork Road (CR 601)[3]. *It was in this meeting house, in the heart of St. Margaret's Parish where Friends lived, that the first monthly meeting for business of the joint Caroline [Golansville] and Cedar Creek Meetings was held on March 12, 1739.*

The meeting house site is located in a copse of trees about 100 yards south of the Golansville crossroads and less than 100 feet west of the highway. Residents who lived nearby reported that the meeting house, of clapboard, was converted into a residence after the Golansville Meeting was "laid down" in 1853....The old burying ground lies a short distance west of the meeting house site, south of CR 601; marked only with periwinkle[4] *and two gravestones of a later time....It is known that Elizabeth Harris Terrell, her husband, Samuel Terrell and their son, George Fox Terrell, as well as other members of this family, are buried in the graveyard in unmarked graves.*[5]

The Quaker records that have been found are as silent about the provenance of the land on which the meeting house sat as they are about its construction. However, an entry in the Caroline County Court Order Book for April 1739 records the purchase of an unspecified amount of land from William Terrell by John Cheadle, David Terrell (William's brother), John Hubbard, Joseph Butler and Nicholas Stone; and what the five purchasers had in common was membership in the Religious Society of Friends. It seems highly likely, then, that this was the land upon which their meeting house was erected.[6]

Forty years later, in November 1779, the Golansville Meeting was deeded one acre of land attached to the meeting house for a burying ground through the will of John Burruss.[7] John Burruss, a Baptist, appears to have been the first preacher to the body that evolved into Carmel Church, Caroline's first Baptist Church. His wife, Rachel was reared a Quaker as the daughter of David and Agatha Terrell....and John [Burruss]...seems to have always been on good terms with the Friends.[8] It was this site that was visited over two hundred years later by Herbert Collins, Arnold Ricks and Virginia Davis, descendants of the early Quakers.

Archaeological Survey of a Golansville Cemetery

Introduction

In February of 1998 David K. Hazzard of the Virginia Department of Historic Resources conducted an archaeological survey of a cemetery at Golansville in Caroline County, Virginia. Questions had been raised regarding the impact of land clearing activity as it might relate to the Golansville Society of Friends Meeting House and cemetery.[9] A survey was conducted and information gathered on the existing cemetery.

Background

In April of 1996, Juan Young purchased a 23 acre parcel of land at Golansville in Caroline County, Va. at the SW corner of the junction of US Route 1 and Cedar Fork Road (State Route {CR} 601), (see site plan). In February of 1997, he had the land cleared of old car parts, remains of a wooden structure, trees and other junk that had accumulated on the property over the past decade or more....

In response to that clearing operation, a local newspaper article headlined "Cemetery razed to make way for house" reported that the "graveyard...was recently bulldozed". The clearing and news article stirred up the emotions of parties interested in both Quaker and Caroline County history, and families tied to the Society of Friends Meeting House and cemetery at Golansville. They believe that this cemetery, and foundation remains 100' to the east adjacent to US Route 1, were in fact, the Golansville Society of Friends Meeting House and cemetery.

Because of the questions raised regarding the possible disturbance of a cemetery, law enforcement officials became involved to determine if there had been any wrongdoing. Robert Hicks from the Virginia Department of Criminal Justice Services, because of the considerable interest in the site and with the prospect of development, followed this up with an application for financial assistance through the Threatened Sites Program of the VDHR in June of 1997. In February of 1998, David K. Hazzard of the Portsmouth Regional Office was asked to conduct a survey of the cemetery. Assisted by volunteers Rich Richardson, John Imlay, and Dale Brown, a two-day study was performed to gain information about the cemetery and to determine whether clearing had caused any damage to the cemetery.

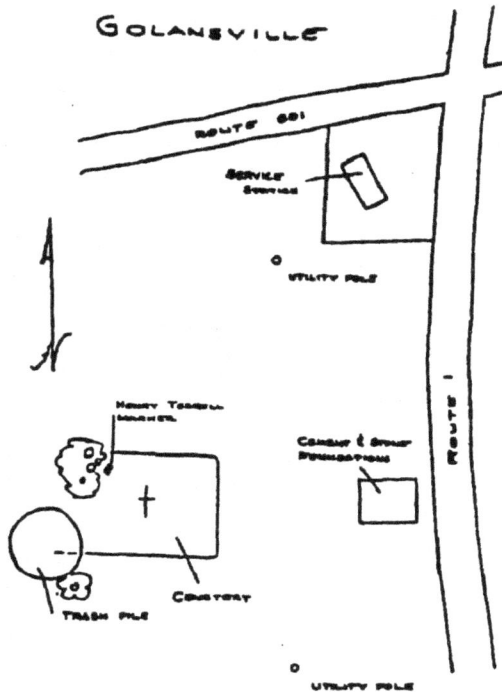

Site Plan

History

Ideally, an archaeological undertaking begins with a thorough examination of the history of a property. In this case, considerable historical information had been drawn together by several individuals before we began our work at Golansville. Historical information was provided by Virginia Lee Hutcheson Davis, Fay Wade, Robert Hicks, and Martha W. McCartney.

The Golansville Society of Friends Meeting House and cemetery was an early religious community/settlement whose primary period of significance was

1739–1853. Existing documentation places this in the vicinity of Golansville. A 1906 deed from the heirs of Joseph and Susan Terrell to A.J. Haley for this area refers to "the family burying ground or cemetery being one hundred feet in length, east and west, and forty feet in width, north and south". Entries in a Terrell Family Bible make references, by name, to several members interred at the east end of the "burying ground" at the "Friends meeting house in Caroline" and at the "Friends meeting house at Golansville". [Editor's note: Both of these entries refer to the same cemetery, the two names being used interchangeably with reference to the Golansville Meeting in the monthly meeting minutes].[10]   Unfortunately, as so often happens, available documentation still does not pinpoint the location of the meeting house and cemetery nor does it provide us with the number and names of all persons interred within the cemetery grounds. [Editor's note: It has not been ascertained that the Terrell Family Bible reference is to the exact same area as the deed describing the Joseph and Susan Terrell's family burying ground. Evidence has not yet been found to delineate the complete area encompassed by the Golansville Meeting House cemetery. Therefore it is not known exactly where Samuel and Elizabeth Terrell and their son, George Fox Terrell were in fact buried (as recorded in their family Bible and referenced in the introduction preceding). One must keep in mind the 1779 gift adjacent to the meeting house site of an additional one acre of land (see *TVF* introduction)].

An article in *Tidewater Virginia Families* discussing the Golansville Quaker Meeting House stated, *The Quaker records that have been found are as silent about the provenance of the land on which the meeting house stood as they are about its construction.*[11] Unwittingly, this statement hints at one of the roles archaeology can play in the resolution of questions regarding history. It often sheds light on where, what and when things occurred in history. [Editor's note: The Society of Friends Monthly Meeting Minutes for Cedar Creek and Golansville for the period in question (1727-1739) have not been found. Except for scattered records (deeds, wills, etc.) continuity of extant county court records for Caroline County for the eighteenth century and the nineteenth century pre-1865 is lacking. The court order books, some plats, chancery court and loose papers, and tax records have helped the reconstruction of what is known about the land and the people of Caroline County].

The scope of our undertaking was focused on addressing questions relating to the graveyard. Consequently, the limited resources provided through the Threatened Sites Program were not directed toward more historical research.

Research Design

The primary goal of the VDHR survey was to confirm the presence of a cemetery and attempt to determine its boundaries. This was to be achieved by removing topsoil at various locations across the area suspected to be the cemetery to reveal soil colorations, configurations, and patterns and orientations suggesting the presence or absence of graves. Peeling back the topsoil and looking at what is revealed beneath it provides valuable clues to the archaeologist important to the understanding of what happened where, when and why. The more the clues, the more complete the picture. A cemetery has its own style of patterning and organization. In a cemetery of the kind expected here, rectangular grave shafts 3-6' deep would have been excavated of sufficient size to receive the coffin containing the deceased. These holes would generally vary in size according to the individual to be interred (infant, child, adult). They would have been buried side by side in rows. Families were sometimes buried in clusters. Graves are usually oriented with the long axis lying east-west with the head of the individual situated to the west.

Holes excavated for interments are dug through the topsoil and into the soils below. These subsoils usually vary in color and consistency as one goes deeper into the ground. Upon backfilling an excavated hole after the coffin has been placed, deeper soils end up closer to the surface contrasting with the soils around them. The uppermost soils are either removed elsewhere or spread along the ground surface. This simple act of excavation, interment and rearrangement of soils leaves telltale remains for the archaeologist.

These remains are referred to as features. That is to say, soils of different colors lying next to one another, different size rectangular shapes with sizes befitting infants, children and adults, orientations of these shapes with long axes lying E-W, and possibly lying next to one another in rows are all indicative of a cemetery. It was assumed that if a number of graves were identified and if they in turn were surrounded by area absent of graves then this would begin to suggest possible boundaries for the cemetery. Evidence of fence lines or walls would be stronger evidence for cemetery limits.

Headstone

If time or personnel permitted, we also planned to gather information on the foundation remains to the east. Circumstances did allow us the opportunity to measure the remains and excavate one test unit. The purpose of that testing was to see if we might find artifacts that would support the historical dates for occupation of the Meeting House....

143

Procedure

The most efficient means of delineating the cemetery was to mechanically remove the topsoil at various locations across the site looking for cemetery-related features. For this purpose machinery and operators were employed from the Virginia Department of Transportation at the Ladysmith residency located a mile to the north of the site.

Excavation began immediately adjacent to a modern-day gravestone marked with the name of Henry Terrell Luck, who was born and died in 1893. A Bobcat (sort of a mini bulldozer) and Gradall (like a smooth blade backhoe) were used to conduct the stripping of the topsoil. Archaeologists closely observed the soils as they were revealed by the machines. As features were uncovered, they were marked with pin flags. Trowels and shovel were used to better define some of the features exposed. These were then plotted on a map and some photographed.

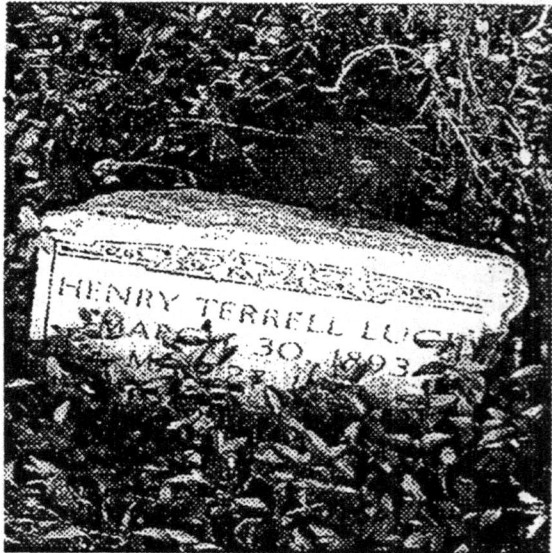

Henry Terrell Luck Marker

The weather was not cooperative. In the days and weeks preceding the machine work, rains saturated the ground. Because people closely concerned with the site were anxious to have something happen as soon as possible, we began at the first opportunity after the rain ended.

The use of both a Bobcat and Gradall were used. Before the Gradall reached the site it became mired 3' deep in the ground. We later brought it to the site from another direction and got close enough to do some excavation on the east end of the cemetery. The rest of the testing was done using the Bobcat. Enough help was available to measure the structural remains to the east and excavate one test unit.

144

Results

It should be noted that periwinkle, a ground cover frequently associated with graveyards, was found in the immediate vicinity of the Henry Terrell Luck grave marker. The archaeological study confirmed the existence of a cemetery at this location and pinpointed approximately 15 grave locations (See graveyard plan). Evidence suggests a minimum of 7 rows were present. Varying sizes of grave shafts (rectangular shapes ranging from 1'x 2' to 3'x 7') indicated the presence of infant, child, and adult burials. All graves identified were oriented with their long axes lying east to west. Graves were generally placed side by side approximately 2' apart within rows, with the rows ranging from 1-2' apart.

Three headstones were discovered *in situ*....One was an unmodified stone while the other two were broken fragments from a cut stone. They all were about 2-3" thick, about 6-8" wide, and of undetermined length. None were marked. Two were uncovered during the excavations to a depth of about 8" below ground surface. The third was discovered approximately a foot behind (northwest of) the Henry Terrell Luck stone. This mark had been mortared to the crude stone behind it whose top was flush with the ground surface. Another stone found lying in front of the Luck stone was broken like the others and about the same thickness but measured in excess of two feet in length. [**Editor's note:** It was not customary for the Friends to use finished gravestone markers, nor to inscribe their gravestones. Since this archaeological work was completed Mr. & Mrs. Wade have recovered some thirty stones of the size that may have been used as marking stones. None of these stones were inscribed, with the exception of one hand-cut stone, post-dating the "laying down of the meeting", inscribed "S B Terrell {---} 1860"].

Possible Grave Marker

Again, the purpose of the survey was not to find all graves present at the site, but to attempt to delineate the boundaries. Based on the locations of the graves found, the cemetery is believed to be rectangular in shape and oriented

145

with its long axis east to west. The limits of the area containing confirmed graves is 60' E-W x 28' N-S. Results of several machine cuts to the north, east and south of the known graves, suggests these graves may be close to what were the cemetery boundaries. The last burial found extends to the edge of the pile of trash at the western edge of the area examined and continues under it. This suggests that the western boundary of the cemetery continues to an undisclosed distance to the west.

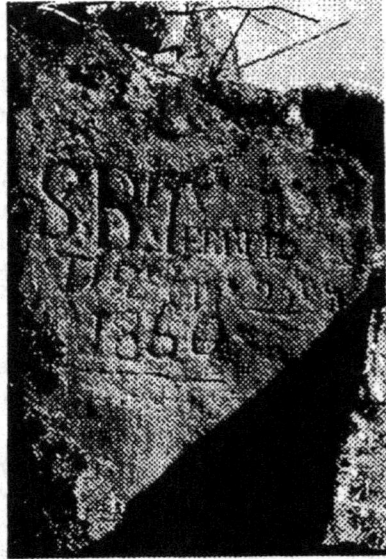

S. B. Terrell Marker
Photograph by Fay Wade

The nearby foundations lying to the east, adjacent to US Route 1, were measured the first day and one 2'x 3' test unit was excavated on the west side of the front (north) steps (see plan view). Topsoil of loose loam came down on poured concrete about 1" below modern grade. The soil was screened through ¼" hardware cloth. Artifacts consisted of cut nails, clear and brown bottle glass, oyster shell and a rubber ring. No evidence was found to suggest a date for the construction phases of the structure. [**Editor's note:** See following this account, the report from James Harrison, archaeologist, in his assessment of the foundation site of the Golansville Meeting House].

A VDHR site inventory form was completed and submitted to the state for recording and assignment of an official state site inventory number. The site has now been officially designated, 44CE322 (the 322nd site recorded in Caroline County in Virginia), and has been entered into the inventory.

A fortuitous result of the work was the visit to the site the first day of our excavation by Wallace Janish, a member of the Caroline County Sheriff's Department. As a child he had resided in the house that had sat on the foundations there. The front faced north (toward CR 601), and there was an outbuilding off the southwest corner of the house. He also told of the room locations and of their use by his family. He even recounted how his mother would take him out to the cemetery to wash tombstones there.

146

Conclusions

The limited archaeological work conducted at the Golansville crossroads did provide some answers to questions raised regarding the presence and nature of a cemetery at this location. It also answered questions regarding what effect clearing operations by the owner in February of 1997 might have had on the cemetery and a stone marker present at the site. What it did not do is establish whose graveyard this was, when it was in existence, and what relationship it might have had to the Golansville Society of Friends Meeting House and cemetery.

Historians, local residents, Quaker descendants and other interested parties have accumulated considerable historical information on the Golansville Society of Friends Meeting House and cemetery. This comes to us in the form of deeds, maps, family Bibles, Friends records, and oral histories. These references which identify actions, list local place names, identify people and even make references to family members in particular locations within the cemetery, bring us tantalizingly close to our desired quest of answering those who, what, where, when and why questions. This recent archaeology provides an anchor from which to cast about looking for answers. Careful study of the foundations to the east might yield more answers that link all these disparate parts into a coherent history of the Quaker presence at Golansville.

While archaeology did not provide the exact boundaries of the cemetery, the minimal dimensions of 60' + x 28' determined to date comfortably fit within the 100' by 40' dimensions stated for the cemetery in the September 1906 deed. For both, the longer dimension was the east-west axis, and the shorter, the north-south axis. At that point in time it is referred to as "the family burying ground or cemetery"[12] [**Editor's note:** It should be reiterated that these measurements refer only to the cemetery designated as the "family cemetery" in the Joseph Terrell deed.]

It was not the purpose of this work to identify all graves within the cemetery and consequently the approximate 15 graves found do not purport to be the extent of graves present. Although an absence of graves was found for a distance to the north, east, and south of the graves identified in this survey, expanding out a greater distance with the same results would confirm the approximate limits of the cemetery. No evidence for the western end of the cemetery has yet been suggested.[13]

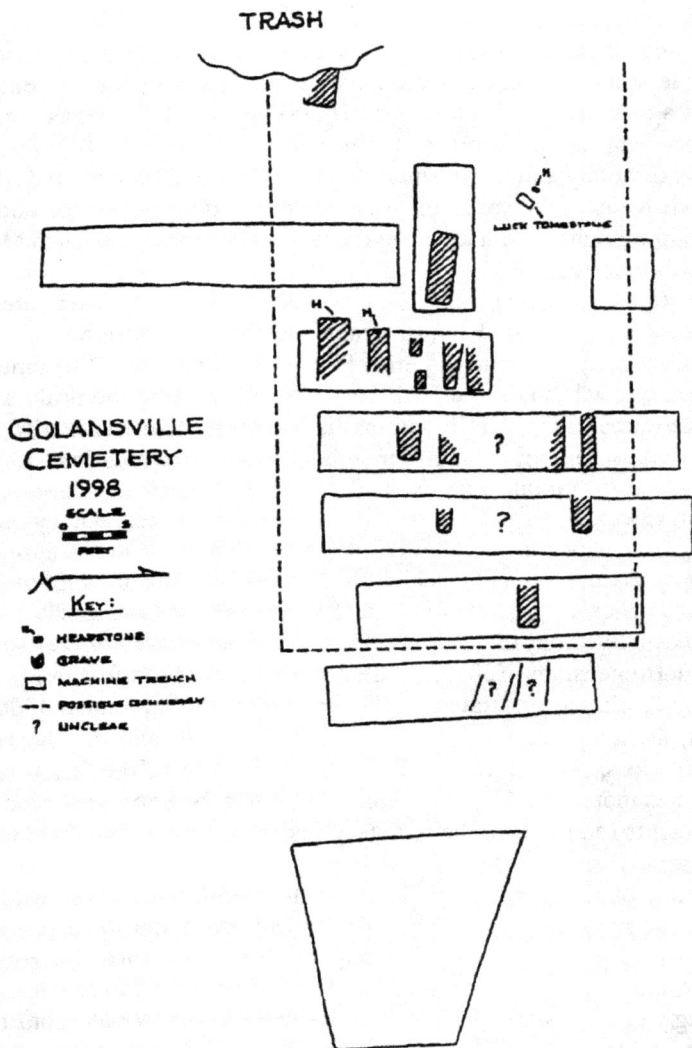

TRASH

GOLANSVILLE
CEMETERY
1998

SCALE
0   5
FEET

KEY:
HEADSTONE
GRAVE
MACHINE TRENCH
POSSIBLE BOUNDARY
? UNCLEAR

Graveyard Plan

148

Golansville Society of Friends Meeting House Site, Reconnaissance-Level Archaeological Survey Golansville, Caroline County, Virginia

James G. Harrison III, Archaeologist, Project Manager

Editor's note: The services of Cultural Resources, Inc., Williamsburg, Virginia, a private archaeological research group were employed by the Golansville Cemetery Restoration Trust to examine the fieldstone and concrete foundation of the Golansville Society of Friends Meeting House site to verify its provenance. Mr. Harrison was assigned this survey and Edward Wade, Fay Parrish Wade and Virginia L.H. Davis met him at the site and participated in the survey under his direction. His report follows, *verbatim* as excerpted, again due to space constraints.[14]

On Wednesday, February 25, 1998, as part of the signed contract between Cultural Resources, Inc. (CRI) and the Golansville Cemetery Restoration Trust, I undertook the field survey of the extant fieldstone and concrete foundation at the Golansville...Meeting House Site....

During this survey, four shovel test pits (STPs), each approximately one foot or larger in diameter, were excavated with the hope of retrieving diagnostic (datable) artifacts and other information to ascertain the age of this foundation and, thus, corroborate the pier arrangement, measuring approximately 33 feet in length east-west by about 17 feet in width north-south, as part of the meeting house which was constructed in 1739 (see schematic [foundation] plan view of the site). In addition, mortar samples were taken from two of the piers (see plan view) for future analysis.

STP 1 was excavated at the western end of the south foundation wall (running east-west) adjacent to a fieldstone pier (see plan view). Two soil strata (layers) were encountered above undisturbed subsoil. Stratum A, .40' thick, consisted of a very dark grayish brown silty loam topsoil and contained nineteenth century and 20th century artifacts, including machine-cut nails (1830-1890s), wire nails (1890s-present), and a 1941(?) penny representative of the post 1853 period when the former meeting house was enlarged and converted into a residence. Stratum B, .80' thick, consisted of a yellowish brown silty clay mottled with brown silty clay and contained artifacts including a hand-molded brick bat and a badly corroded coin. No eighteenth century artifacts were recovered from either Stratum A or Stratum B. Subsoil was represented by a light yellowish brown wet clay.

149

STP 2 was excavated adjacent to and on the north side of a fieldstone pier on the south foundation wall (running east-west, see plan view). Five soil strata were encountered above undisturbed subsoil. Stratum A, .40' thick, consisted of a very dark grayish brown silty loam topsoil and contained eighteenth, nineteenth and 20th century artifacts, including a few wrought nails [eighteenth century] and possible wrought nails (eighteenth century-early 19th century), machine-cut nails (1830s) and wire nails (1890s-present). The wrought nails are probably associated with the construction of the meeting house, while the machine-cut nails and wire nails are representative of the post 1853 period when the former meeting house was enlarged and converted into a residence. Stratum B, .40' thick, consisted of a concentration of very pale brown sandy plaster fragments with charcoal fragments. Stratum C, .35' thick, consisted of a dark brown silty clay mottled with dark yellowish brown silty clay. Stratum D, .40' thick, consisted of a yellowish brown silty clay mottled with brown silty clay and contained mortar and plaster fragments. Stratum E, .40' thick, represented a builder's trench for the fieldstone pier, sandy clay, and contained mortar and plaster fragments. As the builder's trench feature was devoid of any other historic artifacts, this is further evidence that the fieldstone pier portion of the foundation may indeed represent the structural remains of the 1739 meeting house. Subsoil was represented by a light yellowish brown wet clay.

[**Editor's note:** STP 3 and STP 4 were described in the report, but will not be detailed here as they did not contain any identifiable eighteenth century artifacts and appeared to be of the later addition.]

Mortar samples were extracted from two pier locations on the foundation (see plan view). "Mortar samples 1" were taken from the base of the pier in stratum D in STP 2 along the south foundation wall (running east-west). "Mortar samples 2" were taken from the above-grade remains of the pier at the western end of the north foundation wall (running east-rest). Both samples are representative of the mortar used in all the piers, consisting of a sandy, gritty mixture without any visible oyster or mussel shell fragments. [**Editor's notes:** This was a dry mortar and not consistent with mortar mixtures used in later time periods. It is felt by those acquainted with the culture of the Society of Friends that the usual artifacts found at a house site would be absent from a Friends' Meeting House site. The Friends shunned ostentation, and therefore wore no ornamentation. The meeting house was used for business meetings and for worship, and therefore there would have been no housekeeping activities conducted at the location of the meeting.]

Two additional cultural features were noted on the landscape as I was preparing to leave the site at the end of day. Approximately 51' west of the foundation remains is a small pile of hand-molded brick rubble indicative of a possible former dependency. Additionally, about 56' west of the foundation remains is a depression likely representing an old well (see plan view).

In summation, CRI believes, based on architectural evidence and limited diagnostic artifacts recovered during this survey, that the portion of the foundation running east-west containing the fieldstone piers and measuring approximately 33 feet in length east-west by about 17 feet in width north-south is that of the meeting house constructed in 1739. These dimensions also closely match the dimensions of other Society of Friends meeting houses documented in Virginia as stated in the endnotes of the article *Early Caroline County Quakers and Their Meeting House*[15] The concrete additions postdate 1853 when the meeting house was closed, and likely date to the late 19th century or early 20th century when the building was enlarged and converted into a residence.

Notes

1. R. Arnold Ricks, Jay Worrall, Jr, and Herbert R. Collins, *Tidewater Virginia Families: A Magazine of History and Genealogy.* 5(1996): 159-163.

2. William W. Hinshaw, *Encyclopedia of American Quaker Genealogy.* vol. 6. (Ann Arbor: Edwards Bros., 1950) 224; Virginia L.H. Davis, *Tidewater Virginia Families.* (Baltimore: Genealogical, 1990) 486; James P. Bell, *Our Quaker Friends of Ye Olden Times.* (Lynchburg: J.P. Bell Co., 1905) 194-195.

3. In the 1730s Route 1 was a trace of a road running south to north. Cedar Fork Road was known earlier as Polecat Road. It continued southwestward from Golansville, crossing the North Anna River at Butler's Bridge into Hanover County and on to Cedar Creek Friends Meeting House some 20 miles away.

4. Graves may have been unmarked, or marked with ordinary fieldstones. See Herbert Collins, *Cemeteries of Caroline County, Virginia, Vol. 2-Private Cemeteries.* (Westminster, MD: Family Line, 1995) 123.

5. A copy of the Terrell Family Bible is held by VLHD. The original record is in the possession of R. Arnold Ricks, Bennington, VT. There are private family burying grounds throughout this area of Caroline County where other members of the Golansville Meeting are buried. Such ones are the Ness family near Chilesburg and the Chiles family behind the "Chandler Place" at Penola. The Cobb family cemetery, recently restored, is located on a reserved lot at Lake Caroline. The marker of this site incorrectly identifies it as the Golansville Cemetery, which is in error. Herbert Collins, Unpublished Mss. 1996.

6. Caroline County Court Order Book 1739, 531.

7. From the Caroline County Court Order Book entry of May 1778, 83. Deed between John Thompson and William Burruss, executors, indicates the wishes of John Burruss and set aside the one acre of land when James Gatewood, also an executor of John Burruss' estate, purchased the land at auction, setting aside the widow's dower (Rachel Burruss had married Thomas Hackett by this time) and the acre of land to Golansville Meeting. G.H.S. King Papers, Mss1K5823a, Virginia Historical Society, Richmond, VA.

8. Hinshaw 232; T.Elliott Campbell, *Colonial Caroline: A History of Caroline County, Virginia.* (Richmond: Dietz Press, 1954) 201-202, 212.

9. VLH Davis, "*The Importance of Preserving Our History*", *TVF* 6(1997): 3-4.

10. Hinshaw *passim*; Davis, *Tidewater Virginia Families* (1990) *passim*.

11. Ricks, Worrall, Collins. *TVF* 5(1996): 161.

12. Caroline County Deed Book 74, 7.

13. Reference Material (Hazzard, VDHR):

Gilmer Map - 1863.

A Map of the Meeting of Friends in the Provinces of Maryland Virginia, North and South Carolina, Wm. Clifton.

Caroline County Deed Books, 1732-1998 Deed Books.

Harrison, James G. III, Letter to the Golansville Cemetery Restoration Trust, February 28, 1998. Manuscript on file with Cultural Resources, Inc., Williamsburg, VA.

Hicks, Robert, VDHR Threatened Sites Project Proposal. On file with the Virginia Department of Historic Resources, Richmond, VA

Keeney, Jacqueline Hernigle, Archaeological Assessment: Quaker Cemetery, Caroline County. 1997. On file with Virginia Department of Transportation, Fredericksburg, VA.

Ricks, R. Arnold, Jay Worrall, Jr. and Herbert R. Collins. *"Early Caroline County Quakers and Their Meeting House", Tidewater Virginia Families.* 5(1996): 159-163. Publisher Virginia Lee Hutcheson Davis.

Worrall, Jay Jr. and R. Arnold Ricks, *"Early Caroline County Quakers", Tidewater Virginia Families.* continued 5(1997): 221-226.

14. Copies of the report with Fay Wade and Virginia L.H. Davis.

15. Ricks, Worrall, Collins. *TVF* 159-163.

Corner of Grave
(Marked by trowel)

Foundation Plan by Jay Harrison after John Imlay

Land Patents in St. Stephen's Parish, Part II

by Lt Col James W. Doyle, Jr., USAF, Ret.[1]

This is a continuation of the map and discussion presented in the last issue of TVF. It is assumed that all readers will have ready access to that issue, so we will not repeat the preliminary explanations here.

We will start with the comparison of a few of the stream names which appear in the patents with those in common use today. First is the Whorecock Swamp. There are as many variant spellings of this colorful name as there might be explanations for its origin. Certainly, it applies to the portion of Garnett's Creek from its mouth to the fork just north of Maddison's most western patent. The east fork, now called Market Swamp, is almost always referred to as Whorecock. The northern branch, now called Dickeys Swamp, is sometimes Whorecock, and at other times, especially in later years, as Ashawaymanscot Swamp. The many ways that Ashawaymanscot is spelled is a testament to the imagination and creativeness of our ancestors. One not labeled on the USGS maps is Helican Swamp, which branches off Exol Swamp bounding Gresham's land and extending into Lumpkin's patent. Another currently unlabeled stream is Phillips Branch, which rises on the land patented by Ralph Leftwich and runs north to the Dragon. Mantapike Swamp carries on with its ancient name.

To expand on the discussion of the previous issue, it should be emphasized that there is no set of data which could provide a map of the plats at any one time. Instead, we must connect surveys which appear in land patents over a half century, chosen because they fit together to provide a reliable matrix of property lines, located with reasonable accuracy with reference to terrain features. Other researchers, interested in other land owners and their property lines may use this map as a reference grid to reliably locate other surveys. One example is given in the discussion of David Pritchett's patent.

In discussing the individual land tracts, we will carry on the convention of giving references for both *Cavaliers and Pioneers*[2] and Virginia the Land Patent Books.

154

1. Edward Lockey, 1600 ac, 25 Jan 1658, (C&P II:385/PB4:250).
This was Mr. Lockey's home plantation for many years and took its name, *Tower Hill*, from the prominent hill near the center of the tract. The patent names Richard Evans as a neighbor to the west, and Lt.Col. Abrahall to the south. In plotting the surrounding lands, it appears that Abrahall's did not actually form the southern boundary of Lockey's patent, but lay at the east end of Lockey's southern bound. Lockey's various bounds are mentioned in a number of subsequent patents which are discussed below.

2. John Maddison, 320 ac, 4 Jul 1664, (C&P I:467/PB5:223). This patent names the owners of land to the south and west of Mr. Lockey. To the south Richard Morley had recently bought 320 acres from John Pigge and took a new patent to secure his title. Placing the Lockey and Maddison tracts as the map shows satisfies the conditions of those two patents, but results in an overlap of the Pigge patent which is discussed next. This could be explained by a sale of land by Pigge to Maddison, or one could find that the Lockey and Maddison tracts should be placed farther to the west. Maddison sold this land to Isaac Collier who deserted it. It was subsequently patented by John Easterly and Robert Clifford on 22 Sep 1683. (C&P II:268/PB7:325).

3. George Morris, 400 ac 20 Apr 1684, (C&P II:278/PB7:380).
Repatented by Joshua Story, 23 Apr 1688, (C&P II:322/PB7:646). These two patents are identical in wording, which is a reflection on the legal attitude of the clerks who recorded the patents. Every word is copied faithfully, even to include mistakes which were made when the first clerk translated the surveyor's drawing into words. Although the bounds do not fit precisely within the space between the Lockey, Morley and Pigge tracts, it is shown approximately as it should be. From it we may infer the location of lands of the neighboring tracts, as stated in the patent. These include land where Wm. Drumright and Matthew York lived, land of Jno. Symonds, Mr. Collier, and land which John Bowles bought of Col. Robert Abrahall. The approximate locations of these are shown on the map.

4. John Pigge, 700 ac, 5 Sep 1658, (C&P I:370/PB4:1870. This is the last of four patents issued over a two month period to Axoll & Haines, Pigge and Leftwich. These four tracts line up with unusual precision, each making reference to the next in line, and without those minor discrepancies of a few degrees which are common in the bounds of neighboring tracts. From this, we may assume that the owners cooperated in having the same surveyor lay out the lines in a single project.

5. Ralph Leftwich, 300 ac, 10 Aug 1658, (C&P I:369/PB4:184). This tract is significant in that it is an example of how owners tended to patent tracts with neat geometric bounds, and later sold and bought land to define their bounds along natural barriers such as streams. The logic of this is obvious, in that tending to fields on opposite sides of a stream presented problems. It is also an example of how bits of data from multiple sources can be merged so that the sum of the information is greater than the parts. Leftwich sold a sliver of land to David Pritchett, who combined it with other land formerly belonging to John Pigge and secured a new patent as described below. The result of overlaying the two surveys is that we may be confident that the northeast corner of the Leftwich tract is located with unusual precision, probably within 100 feet, or about five times the width of the survey line. From data in the Pritchett patent, we may conclude that Ralph Leftwich was living on 9 Jun 1708; probably living in 1713.

6. David Pritchett, 175 ac, 13 Nov 1713, (C&P III:133/PB10:91). The patent is specific in saying that the 175 acres includes 45 acres bought from Ralph Leftwich on 9 Jun 1708, and the remainder being new land for which he paid three headrights. Three significant points are named in the Pritchett patent. They are: 1) a great ash standing on the northwest side of *Axell Swamp* at the mouth of a great branch (most southerly corner); 2) to a corner white oak of William Drumright and Jacob Lumpkin on the east side of Phillips Branch (most northerly corner); 3) and a "notch" which goes down Ferguson's line [formerly Pigge's] SSW 22 poles and N 63^0 W 20 poles along Leftwich's line, it being a corner of the land Pritchett bought off Leftwich. With these constraints, there is almost no latitude in placing the Pritchett tract as is shown. By extension, all of the bounds in this area are felt to be very accurate.

7. John Pigge, 300 ac, 10 Jul 1658, (C&P I:368/PB4:182). There is nothing remarkable about this tract other than the inference that the "bulge" of Pritchett's tract must have been deserted by Pigge or some subsequent owner before being taken up by Pritchett as "new land" in exchange for headrights. Likewise, one may infer that by some chain of conveyances, part of Pigge's tract to the south of Pritchett must have come into the hands of a man named Ferguson.

8. John Maddison, 300 ac, 28 Aug 1658, (C&P I:369/PB4:184). The southwest corner of this patent is described as a red oak by the Whorecock Swamp. From this point, one can trace interconnecting surveys which extend all the way to the mouth of Exol Swamp, where it runs into the Dragon. His neighbor to the west was Robert Abrahall, who bought 1000 acres from Thomas Peck.

9. John Maddison, 200 ac, 13 Sep 1664, (C&P I:515/PB5:372). Although this tract fits nicely with those on the west, south and east, there are difficulties in matching it with the surveys to the north. To start with, the tip of the spike is said to be on Lockey's line, but two other surveys of Maddison and the 80 acres of Baggbe would then overlap Lockey. There appear to be several instances of sloppy survey work in this area. Perhaps the surveyors did some guesswork rather than wade in the swampy area where the fish hatchery is now located.

10. John Maddison, 300 ac, 18 Mar 1662, (C&P I:469/PB5:232). From the description of the eastern bound of Maddison's 200 acres, above, one may conclude that John Maddison lived on this tract in 1664. Exactly where his house was is open to question, but one might assume that it was near the road which runs across the southern side of the tract. The patent says it is renewal of patent dated 9 Aug 1659.

11. John Maddison Jr, 430 ac, 16 Apr 1683, (C&P II:255/PB7:246). This patent includes the 300 acres patented on 18 Mar 1662, and 130 acres for three headrights. This would imply that the 200 acres to the west had been lost due to desertion or other cause. Again, the survey lines are confusing, and the best fit is shown.

12. Robert Baggbe, 80 ac, 27 May 1673, (C&P II:126/PB6:455). This is a small, simple tract. Yet, the survey lines do not close and the angled bound doesn't match the line along Maddison as it is supposed to. It is shown as a "best fit" without further comment.

13. Abrall and Pigg, 1280 ac, 10 Jul 1658, (C&P I:366/PB4:174). This patent has only a vague description of the bounds, but from subsequent patents one can conclude that they soon divided the land equally; Pigg taking the western half and Abrahall taking the rest.

14. Robert Chamberlaine, 320 ac, 22 Sep 1682,
(C&P II:244/PB7:187). The patent states that this land was formerly granted to Abrahall and Pigg (see above), and sold by Pigg to Robert Morley from whom it escheated on 10 Oct 1681. One must wonder if Morley lost his land as a result of being involved in Bacon's Rebellion. His neighbor, Anthony Arnold was, for sure.

15. ?Anthony Arnold? There is no clue to Anthony Arnold having owned this land other than the mention of Arnold in the Chamberlaine patent, above, and the Morris patent, below. Arnold was one of the most well-known of Bacon's rebels, having been hanged in chains at West Point. It would not be surprising that people didn't even mention his name after that for fear of being associated too closely with a rebel. The bounds have been drawn to enclose what is presumed to be the remaining 320 acres of Pigg's half of the Abrahall & Pigg patent.

16. George Morris. Please refer to TVF:7.2, p.82.

17. John Maddison, 800 ac, 28 Aug 1657, (C&P I:350/PB4:112). This is Maddison's second patent, and one of the first which is supported by an accurate survey. This patent mentions Maddison's own 600 acres (see #24) as a neighbor to the south and west, and both of these patents mention Adam Holland as a neighbor to the east.

18. John Maddison & Richard Owen, 100 ac, 16 Apr 1683,
(C&P II:255/PB7:245-6). The specific landmarks mentioned in this patent leave little doubt as to the location of this tract at the northwest corner of the crossroad at Stevensville. From it, the placement of the surrounding tracts seems certain. One can only speculate on the reason Maddison, who owned over 2000 acres, would become a partner with Owen in acquiring 100 acres.

19. ?John Maddison? Although no patent has been found to match this tract, the land to the east was part of a patent to John Maddison (see below). The patent of Maddison and Owen mentions Jacob Fleepo as owning the land at the southeast corner, and Mr. Hansford along the Indian Path on the south. John Hansford had deserted his 950 acres to the east of Abrahall's large tract by 1653, but no other patent data has been found to indicate that he owned land in this area. There is no other known reference to Fleepo, so he may have died or moved before securing a patent. In Edward Eastham's patent, Peter Deshasero is named as owning land to the west of Eastham. Peter Deschazaut, Junr., (decd) is mentioned as having land elsewhere in St. Stephen's Parish in 1699. (C&P III:220)

20. Edward Eastham, 280 ac, 23 Apr 1681, (C&P II:218/PB7:76). The patent says this land was part of a patent to John Maddison, who sold to Eastham on 8 Apr 1680. The eastern line of this tract is said to be the *side line of Maddison's devidend.* Other neighbors mentioned are Maj Morris and Peter Deshasero.

21. Edward Eastham and John Page, 48 ac, 20 Oct 1688, (C&P II: 328/PB7:681-2). From the bounds mentioned, one may infer that Page had bought land from Abrahall, since both ends of the southern bound are said to be by his plantation. The southeast tip is mentioned as a corner white oak of Maj. Morris on Hoghouse Branch; exactly as this point is described in the Morris patent.

22. ?Eastham?. No patent data has been found to match this tract, but it seems to have been owned by Edward Eastham, who is named in the Morris patent as having a common bound with Morris along the Hoghouse Branch; apparently a branch of Mantapike Creek.

23. Robert Abrahall, 1200 ac, 20 Oct 1675, (C&PII:169/6:585). The Abrahall patent states that this land was *formerly granted to Wm. Lewis by pattent dated 25th of May 1645.* The Lewis patent has not been located. Abrahall's survey is probably identical to that of Lewis, and retains much of the vague wording characteristic of the earlier patents and names neighbors who had since deserted or otherwise disposed of their land. His neighbor to the east, John Sandford [Hansford] had long before sold to Richard Tunstall. Although Holland had probably moved on, the Abrahall patent names him as a neighbor to the south.

24. John Maddison, 600 ac, 4 Jan 1653, (C&P I:280/PB3:217). This is Maddison's first patent in the area, and as was the usual practice of that era, the bounds are very general, *beg at Col. Taylor's Cr., running down the river E. to Mr. Adam Holland's Cr., thence NNE.* This is the one instance where Garnet's Creek was referred to as Taylor's Creek, and Mantapike Creek was referred to as Holland's Creek.

25. William Banks, 1079 ac, 21 Apr 1690, (C&PII:341/PB8:36). This is the plantation traditionally known as *Mantapike.* The whole 1079 acres was apparently claimed by Edward Diggs on 18 Mar 1653. He assigned it to Holland, who assigned it to Banks. The Banks patent states that a resurvey showed more land, for which additional headrights were submitted. The survey is so closely linked to the terrain features that there can be little doubt that the tract is plotted accurately on the map. The admission that a survey revealed more land than was originally claimed is not unusual. People with the power and status of Diggs could usually win a legal dispute by saying that their patent was as big as they wanted and located where they wanted. Subsequent owners — buyer beware — would have to straighten it out as best they could if a problem arose. Looking at the original vague patent of Diggs, one might speculate that the Holland land was also a part of the Diggs patent, and that Diggs assigned that land to Holland. If so there is no concrete evidence such as exists here in the Banks patent. Having introduced this conjecture, it may be appropriate to point to another inconsistency which may shed light on the hectic land dealings of the frontier as they existed in the mid-1600s.

Consider that the Banks patent mentions Robert Abrahall as having the land to the southeast, where (John) Broach is shown on the map. The Broach patent specifically states that the western boundary of his land was *Mantipike Swamp*. Taken literally, this survey would place the Broach land right in the middle of the Diggs patent, the same land which was included in the Banks survey just six months later. Was Broach unaware of the assignments from Diggs to Holland to Banks? Did he, in fact, have a valid patent for any land on the Mattaponi River? I don't know the answer, but have squeezed Broach in where the Banks and Abrahall surveys leave a gap. That tract does not measure up to the 342 acres patented by Broach, and so must be regarded as tentative.

26. Adam Holland. The original patent for this land has not been identified. There can be little doubt that Adam Holland once owned this land, however he acquired it.

Notes

1.. 2923 Tara Trail, Beavercreek, OH 45434. JWDoyleJr@aol.com
2.. Nell Marion Nugent, *Cavaliers and Pioneers vol I*, (Baltimore: Genealogical Publishing, 1983); vol II & III, Richmond: VSL, 1977, 1979). passim.

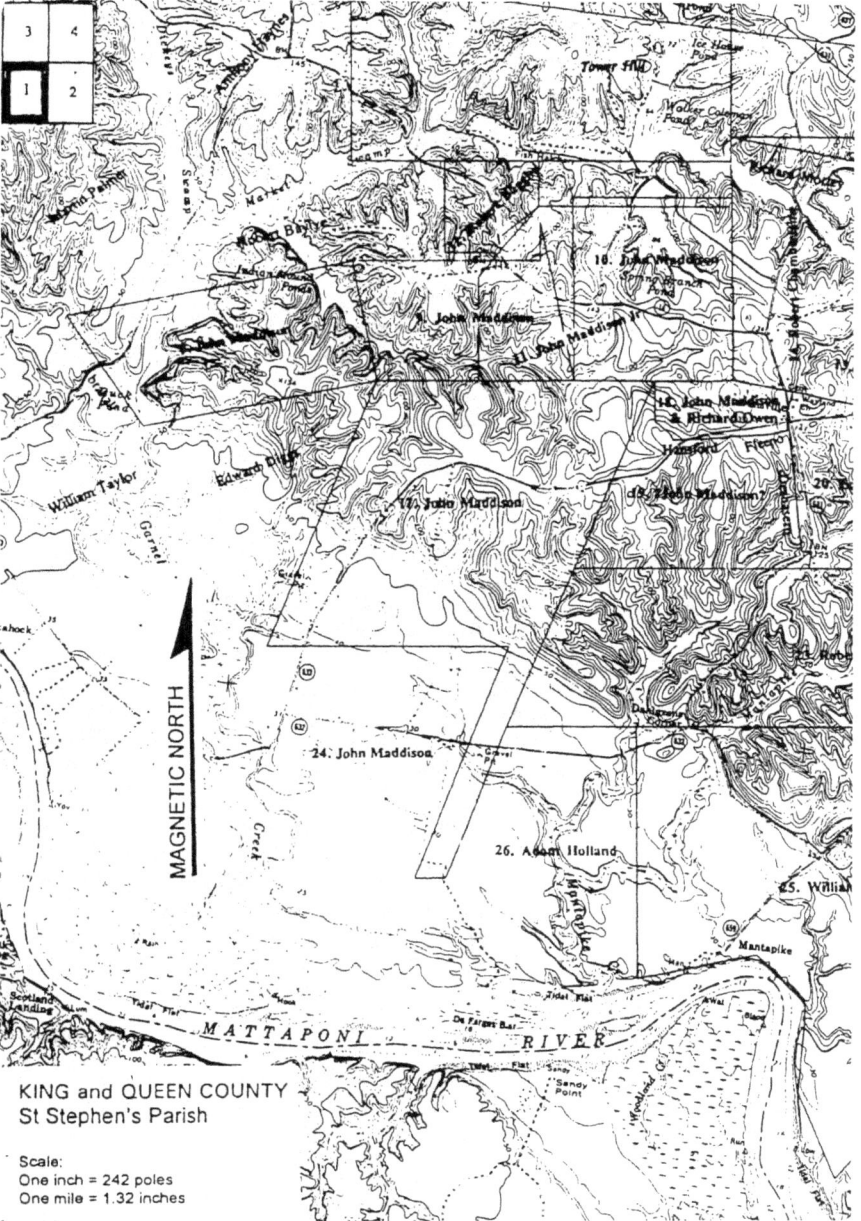

KING and QUEEN COUNTY
St Stephen's Parish

Scale:
One inch = 242 poles
One mile = 1.32 inches

3
4
1
2
Tower Hill
Ice House Pond
Walker Coleman Pond
10. John Maddison
Spring Branch Pond
11. John Maddison Jr
Anthony Arnold
13. Abrahall and Pigg, 1280 ac
George Morris
John Maddison
& Richard Owen
Hansford
20. Edward Eastham
Eastham
23. Robert Abrahall
26. Adam Holland
25. William Banks
Mantapike
RIVER
Sandy Point
John Broach
Robert Abrahall
Hansford
Richard Tunstall

163

3
4
1
2
Mr. Collier
Jno. Symonds
John Bowles
Wm. Drumright and Mathew York
Jacob Lumpkin
William Drumright
6. David Pritchett
Phillips Branch
Daisy
4. John Pigge
2. John Maddison
Edward Lockey
Ice House Pond
Tower Hill
Walker Coleman Pond
5. Ralph Leftwich
7. John Pigge
Richard Moody
10. John Maddison
Spring Branch Pond
11. John Maddison Jr
16. George Morris
18. John Maddison
& Richard Owen
20. Edward Eastham
19. John Maddison

The Pollard Families of King William and King and Queen Counties

Peter McDearmon Witt, PhD[1]

Robert Pollard (*fl.*[2]1700) so-called "of *Bruington*," King & Queen County has been since 1833 generally acknowledged as the progenitor of various Pollard families of the Virginia Tidewater.[3] Throughout the eighteenth, nineteenth and early twentieth centuries Pollards lived in the basin of the York River, and two large families emerged which are for convenience referred to as the "King and Queen" and the "King William" Pollards after the sister counties along the Mattapony River. Neither family confined itself to their eponymous counties but during the same time period ventured to neighboring Hanover, Caroline, Spotsylvania, Orange counties and further west. Indeed they criss-crossed the Mattapony itself; King and Queen Pollards living in King William and vice versa. Not surprisingly they also favored the repetition of common christian names for their descendants. Particularly with respect to the King William Pollards this has led to confusion of bloodlines.

The most extensive information concerns the King and Queen Pollards, who have preserved knowledge of the line of Joseph Pollard (1701-1792) of King and Queen and Goochland counties for a century-and-a-half. According to tradition, Joseph is a son of Robert Pollard of *Bruington*, and his wife [Elizabeth] Baylor, "the daughter of a large merchant [John Baylor II] of King and Queen".[4] This is the family of Virginia's governor John Garland Pollard, as well as numerous county clerks of King and Queen and Hanover counties. The King William family descends from Robert Pollard (born c.1699) of King and Queen *sic*, brother of Joseph, and produced the nineteenth-century Pollard county court clerks in King William County, hence the name.

The focus of this article is principally an attempt to sort out some descendants of Joseph's brother, Robert, and to place other Pollard families of King William and Hanover counties, who do not seem to fit the received pedigree. Because there is little direct documentary evidence (the"burnt county" syndrome) the following is speculative, not to say "creative." Indeed the reader is warned that I discuss individuals who are nowhere (to my knowledge) documented nor even named by tradition.

The Tradition

In the latter part of the last century the Rev. Dr. Robert Douglas Roller of Charleston, West Virginia began reviewing his father's researches into the Pollards, and among his papers was a genealogy written in 1833 by Robert Pollard (1763-1836) clerk of King and Queen. This genealogy, published in

Tyler's Quarterly has been the starting point for all subsequent researches.[5] It states that Robert of *Bruington* had three sons and at least one daughter. One son "went to sea and was not heard from." Joseph (1701-1792) "another son" had two sons and six daughters, and Robert "brother to the said Joseph" had four sons and four daughters.

The tradition appears solid with respect to the children of Joseph's son, William Pollard (died 1781) of *Buckeye*, Hanover County, although I begin to think that Joseph may have had sons other than the William (died 1781) and Thomas (born 1741) alone attributed to him. (I shall return to that suggestion in a second article, *Other Pollards*).

For the descendants of Joseph's brother, Robert (born c.1699) the tradition, I believe, confuses two generations, conflating Robert's children and grandchildren of the same names, as well losing sight (perhaps) of another of Joseph's siblings who died young. It is well to remember that it was Joseph's descendants not Robert's, who compiled the genealogy more than a hundred years after the subject generation was born.

These are the relevant paragraphs in the article in *Tyler's Quarterly* which deal with Robert Pollard (born c.1699):

Sixth. *Robert, another son of the first named Pollard and brother to the said Joseph, settled in King and Queen near Bruington meeting house, and said Robert had 4 sons and 4 daughters.*

Eighth. *Robert (the brother of Joseph) - his children, Robert died young, leaving two sons Richard and Robert, Richard died in King & Queen, had two sons and six daughters. Robert died in King William, had 4 sons and 4 daughters. Richard, another son, removed to Culpeper.*

Ninth. *John, another son died in King and Queen, had 7 sons and 2 daughters.*

Tenth. *Benjamin, another son, settled in Norfolk and had one son and one daughter.*

Eleventh. *Daughters, one married Mitchell lived in Mecklenburg. One married Gaines lived in Orange. One married Smith lived in King & Queen. One married Garlick lived in King & Queen.*

My contention in this article will be that the eighth paragraph errs in naming "Robert [who] died young" as a son of Robert (brother of Joseph) and further that the paragraphs ninth, tenth and eleventh more accurately describe grandchildren of Robert, the brother of Joseph.

The Family of Nancy Pollard Garlick

In order to verify these statements, let us look at the letter of a granddaughter of the last named daughter. Among the Kean-Prescott papers in the Southern Historical Collection of the University of North Carolina[6] a letter of Elizabeth Garlick Hill recites "the little [she had] learned" concerning the family of her grandmother, Nancy Pollard who married John Garlick (died 1803) of *Whitehall*, King and Queen County. The letter is dated 17 June 1881 and names three brothers of Nancy Garlick and two sisters: John who married Miss Quarles; Ben, Richard, Mrs Smith and Mrs Gaines of Orange County.

This is what I know about Miss Hill's grandmother's family:

Nancy Pollard married John Garlick, the son of Samuel Garlick (died 1772) and his wife Mary Camm (1727-1797). In 1780 John Garlick was appointed a justice of Caroline County; he died around 1803 the master of *Whitehall* in King and Queen. Because he was a minor child at the date of the writing of his father's will (1765), but an executor in 1772, I have placed his birth around 1750. I assume that Nancy Pollard was about the same age or younger than her husband, and one source gives her birth year as 1756.[7]

John Pollard, the brother of Nancy Garlick, married Dorothy Quarles, the daughter of Roger Quarles (born 1720) and his wife Mary Goodloe (born 1728) of Caroline County.[8] I know of only five children, three sons and two daughters. The birth dates of three of Dorothy's children make it likely she was born in the late 1760s: Joseph (1783), Richard (1790) and Keturah (1794). Assuming that John Pollard was her age or older, he was born in the late 1750s or early 1760s.[9]

Ben Pollard married Abigail Taylor in 1784 and lived in Norfolk according to an account of the family recorded in the *Richmond Times Dispatch Genealogical Column*. This marriage date would normally indicate a birth date also in the 1760s. Benjamin Pollard accompanied Camm Garlick, brother-in-law of his sister Nancy, to England where the latter went to claim an inheritance in 1781.[10] Miss Hill discusses only a son Ben, "the only one of his children whom I ever saw."

The **Richard Pollard** who was the brother of Nancy Garlick does not seem to have married. Miss Hill records that he had been captured by Algerine pirates and "worked like a galley slave: that is about all I know of **him** except that he was finally restored to his home & country." The Barbary pirates were active in the Mediterranean until the U.S. Marines put an end to their depredations early in the nineteenth century.

Susan Pollard may have been the name of a sister of Nancy Garlick.[11] Miss Hill says, "My G. mother had two sisters one of whom married a Mr. Smith; the other Mr. Gaines of Orange. Aunt Smith left two daughters ...."

Mildred Bland Pollard married James Gaines (born 1766) the son of James and Mary (Pendleton) Gaines. She was the grandmother of Major John Pollard Gaines of Charlotte County.[12] I assume that Milly Pollard Gaines is about the same age as her husband, again born in the 1760s.

What we know of the six children named by Miss Hill shows that they were born roughly in the decade 1755-1765, and in consequence I think it is reasonable to suppose that their father was born in the decade 1720-1730, rather than c.1699 as indicated for Robert Pollard, brother of Joseph. In other words, these are Robert (c.1699) Pollard's **grandchildren**. Miss Hill's letter nowhere says who Nancy Garlick's father was. There is however, a contemporary document that suggests an answer. Samuel Garlick (died 1772), father-in-law of Nancy, penned a brief note (undated) to Robert Hill, his eldest daughter Hannah's husband. The note concerns business, but has this postscript: " Mrs Ben Pollard died 7th instant in child bed w/her seventh child.[13] I wonder whether this Benjamin Pollard is not the father of the six children described by Miss Hill. Samuel Garlick's note places a young family of Pollards in his neighborhood of an age to furnish his son, John (born c.1750) with a wife.

Two further discrepancies then attach to the tradition given in the *Tyler's* article list. Instead of four sons and four daughters; three of each. Miss Hill does not mention any great-aunt Mitchell. More significantly she does not list a brother, Robert for her grandmother Nancy (Pollard) Garlick, but says instead "Mr Bob Pollard of King William & clerk of the county court must have been my G.mother's nephew as I always heard he was first cousin to my mother, but I do not know his father's name." Let us look at this Robert Pollard (1756-1819), the first clerk of the name in King William County.

It is immediately apparent that he is of the same generation as Nancy Garlick and her siblings. On that fact alone I think it more likely that he would be her brother rather than her nephew. But Miss Hill knows he was not a brother. An explanation that removes Miss Hill's difficulty is at hand: her mother, Mary Garlick (daughter of Nancy Pollard) was first-cousin "once-removed" to the clerk Robert Pollard (1756-1819) through her grandmother, Mary (Camm) Garlick (1727-1797). The latter was a sister of the clerk, Robert Pollard's mother Ann (Camm) Cluverius (pronounced Cliveers) Pollard Booker (1723/4-1770).[14]

Will of Robert Pollard Jr

The father of the clerk of King William County Court left a will that was proved in King and Queen County in 1757.[15] The future clerk, Robert is referred to as "my Infant unbaptized son," but he is mentioned by name in both his grandfather John Camm's will and his mother, Mrs Ann Booker's will.[16] This is the will in its entirety:

IN THE NAME OF GOD AMEN I Robert Pollard junr being
very sick and weak doe make and appoint this my last Will
and Testament and dispose of my worldly Estate as followeth

168

Imprimis I give unto my loving Wife Anne Pollard all my whole
Estate during her naturall life or widowhood and after her decease
or marriage I give to my son Richard Pollard my Land and
Plantation whereon I now live which my Father gave me —
I give unto my Infant Son unbaptized my Land and Plantation
that I purchased of William Pollard and my Will is that all the
remainder be equally Divided   [amongst my loving wife Anne Pollard   ]
[an]d my Two Sons above name[d .... Given under my   ]
Hand and seal this 25ᵗʰ Day of J[anuary? 175 . I appoint Obadiah   ]
Marriot and John Pendleton E   [x(ecut)ors   ]
Signed sealed and published   [   ]
in the Presents of - - - }   [[Ed. note: apparently a]
                              [square piece of the paper was]*
Robert Pollard   [cut from the copied document]]*
Milly Pollard   [   ]*

At the Court held for King and Queen county the [..] Day of October 1757
This Will was presented in Court by John Pendleton one of the Ex(ecut)or
theirin [sic] named who made oath thereto and same being proved by
the oaths of several witnesses thereto subscribed is admitted to record
and liberty is reserved for Obadiah Marriot the other Executor mentioned
in the said Will to join in the probate if he thinks proper

Test(e) John Tunstall Cl(er)k

A Copy Test[e] Richd Tunstall jr
D

John Tunstall Cl(er)k

Several observations can be made here. First of course, Robert Pollard Jr of King & Queen County would be called "junior" as the younger of two living Robert Pollards of King & Queen, not because his father was named Robert. Indeed the other living Robert Pollard of King & Queen, **senior**, is likely the witness of that name to this very will. And who is this? I suggest that he is the Robert Pollard (born c.1699) who was the brother of Joseph (1701-1792), the putative ancestor of all the "King William" clan. If the witness is Joseph's brother, who then was Robert Pollard Jr's father?

Robert Jr is a young man. Although we do not have his birth date, his wife, Anne was born 5 January 1723/4[17] and we may assume he was her contemporary. He named his eldest son, Richard and willed to him the land his father gave to him. His father-in-law John Camm's will also names grandson, Richard Pollard before grandson, Robert. I suggest that Robert **Jr** (died 1757) was the son of a **Richard** Pollard, contemporary with Robert (born c.1699) and Joseph (1701-1793). Perhaps he is the son "lost at sea."[18] If [Richard] were lost at sea as a young man (at any rate he died young), I do not think it is too much of a stretch to imagine that his descendants forgot his name, especially if an only son, Robert Jr (died 1757) predeceased an uncle Robert (born c.1699).

Children of Robert Pollard (born c. 1699)

Consider these candidates for children of Robert Pollard (born c.1699):

1. **Robert Pollard (fl.1760)** of St Peter's Parish in New Kent County[19] is of an age to be of this omitted generation since his children, Ann (1756) Frances Poindexter (1759), George (1769) and [—] (177-) are of an age to be grandchildren of Robert (born c.1699).

2. **Richard Pollard (died 1770)** of Culpeper County is, I believe the only accurately reported son of Robert (born c. 1699). His children are also contemporaries of the New Kent County Pollards: e.g. his son Robert Pollard (1756-1842).

3. **John Pollard** and Ann Pollard witness Richard's Culpeper County will in 1769. Could this be a brother? I submit that this is the John Pollard reported as the son of Robert (born c. 1699). A Robert Pollard (born 1762) who enlisted for the Revolution from Hanover County might be a son. This is probably the Robert who is later of New Kent County, and who named his eldest son John.

4. **Benjamin Pollard** is mentioned in the note from Samuel Garlick to Robert Hill written sometime before 1772. I think he is the likely parent of Nancy Garlick and her siblings.

5-8. **Pollard daughters**, one of whom may have married a Mitchell.

The Wife of Robert Pollard (born c.1699)

I posit a wife, Milly Bland for Robert Pollard (born c.1699) on this evidence: the putative granddaughter Mildred Bland Pollard who married James Gaines (born 1766) of Orange County and the witnesses Robert Pollard and Milly Pollard to the will of Robert Pollard, Jr (c.1724-1757). According to Dr. Malcolm Harris's *Old New Kent*, the Blands lived in the same area (*Pepetico*) of King and Queen County as the original 1668 grant to Robert Pollard, so a Bland wife makes sense.

Conclusions

To recapitulate: I believe that Robert of *Bruington*'s son, Robert (born 1699) married Mildred Bland and had four sons, Robert, Richard, John and Benjamin, as stated in the tradition. The individuals mentioned in the *Tyler's* article; however, are in the main, Robert and Milly Pollard's grandchildren. In particular the "Robert [who] died young" referred to as his son, is more likely the son of another brother of Joseph, perhaps named Richard. This is the ancestor of the King William County Court clerks.

Notes

1. Peter McDearmon Witt is a practicing architect in Richmond, Virginia and a researcher in Virginia history and society. Trained in Classical Studies (PhD, Duke University, 1977) Peter Witt has lectured on Virginia architecture and genealogy. He was editor of the *Magazine of Virginia Genealogy* in 1990-1991.

2. fl.(*floruit* = flourished).

3. Another family of Pollards originating in Lancaster County with Robert Pollard who married the widow of Vincent Standford can be identified. His son Robert who died testate in Lancaster in 1711 cannot be Robert of *Bruington*. This family can with some ease be traced through extant records of Lancaster and other Northern Neck counties. See Malcolm H Harris, *Old New Kent County History* (West Point: privately printed, 1977) 435.

4. 31 Jan. 1929, letter of Ben R. Roller to Mrs Mary (Pollard) Clarke in the possession of Mrs C. C. (Jessie Pollard) Dodge of Lively, Virginia, regarding researches made in 1846-48 by Congressman Joseph Rogers Underwood, a descendant of one of Joseph Pollard's daughters.

5. *Tyler's Quarterly*, 10:58-60; *Richmond Times-Dispatch, Genealogical Column*. 1 January 1905.

6. SHC, University of North Carolina, Chapel Hill, NC. #2851. Letter dated 17 June 1881, addressed to "cousin Betty [Hill]."

7. J.H. Walker, The *Chart of Garlick & Related Families*. (June 1, 1955) gives her life span as 1756-1819. Copy in the possession of Peter Witt.

8. *Virginia Magazine of History and Biography (VMHB)*. 38:362; Harris, 679ff, 758ff; Also letter of Alexander Brown to Dr. John Pollard 18 December 1894, in possession of Mrs C.C. Dodge.

9. *William & Mary Quarterly (W&M Q)*. (2) 8:46-7.

10. Beverley Fleet, *Virginia Colonial Abstracts, vol.II*. (Baltimore: Genealogical, rep. 1988) 483.

11. Alfred Bagby, *King & Queen County, Virginia*. (New York & Washington: 1908) 363 records that Thomas (son of Philip) Walker married Joanna Mann "early in the last century". Her grandmother was Mrs Smith (nee Susan Pollard).

12. *Tyler's*, 3: 211-2.

13. Fleet, 2:486.

14. Camm Bible record gives the birthrates of the children of John Camm (d.1767) and Mary Bullock (1703-1753) of *North Bank* in King & Queen County. *W&M Q* (1) 14: 130-1.

15. Copy of the will is in the Virginia State Archives. Acc. No. 23553 68-1751, Richmond, VA.

16. John Camm's will was found at *North Bank* in 1934: Fleet, 2: 337-8. Ann (Camm) Cluverius Pollard Booker's will was proved in Essex County, 18 December 1775, Will Book 13, 29.

17. Camm Bible, *op. cit*.

18. There is a tradition that Robert Jr's father married a sister of Samuel Garlick (d.1772): e.g. an (c.1950) manuscript of the Pollard lineage of Mary Douglas Causey Kendrick, copy in the possession (1996) of Mrs C.C. Dodge; See I.V. Hall, *"The Garlicks: Two Generations of a Bristol Family 1692-1781,"* The *Bristol and Gloucestershire Archeological Society*, England; *Transactions* 80(1961): 132-156; Edward Garlick's 1745 will at Canterbury mentions no Pollards, but they, now long dead, could have been provided for at the time of a marriage.

19. C.G. Chamberlayne, ed., *The Vestry Book and Register of St. Peter's Parish, New Kent and James City Counties, Virginia, 1684-1786*. (Richmond: Library Board, 1937). 592, 593, 595.

King George County Land Tax Records, 1787

Ed. note: The year 1787 was chosen because the first recorded year of the King George Land Tax Records (1782) was barely legible. The years 1783-1786 listed only the alterations; that is the transfer of land ownership. The list for the year 1787 is the first complete and generally legible listing of land ownership [with unusual names, researchers should check the original].

Transcribed by VLHD.

A List of the Land Tax within the District of George Strother Commissioner for the County of King George, 1787.

Persons' Names	No. Acres	Persons' Names	No. Acres
page 1		William Brown	72½
Lawrence Ashton	223	Hannah Corbin	400
Jacob Anchison	14½	Francis Conway	700
John Ashton Jun[r]	500	Landon Carter	1951
Est John Ashton	150	D° of Abner Waugh	525
Berdett Ashton	350	Thomas Casson	100
John Ashton Sen[r]	465	Charles Carver	100
John Atwood	50	Oswell Crismond	[blot]
Jack Berry	300	Est of James Cash	250
William Berry	100	Benjamin Clift	200
William Boon	250	Robert T Dade	627
D° of Wm Green	557	John Dishman	240
Est Wm Bernards	1650	James Dishman	400
John Bryant	100	d° of John Peck	150
Thomas W Berryman	100	Saml Dishman jr	200
Catherine Baker	175	Est of John Dickenson	50
Catherine Bennett	250	James Dunlop	200
Jesse Bunting	198	Samuel Dishman Sen[r]	300
Est William Benjamin	600	page 2	
Sarah Benjamin	598	Mildred Edwards	44
William Bennett	200	Daniel Edrington	300
D° of Joseph Rollings	14	James Edwards	87
John Bailey	100	Torrence Edrington	85
Stephen Bailey	116	George Fitzhugh	100
Thomas Berry	520	Danl McCarty Fitzhugh	473

Robert Frank	50	D° of James Wilkerson	225
James Frank	50	D° of Original Wroe	40
Hugh Gordon	100	D° of Joseph Gains	150
Thomas W Green	500	John Lewis Dec^d	337
Elizabeth Hughes	60	John Lovell	218
Joseph Hutt	140	William Lovell	100
Landious[?] Harrison	150	Maham[?] Lewis	100
Jonathan Hilton	150	Est of Moses Marders	100
William Horton	30	page 3	
Est William Hughs	50	Robert Manning	50
D° of Benja Edrington	50	Richard Muse	163
Benjamin Johnson	411	Mary Marshall	150
D° of George Reding	90	Rush Marshall	71
D° of James Brown	100	Edward Massey	100
D° of Wm Reding	420	Elizabeth Massey	50
D° of Wm Green	543	George Marshall	251
D° of Ross Dade	400	James Marshall	199
D° of Wm Grigsby	100	D° of Chs Willis Est	100
D° of Rawley Marders	122	Est of James Marders	222
Catherine Jett	30	D° of Wm Gunn	100
Colbert Jones	200	Robert Massey	200
George Johnson	200	William Monroe	100
John I Johnson Senr	70	Jesse McKenney	100
John Johnson (Tay,[?]	70	Betty Monroe	46
Peter Jett	175	James Monroe	300
Frances Jett	175	William Massey	100
D° of Joseph Hutt	200	William Nelson	100
John Johnson	226	Samuel Oldham	500
Gabriel Johnson	219	D° of Aaron Webb	100
John Jett	200	D° of Abra. Prim	100
Wm Storks Jett	800	Aaron Owens	100
Frances Jackson	200	William Price	100
James Kay Senr	120	William Park	148
James Kay Junr	75	John Pollard	166
Samuel Kendall Senr	200	John Pittman	100
Samuel Kendall Jr	85	John Price Senr	625
Jeremiah Kirk	212	John Price jr	100
Hezekiah Kirk	200	William Piper	442
Woffendall[?] Kirk	245	Isaac Pittman	470

Ann Peper	100	John Thornley	318½
Est of John Price	130	Aaron Thornley	283
Jane Potes	60	D° of Eliza Arnold	8
Mildred Rogers	60	D° of John Wren	100
John Rogers	107½	D° D°	37
Est of Alexr Ross	610	D° Thomas Turner	133
John Ross	94	Ann Thornley	200
Francis Ross	200	Elizabeth Thornton	778
Cayton Ross	100	Francis Thornton	1165
Joseph Rollins	[blot]	Thomas Thornton	4164
Est of Price Roach	100	D° of Mary Tankersley	200
Est of Wm Smith	150	Thomas Wray	126
Rosamond Stewart	125	Samuel Wharton	38
William Shropshire	98	Gerrard Wilkerson	123
William Skinker	580	Est Thomas Wilkerson	210
Saml Skinker Est	532	Thacker Washington	2160
Margaret Strother	121	D° of George Wardon	600
Col° John Skinker	1275	John Wilkerson	140
Mary Stigler	100	Grace Wroe	70
Charles Stewart Est	732	Original Wroe	30
John Strother	170	Lovett White	298
		Benja Wilkerson	95
page 4		D° Davis Galloway & Co	107
George Strother	100	Elizabeth White	150
Amey Settler	50	James Wisdom	125
Thomas Settler	135	James Wilkerson jr	188
Frances Storke	225	Charles White	295
Thomas Smith	560	James Williams	139
Frances Spillman Est	240	Mary Wren	[blot]
Elizabeth Smith	140	Charles G Jones	200
Est of Col° Jno Taylor	1400	William Jones	100

Imprimis

[signed]   Y Johnson

[signed]

[dated] June 5, 1787 King George Office

page 5
List of the Land Tax within the District of Rice W^d Hooe Commissioner for the County of King George

Est Phillip Alexander	1066	Ann Fowke	162
Joseph Armstrong	200	Charles Fowke	482
Est Lucy Alexander	50	Will Fitzhugh	
Susannah Alexander	1100	Chatham	2070
Henry Alex^r Ashton	1190	Will Fitzhugh	
d° d° of Jno Tyler	226	Marin	1973
William Alexander	327	Jno B Fitzhugh	350
Estate of Burgis	100	Mary Grant	220
Revd Robt Buckham	500	Richmond Grigsby	[blank]
Laurence Brooke	747	Alexander Hansford	226
Jno Bunbury	260	d° d° of Mary Jones	200
William Bunbury	150	Stephen Hansford	80
Elizabeth Bunbury	150	d° d° James Monteith	156
Richard Brent	1200	d° d° of Elz Hansford	120
William Champ	342	Peter Hansbrough	800
James Cross	201	Estate Gerrard Hooe	1000
Jno Taylor Corbin	600	d° d° of Elz Yates	300
Mildred Clifton	165	William Hooe Junr	90
Robert Clift	80	d° d° of Jno Hooe	325
Jno Clift	30	Valentine Hudson	50
Mott DJarrnitt	70	Ann Hooe	200
James Davis	160	Estate Seymour Hooe	558
d° d° of Saml Mardis	130	Rice W^d Hooe	800
Mary Doniphan	200	William Hooe Jun	560
Alexander Doniphan	4[blot]	d° d° of Pratt	512
Phillip Townd Dade Esq	950	William Hudson	[blot]
Est Ewd Dade	200	Joseph Jones Esq	832
Estate [Baldwin] Dade	350	Nathl Jones	739
Nathaniel Elkins	86	Jno Kibble	330
Zachariah Elkins	50	Jno Lunley	181
Jeremiah Elkins	50	William Murphey	253
page 6		Jno Morton	200
Est Col° Henry Fitzhugh	1843	George Morton	100
Henry Fitzhugh Jr	530	George Mifflin	71
Jonathan Finnel	50	[last name on page illeg]	

page 7

175

Nehimeah R Mason	298	Will G Stuart (Dr)	905
Robert Massey Jun	343	d° d° Fitzhugh Marmion	79
Daniel McCarty	400	d° d° Phillip Stuart	500
Thomas Massey	300	Estate Jno Stuart	506
Robert Massey Jun	198	William Stewart	360
Thomas Moss Est	66½	Robert Stith	743
Pisgismand Massey	375		
Jno Moss's Estate	133	page 8	
John Marcus	93	John Talliaferro Hays	613
Estate Thos Oliver	135	d° d° of Wm Bruce	150
Rhueben Owens	350	d° d° Joseph Jones Est	498
Greenlees S Orr	400	John Turner	100
John Peed	212	d° d° Jno Talliaferro	1043
Anthony Price	200	d° d° Gieorde[?] King	125
Margaret Pratt	1484	William Thomson	50
Jno Pratt	283	William Thornton Esq	400
Richd Potes	170	James Went	105
d° d° Richd Brown	166	Estate Gerry Waugh	1100
William Quarles	533½	Jno Waughs Estate	1200
Moses Rowley	75	Michael Wallace	1126
Ann Rowley	300	Lewis Willis	1955
Will Smallwood (Gov)	500	Walter Williamson	196
d° d° of Jno Mercer	[blot]	Rob. Washington	576
Revd William Stuart	400	Laurence Washington	1177
d° d° Glebe	200	Estate Jno Washington	490
d° d° Passpatansy	100	Estate Nathl Washington	300
d° d° Nick	200	Elizabeth Yates	250
Theodosiah Short	750		

King George Office   [signed] *Johnson*

May 28th 1787
A true Copy

King George County Land Tax Records, 1787, Reel 162, Archives and Information Services, The Library of Virginia, Richmond, VA.

Pay Roll of Persons at the State Magazine, 1788

     A loose paper, probably filed among the State Auditors Office Records, listing the personnel assigned to the state magazine, the facility that manufactured and repaired weapons. Listed are the superintendent, the artificers, or artisans and craftsmen; the armourers, or those who manufactured or repaired arms; and the laborers. The list is recorded in chart form, with the individual's name, occupation, the time period of employment for which pay is requested, the number of lost days and the amount of pay due. Elias Langhorn was the superintendant. It is thought that the state magazine was the *Point of Forks Arsenal* in Fluvanna County.   VLHD

Payroll of the Superinten^{dt} & Artificers, labourers etc at the State Magazine imployed by Elias Langhorn Superintend^t October the 1st Ending the 31st Decemb^r 1788 Inclusive

Name	Characters	Total Pay (exc. of lost das.)	Comments	
Elias Langham	Superintdt	£37/10	no lost days	
Ro. Fowler	Armourrer	12/10	6 lost days	
Jon. Hays	do	12/10	8 do	
Jno. Barlow	do	10/10	3 do	
Thos. Dawson	do	10/10	10 do discharged Jan 1 89	
Thos. Gray	do	9/10	2 do	
Jno. Heekle	do	9/10	3 do	
H. Wade	do	2/4/5	1 do dischged 10 Nov 88	
Geo. Burton	Smiter	4/1/5	none	
Wm. Farris	Carpenter	9/1/5	4 lost days	
Wm. Quarles	do	9/1/5	2 do	
Wm. Sutton	do	9/1/5	none	
Roger Quarles	do	9/1/5	do	
Jno. Robinson	Labourers	4/10/5	6 do dischged 1 Jan 1789	
Jas. Hawkins	do	3/12/5	1 do	do
Negro Zadock	do	3/15/5	none	do
Jas. Rice	do	4/4/5	7 lost days	do
Reubin Wood	do	4/10/5	3 do	do
Negro Derry	do	1/10/5	3 do	Nov. 1-Nov 30
Richd. Merritt	Armourer	(name added as footnote)	engaged Feb 1 89	

Loose Papers, The Library of Virginia, Richmond, Virginia.

This transcription is taken from a xeroxed copy of a bound and stitched book measuring 6½ x 6½ inches with the above heading; containing in all 167 pages, exclusive of a complete index of the names in the front of the book. Essex County Circuit Court Clerk's Office. This transcriber has a good knowledge of the names of the earlier (and long-time) residents of Essex County, and in fact many of these same names can still be found in the county. Even so, some names are difficult to read; if there are questions it is suggested that the originally xeroxed copy be consulted. VLHD

A Register of Free Negroes in the County
Essex County Circuit Court Office State of Virginia

By virtue of an act of the General Assembly this State passed 25th January 1803 entitled "An act more effectually to restrain the practice of negroes going at large" I have registered the bearer (who states himself to be a resident of this County) as follows No. 1 **General Webb**, emancipated, appearing by the will of Moore Fauntleroy recorded in Richmond County Court and the certificate of Robert Fauntleroy the executor of the said Moore, a dark Mulattoe, about twenty years of age and statue five feet eight and one half inches — Given under my hand as Clerk of the said court of Essex County the 30th of November 1810.

[signed] *John P. Lee*

[Note: until stated otherwise, each of the following entries have been recorded with the following heading: *State of Virginia, Essex County Court Office, By virtue of an act of the General Assembly of this State passed 25th January 1803 entitled "and act more effectually to restrain the practice of negroes going at large"...]*

......I have registered the bearer (who states herself to be a resident of this county) as follows No. 2 **Eunice Bailey** born free appearing by certificate of James Ball a Justice of the Peace for Lancaster [County] colour bright

Mulattoe about [blank] and Stature four feet two inches — Given under my hand as Clerk of the said court of Essex County the 30th of November 1810.
John P. Lee

I have registered the bearer (who states herself to be a resident of this county) as follows No. 3 **Mary Jones,** born free ~~appearing~~ [blank] colour dark Mulattoe about sixty years of age and five feet two inches — Given under my hand as Clerk of the said court of Essex County the 7th of December 1810. certified correct   John P. Lee

I have registered the bearer (who states ~~him~~ herself to be a resident of this county) as follows No. 4 **Chancey Jones** born free appearing by the affidavit of Richard Banks [blank] colour dark Mulattoes about 33 years of age and Stature five feet three inches and three quarters of an inch — Given under my hand as Clerk of the said court of Essex County the 7th of December 1810.   John P. Lee
1818 Aug 17th Ex[ecute]d by the Ct and certified correct.
Wm.B. Matthews Cl

I have registered the bearer (who states herself to be a resident of this county as follows No. 5 **Mildred Atkinson** born free appearing by the copy of her Register signed by Ro. S. Chew Clk [illeg] coloring a dark Mulattoe about fifty three years of age and Stature 5 feet 5 inches — Given under my hand as Clerk of the said court of Essex County the 8th of December 1810. certified correct   John P. Lee

I have registered the bearer (who states herself to be a resident of this county) as follows No. 6 **Nelly Webb** appearing by cert. of the Clerk of Richmond Cty to have been emancipated by William Fauntleroy colour brown Mulattoe about 49 years of age Stature 5 feet 1¾ inches — Given under my hand as Clerk of the said court of Essex County the 8th of December 1810. [notation in margin] with no other mark or scar on her face head or hands except a scar on the side of the upper joint of the left thumb caused by a cut. certified correct   John P. Lee
Essex Court held 20th May 1811

I have registered the bearer (who states herself to be a resident of this county) as follows No. 7 **Lanah Webb** born free appearing by the affidavit of **Nelly Webb** the mother who was emancipated by William Fauntleroy colour a dark Mulattoe ~~eight~~ six years of age and Stature three feet 8 inches — Given under my hand as Clerk of the said court of Essex County the 8th of December 1810.
certified correct   John P. Lee

I have registered the bearer (who states herself to be a resident of this county) as follows No. 8 **Mary Webb** born free appearing by the affidavit of

179

Nelly Webb the mother who was emancipated by William Fauntleroy colour a dark Mulattoe eight years of age and Stature four feet 1¼ inches — Given under my hand as Clerk of the said court of Essex County the 8th of December 1810. certified correct   John P. Lee

I have registered the bearer (who states herself to be a resident of this county) as follows No. 9 **Sally Hollinger** born free appearing by a certificate of her enrollment by the Com[missione]r of the Revenue colour a dark Mulattoe about sixty[?] years of age a scar upon the upper part of her nose and Stature five feet two and one quarter inches — Given under my hand as Clerk of the said court of Essex County the 8th of December 1810.
certified correct   John P. Lee

I have registered the bearer (who states herself to be a resident of this county) as follows No. 10 **Judy Hollinger** appearing by a certificate of her enrollment by the Com[missione]r of the Revenue colour a bright Mulattoe about 44 years of age a scar on the eyebrow of the left eye and Stature five feet two and one quarter inches — Given under my hand as Clerk of the said court of Essex County the 8th of December 1810.
certified correct   John P. Lee

I have registered the bearer (who states herself to be a resident of this county) as follows No. 11 **Sally Hollinger Junr** daughter of **Judy Hollinger** appearing by a affidavit of **Sally Hollinger Senr** to be born free colour a dark Mulattoe nine years of age and Stature four feet five and one quarter inches — Given under my hand as Clerk of the said court of Essex County the 8th of December 1810. certified correct   John P. Lee

I have registered the bearer (who states himself to be a resident of this county) as follows No. 12 **Thos Hollinger** son of **Judy Hollinger** appearing by a affidavit of **Sally Hollinger Senr** to be born free colour a dark Mulattoe about 7 years of age and Stature 3 feet 10¾ inches — Given under my hand as Clerk of the said court of Essex County the 8th of December 1810.
certified correct   John P. Lee

I have registered the bearer (who states herself to be a resident of this county) as follows No. 13 **Judith Day** born free appearing by certificate of the Clerk of Essex colour dark Mulattoe about 30 years of age and Stature 5 feet 1¾ inches — Given under my hand as Clerk of the said court of Essex County the 8th of Dec 1810.
certified correct   John P. Lee

I have registered the bearer (who states by his mother to be a resident of this county) as follows No. 14 **Cole Day** born free appearing by the affidavit of **Judith Day** her mother colour bright Mulattoe about ten years of age and

180

Stature 3 feet 10¾ inches — Given under my hand as Clerk of the said court of Essex County the 8th of December 1810.
certified correct   John P. Lee

    I have registered the bearer (who is stated by **Judith Day** her mother to be a resident of this county) as follows No. 15 **Lucy Day** born free appearing by the affidavit of the said **Judith Day** his mother colour dark Mulattoe about 5 years of age and Stature 3 feet 5¼ inches — Given under my hand as Clerk of the said court of Essex County the 8th of December 1810. certified correct   John P. Lee

    I have registered the bearer (her mother who states by self to be a resident of this county) as follows No. 16 **Maria Day** appearing by the affidavit of **Judith Day** her mother colour dark Mulattoe about 3 years of age and Stature 2 feet 10 inches — Given under my hand as Clerk of the said court of Essex County the 8th of December 1810.
certified correct   John P. Lee

    I have registered the bearer (who states himself to be a resident of this county) as follows No. 17 **William Lewis** emancipated appearing by deed of emancipation recorded in Essex Ct from Edwd Noel colour a shade lighter than a black about fifty years of age and Stature 5 feet 5¾ inches — Given under my hand as Clerk of the said court of Essex County the 8th of December 1810. certified correct   John P. Lee

    I have registered the bearer (who states herself to be a resident of this County) as follows No. 18 formerly **Betty McGuy, Betty Soleleather** appearing by certificate of the Clerk of Richmond County to be born free colour bright Mulattoe, about 21 years of age scar upon the right arm and above the elbow and Stature five feet 5¾ inches — Given under my hand as Clerk of the said court of Essex County the 8th of December 1810.
certified correct   John P. Lee

[Note: beginning with this entry the statement *By virtue Etc (as before to the word follows)* is shortened to read]:

    No. 19 **Mary Soleleather** free born it appearing by the statement of Thomas Brockenbrough in person that she has always passed as a free born person — colour a shade lighter than a black about 39 years of age and Stature four feet 11 inches — Given under my hand as Clerk of the said court of Essex County the 8th of December 1810.
certified correct   John P. Lee

    No. 20 **Thos Soleleather** son of **Mary Soleleather** born free it appearing by the statement of Thomas Brockenbrough in person that his mother has always passed as a free born person — colour dark Mulattoe about

15 years of age and Stature five feet ¾ inches — Given under my hand as Clerk of the said court of Essex County the 8 December 1810.

Essex Ct 18 December 1815 Examined by the court and certified correct with the amendment that his Stature be changed to 5 feet 11 inches and his age to 20 years.   John P. Lee

No. 21 Son of **Mary Soleleather** born free **Philip Soleleather** appearing by the statement of Thos Brockenbrough in person that by said mother has always passed as a free born person colour dark Mulattoe about 18 years of age and Stature five feet 7 inches — Given under my hand as Clerk of court of Essex Cty the 8 December 1810.   John P. Lee

No. 22 Daughter **Mary Soleleather** born free **Mary Soleleather** appearing by the statement of Thos Brockenbrough in person that by said mother has always passed as a free born person colour very dark Mulattoe about 9 years of age and Stature four feet 3¾ inches — Given under my hand as Clerk of the said court of Essex County the 8th of December 1810.
                                                                             John P. Lee

No. 23 =Soleleather daughter **Mary Soleleather** born free **Nancy [Soleleather]** appearing by the statement of Thos Brockenbrough in person that by said mother has always passed as a free born person colour very dark Mulattoe about 7 years of age and Stature three feet 7¼ inches — Given under my hand as Clerk of the said court of Essex County the 8th of December 1810.
                                                                             John P. Lee

No. 24 =Soleleather daughter **Mary Soleleather** born free **Charlotte [Soleleather]** appearing by the statement of Thomas Brockenbrough in person that by said mother has always passed as a free born person colour very dark Mulattoe about five years of age scar on the right cheek and Stature three feet three inches — Given under my hand as Clerk of the said court of Essex County the 8th of December 1810.

certified correct   John P. Lee

No. 25 **Milly Jones** daughter of **Mary Jones** appearing by the statement of Thomas Brockenbrough in person that she has always passed as a free born person colour a light black with a small mole on the upper part of the nose on the right side about 25 years of age and Stature five feet 3 inches — Given under my hand as Clerk of the said court of Essex County the 8th of December 1810. certified correct   John P. Lee

at a court held April 1817 Wm B Matthews Clk

No. 26 **Sukey Hollinger** appearing by the statement of Thomas Brockenbrough in person that she has always passed as a free born person colour dark Mulattoe about 35 years of age small care[?] under the right eye

near the nose and Stature five feet 5½ inches — Given under my hand as Clerk of the said Court of Essex County the 8th of December 1810.
certified correct   John P. Lee

No. 26[sic] **Wm Hollinger** born free appearing by the statement of Thomas Brockenbrough in person that **Sukey Hollinger** his mother has always passed as a free born person colour bright Mulattoe about 13 years of age and Stature four feet 3½ inches — Given under my hand as Clerk of the said Court of Essex County the 8th of December 1810.
certified correct   John P. Lee

No. 27 **Smith Hollinger** born free appearing by the statement of Thomas Brockenbrough in person that **Sukey Hollinger** his mother has always passed as a free born person colour dark Mulattoe about 16 years of age and Stature five feet 3 inches — Given under my hand as Clerk of the said Court of Essex County 8th of December 1810.
certified correct   John P. Lee

No. 28 **Henry Hollinger** born free it appearing by the statement of Thos Brockenbrough in person that **Sukey Hollinger** his mother has always passed as a free born person colour bright Mulattoe about 8 years of age and Stature four feet — Given under my hand as Clerk of the said Court of Essex County 8th of December 1810. Passes as free born person.
certified correct   John P. Lee

No. 29 **Mary Hollinger** free born it appearing by the statement of Thos Brockenbrough in person that **Sukey Hollinger** her mother has always passed as a free born person colour bright Mulattoe about five years of age and Stature three feet 3¼ inches — Given under my hand as Clerk of the said Court of Essex County 8th of December 1810.
certified correct   John P. Lee

No. 30 **Jenny Rollins** it appearing by the statement of Thomas Brockenbrough in person that her said mother has always passed as a free born person colour bright Mulattoe about 25 years of age a defect in her left side and a small scar on her right cheek and a large scar on her left cheek and about five feet 2¼ inches — Given under my hand as Clerk of the said Court of Essex County 8th of Dec 1810.

certified correct

To be continued

Contributed by June Banks Evans[1]

Lunenburg County Will Book 4, 1791-1799.
p. 75b+ 4 Dec 1794 (Lunenburg Court Order Dec 1793) Inventory/appraisal Essex Co estate of **Thos. Bridgforth** decd: Negroes: Reubin, John, Harry, Charles, Bander, Billy, Bob, Will, Beck, Rachel, Barnet, Nanny, Sarah, Sukey, Betty, James, Billy, Lucy, Prince, Winney, Sam, Mary and Phillis. Livestock and assorted farming tools, total value £1093/3/9.
Recorded 8 Dec 1795. Appraisers: **Henry Garnet, H.B. Brooks, C. Boughan**

p. 116b Marriage in Lunenburg County (entry headed Nottoway County)
5 Sep 1795 **Thomas Blackwell & Mary Bridgeforth** of Lunenburg.
Recorded 10 Dec 1795. Signed **Jno. Jones**

p. 246a+ 1 Dec 1794 Acct/Sales personal estate **Thos. Bridgforth** in Essex County: To **Humphrey B. Brooke**, sheep, brandy, £17/17/9; **Robert Parker**, brandy, wheat, £39/13/10; **Ambrose Pitts**, livestock, wheat, £41/1/10; **Caleb Noel**, corn, mare, £28/12/0; **Edwin Noel**, livestock, £6/0/6; **Thomas Anderson**, heifers, £4/0/6; **Jno. Hungerford**, livestock, £5/5/0; **William Rouse**, horse, brandy, pork, £12/11/6; **Thomas Boulware**, pork, £9/12/3; **William Tussman**, cows, £4/3/10. Value £169/8/0; received of overseer in Essex for sundries, £37/4/7; received of **Jno. Butler** for shoemaking £1/2/9. Recd 9 May 1799.

p. 248+ 11/12 Dec 1795 Acct/Sales estate of **Thomas Bridgeforth** in Essex County to **James Bridgeforth**, livestock, farm items, rent of land/plantation 1 yr, £204/15/7½; **James Micou**, livestock, corn, £37/4/2; **William Weatherford**, livestock, £2/14/10; **William Wright**, livestock, farm tools, £/10/0; **Thomas Blackwell**, cart wheels, gear, £7/2/2; **Thomas Fog**, tools, £/6/6; **Ralph Rouzer**, spades, £/10/0; **Robert Parker**, tools, corn, £27/7/2; **Mr. John Matthews** bound himself to deliver **Mr. James Micou**'s bond due in 12 mos; **Reuben Atkinson**, irons, £/13/; **Thomas Noel**, gun, fodder, £4/0/1; **Barker Spindle**, furniture, hhds, £3/8/8; **Vincent Meadow**, brandy (said Meadow not appearing, brandy sold to **Humphrey B Brooke**); **Thomas Boulware**, brandy, fodder, £18/3/1; **Alexander Somervail**, brandy, £11/1/3; **Augustin Baughan**, bricks, wheat, £10/19/0; **James Adams**, wool, £/14/3½; **Jeremiah Upshaw**, corn, £96/3/4. Recorded 9 May 1799.

Lunenburg County Deed Book 24, 1815-1819.
p. 179 22 Oct 1816 (King and Queen Co) **Peggy**, wife of **Richard Dunn**, relinquished her dower right in 92 acres in Lunenburg Co, sold to **Horatio Winn**, 5 Feb 1813. Recorded 14 Nov 1816. Lunenburg County. Signed: **Humphry Walker, R B Hill** J/P.

Lunenburg County Will Book 4, 1791-1799 & Lunenburg County Deed Book 24, 1815-1819. Abstracted by June Banks Evans. Purchase from Bryn Ffyliaid Publications, 300 Lake Marina Dr #16BW, New Orleans, LA 70124.

* * * * *

To Be Sold: Land Tracts, 1788
Elizabeth City County

TO BE SOLD On the premises in Elizabeth City County, the following Tracts of Land, or so much thereof as will discharge the Revenue and additional Taxes for 1786, and necessary expenses attending the advertisement, sale, and Etc., viz.

Elizabeth Allen, 17 acres   **Barthia Allen**, 33 acres
George Bains, 50 acres   **Thomas Baylis sen**, 90 acres
Stephen N. Haynes, 200 acres   **Mary Houle**, 27 acres
Martha Jiggitts, 49 acres   **Catharine Mercer**, 150 acres
Margaret Mossom, 15 acres   **Samuel Sandefer**, dec'd. 25 acres
Thomas Skinner (orphan), 100 acres   **Mary Williams**, 95 acres
John Williams, 97 acres   **John Yeargain**, 65 acres
[blank] Yeargain (orphan), 35 acres   **William Armistead**, 1 lot
Robert Boyd, ½ ditto   **John Williams**, ½ ditto
Timothy Baker (orphan) part ditto   **Alexander Brodie**, ¼ ditto
Michael Conneil, dec'd. ¼ ditto   **Charles Cooper**, ¼ ditto
William Davis, sen, ½ ditto   **Elizabeth Jones**, ½ ditto
Henry Irvin, dec'd., ½ ditto   **John Lawson**, ½ ditto
British Property, 1 lot   **John Plauket**, ¼ ditto
[blank] Selden (orphan) part of ditto

The sale to begin in Hampton, January 1st 1789 and to continue from lot to lot, and from tract to tract until the whole is disposed of.

[signed] George Wray, late sheriff

The Virginia Independent Chronicle, Richmond, VA, Wed. 12 Nov 1788, 3:3.

Transcribed by Dr. Benjamin B. Weisiger, III
Contributed by Minor T. Weisiger

Continued from Volume 7, Number 2, page 122.

The entries from the Henrico Will Book 1, 1781-1787, as abstracted by Dr. Benjamin B. Weisiger (1924-1995), ended with page 199. His abstractions of county records were both meticulous and prolific. Your editor has continued the abstraction of this will book, hopefully, as accurately as Dr. Weisiger. These records, continuing, will be a feature of Tidewater Virginia Families: A Magazine of History and Genealogy to the completion of Will Book 1.

Abstracts of the wills following give the page number in the will book on which the will is first entered. Names are entered in bold using the format of Dr. Weisiger. (VLHD)

p.308 Will of **Mary Whitlock**, co and Parish of Henrico, "sound mind and memory, but sick and weak of body".
Imprimis to son **John Whitlock** items.
Item to daughter **Elizabeth Werner** two Negroes, Fillis and Charlie, items.
Item to daughter **Sarah Whitlock** two Negroes, Doctor and Milley, items.
Item to son **Thomas Whitlock** two Negroes, Sal and Sam.
Item to daughter **Sarah** remainder of estate.
Executors: **Samuel Gathright, Sen., William Gathright, Sen.**
14 Jan 1786   signed **Mary X Whitlock**
Witnesses: **John West, Elizabeth Smith**
Recorded 3 July 1786
Proved by **John West** and **Elizabeth Smith.**

p.310 Will of **Michael Johnson** Henrico Co "sick and weak, perfect sense and sound memory".
Item to sons **Benjamin Johnson, David Johnson, Thomas Johnson, James Johnson, William Johnson,** daughters **Alice Johnson, Martha Johnson, Sarah Johnson, Frances Johnson** and **Jane Johnson** all lands to be sold and money equally divided. Legacy given deceased wife by her father also divided. Those of age may choose guardians, others under care of executors.
Executors: **Benjamin Johnson, David Johnson, John Miller, John Hughes.** 23 Dec 1785.   signed **Michael Johnson**

Witnesses: **Winney X Bowles, Martha X Bowles, David Bowles.**
Recorded Henrico Co, no date.
Proved by **Winney Bowles, Martha Bowles, David Bowles.** Motion by executors. Securities: **John Price** and **William Gathright.**

p.313 Will of **Peter Bailey** parish and co of Henrico, "ill and weak, but sound and composed mind and memory".
Item to daughter **Sarah Bailey** Negro Phebe; plantation to be sold, money divided among three sons, **John W Bailey, Peter Bailey, Joseph Bailey.**
Estate lent to wife **Frances Bailey** to support and bring up children.
Frances Bailey to be executrix.
10 Mar 1786.   signed **Peter Bailey**
Witnesses: **John Ferris, Elizabeth Ferris, Richard Bailey**
Recorded 3 July 1786
Proved by **John Ferris, Elizabeth Ferris, Richard Bailey.**
Frances Bailey executrix, posted bond.

p.314 Inventory of **William Gathright**, dec'd. Negroes Joe, Peter, Betty, Amey, Sue, Sall, Fanny, Doter, Milley, Peg, Nancy, Mark, Ben, Sam, Jeffrey, Isam, Betty, Siller, Ned, Isaac, Abram, Nat, Jenny, Stephen, Charles, Mark, Jenny, Jude, Milley. Value £1632/9/6. Appraisers: **Benjamin Hobson, Thomas Childrey, Benjamin Goode.** Returned 4 Sep 1786.

p.316 Will of **Elizabeth Price**, Henrico Co sound and perfect mind and memory.
Item to son **Peter Price**, Negro Will, son of Rachel.
Item to support of children until daughter **Sarah Price** comes of age 12 then equally divided among children. That part of father's estate left to be divided at my mother's death, be equally divided as above.
Executors: sons, **Peter Price, Lewis Price** and brother **Barret Price** and **Obediah Smith** of Chesterfield. 16 July 1786   signed **Elizabeth Price**
Witnesses: **James Price, Elizabeth X Kelley, Susannah W Price**
Recorded 2 Oct 1786
Proved by three witnesses. **Peter Price** executor posted bond.

p.317 Inventory of **Mary Whitlock**, dec'd.
Negroes Sam, Sally and child, Doctor, Milley, and Charles. Value £217/7/3.
Appraised by **Moses Woodfin, Thos Binford, Samuel Gathright.**
Returned 2 Oct 1786

p.318 Will of **Matthew Harbert,** Henrico Co, "sick and weak, perfect mind and memory".

Item to son **John Harbert** 1 shilling, having received already what is sufficient.

Item to daughter **Martha Whitlow** plantation and land where she lives 400 acres of Wood's Creek in Charlotte Co, which I had of **Smith Blakey.** At her death to **Frank Camp**'s children.

Item to son **William Harbert** planation, 400 acres; Negroes to son **William:** Frank, Judy, Ben, Sall, Jenny, Rose, Pompey, Easter, Else, Davy, Martain, Edy, Rachel, Abram second, Jenny Junr. Stock, household goods, he to maintain beloved wife **Martha.** Executor: **William Harbert**

2 Sep 1786   signed **Matthew X Harbert**

Witnesses: **Thos. Pinchback, Thos. Johnson, Sen., William Pinchback, Philip Williams, John Blackey.**

Recorded 1 Jany 1787

Proved by **Thomas Pinchback, Thomas Johnson, Sr, Jno Blakey. William Harbert** motion.

Securities: **Thomas Johnson, Jno Blackey, John DePriest.**

p.320 Will of **Patrick Wright** city of Richmond, "weak in body, sound and disposing mind".

Imprimis Interest and profit from estate for use of beloved wife **Lucy** support and support of children. In case of death of both children before 21, whole profits to wife. Wife to have house and lot in Portsmouth and co of Norfolk, also Negro Fanny.

Item real estate sold at discretion of executors except houses and lots in city of Richmond, house and lot in Portsmouth and 2 lots in Borough of Norfolk, purchased of **Richard Evers Lee.**

If children and wife die one moiety to children of brother **John Wright** and other moiety to children of friend **Richard Evers Lee.** Lease on coal pits of **Thomas Short** in Chesterfield, executor can dispose of or retain.

Books of **Patrick Wright** & Co not to be delivered to anyone unless they indemnify estate.

Executors: **George Muter, George Kelly** and **Richard Evers Lee**

8 Dec 1786   signed **Patrick Wright**

Witnesses: **Charles Hay, John Cunliff, John McColl**

Recorded 1 Jan 1787

Proved by above three. Motion by **George Kelly** and **Richard Evers Lee**

Securities: **Gabriel Galt, Alexander McRoberts**   **Adam Craig**, clerk

p.322 Will of **William Coutts**, Henrico, clerk, "sick and weak, but perfect sense and memory".

Imprimis executors to sell land, lots in Richmond, Islands in James River and ferries as advantageous.

Item to Mrs. **Margaret Barnes** house I live in (Richmond), Negroes Sylvia and Monimia and children of Sylvia and Stephen the son of Monimia.

Item to **Reuben Coutts** son of my brother **Patrick Coutts**, dec'd. right to the reversion of the south ferry except lot belonging to **William Byrd.**

Item freedom to Isiah (sic), son of Monimia and sent to school £50 to set him up in trade.

Margaret Barnes and **Patrick Barnes, Patience Barnes** supported by estate.

Executors: **John McKeand, Benjamin Lewis, Alexander McRoberts, James Buchanan, John Marshall.**

12 Jan 1787   signed **William Coutts**

Witnesses: **Gilbert Hay, John Bryan, Thos. Williamson**

Codecil: to brother **John Coutts** of Aberdeen £1000. To **Leslie (blank,? Coutts?)** £200. Any remainder divided between Mrs. **Margaret Barnes** and her daughter **Patience Barnes.**   Teste **William Foushee**

Codicil to executors £500 divided among those who act.   **William Coutts**

Recorded 5 Feb 1787

Proved by **John Bryan** and **Thomas Williamson, William Foushee.** Motion of **Alexander McRoberts** and **John McKeand**, executors.

Securities: **William Duval, Smith Blakey, Samuel Williamson.**

                                                            Benjamin Pollard D C

p.328 Inventory of **Joseph Brown**, dec'd. Appraised by **William Henley, Thomas Ellis, Jacob Smith, John Ellis.** 3 Feb 1787. 1 Negro woman no value given. Sworn by **Thomas Prosser**, magistrate.

Returned 5 Feb 1787.

p.332 Will of **Thomas Childrey**, Henrico Co, "weak in body but sound sense and memory".

Item to wife **Nancy Childrey** all estate, lands, Negroes, stock and furniture during her lifetime. At death equally divided among five sons, **Stephen Childrey, Thomas Childrey, Charles Childrey, William Childrey** and **John Childrey.**

Executors: friends, **John James Woodfin, William Gathright, Sr, Noble Jordan.**

14 Nov 1786   signed **Thomas Childrey**

Witnesses: **Moses Woodfin, John Edwards, Joseph Francis**

Recorded 5 Feb 1787

Proved by witnesses, **William Gathright**, executor, motion.
Securities: **Anselm Gathright** and **William Binford**

Adam Craig C C

p.334 Will of **Sterling Thornton** Henrico Co, "low health but perfect mind".
(1) to son **Francis Thornton** Negroes Charles and Arthur and equal share of estate.
(2) to daughter **Rebecca Thornton** Negro Moll and equal share of estate.
(3) to daughter **Ann Thornton** items and equal share of estate.
(4) desire land I live on to be sold and proceeds to children.
(5) residue of Negroes and estate be sold.
(6) brother-in-law **Richard Cock** of Surry and friend **Thomas Pleasants** and **John Pleasants** of Henrico executors.
Thomas Pleasants and **John Pleasants** to be guardians of children.
18 Feb 1787   signed **Sterling Thornton**
Witnesses: **Peter Sharp, John Williams, Benjamin Perkins** and **Benjamin Fussell.**
Recorded Henrico 2 Apr 1787
Proved by **Peter Sharp, John Williams, Benjamin Perkins. John Pleasants** executor, motion.
Securities: **Turner Southall** and **John James Woodfin.**

p.336 Inventory and appraisement of estate of Revd. **William Coutts**, dec'd.
Negroes: Izreal (sic), Young Izreal, Jesse, Phillip, Peter, Josiah, Tom, Hagar, Monimia, Sylvia and Billy, Mary, Nanny, Nancy, John, Jack, Betty, Stephen, Molly. Appraiser **Martin Burton** Value £1044/7/-.
John Hague, Pleasant Younghusband.
Returned 13 Feb 1787.

p.340 Inventory of estate of **John Parker**, dec'd. 28 Mar 1787. Negro Will Value £117/3/2. Appraised by **John James Woodfin, Thos Jordan, Banks X Wade.** Returned 4 June 1787   **Adam Craig** C C

To be concluded

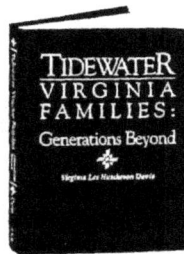

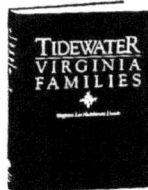

191

BOOK REVIEWS:

Mark D. Herber, *Ancestral Trails: The Complete Guide to British Genealogy and Family History.* xiv, 674 pp., index, illus., charts, documents, maps, coated paper, cloth. 1997. $34.95, plus $3.50 ship. This outstanding, comprehensive book on English genealogical research is compiled in association with the Society of Genealogists, London, England. Mr. Herber's own genealogical research provides the introduction to research among the British repositories. It includes a detailed description of each of various sources of records and how to best utilize them. This reviewer immediately became caught up in following the sources necessary to identify some personal ancestors from across the water, and became hopeful, that under Mr. Herber's direction some illusive persons may be identified. He presents detailed descriptions of available records; civil, census, parish, wills, estates, shipping, professions, trades military, as well as many others; each in an entire chapter. Sources of information about births, marriages, divorces and deaths are included, as well as directories of archives, libraries and family history societies. This compilation offers the researcher the most complete, easily accessed and authoritative guide to British genealogical research this reviewer has found. (it is also an inexpensive book, unusually well-presented). #2691. Genealogical Publishing Co, 1001 N. Calvert St, Baltimore, MD 21202-3897.

Lyon Gardiner Tyler, *Encyclopedia of Virginia Biography, 5 volumes.* 2296 pp., 279 full-page plates, index, cloth. (1915) repr. 1998. $250.00 for the set, plus $8.50 ship. Volumes 1 and 2 present biographical sketches of notable Virginians from the colonial period of the 17th and 18th century. Volumes 3, 4 and 5 present more detailed biographies of Virginians of note of the 19th century. Earlier sketches present available information of birth date and place, parents, spouse and antecedents to the early immigrant, as well as notable contributions to the colony. Later biographies present the vital records of the individual as well as education, and more detailed accounts of careers, military and political service. Many full page portraits, with the individual's signature are included. Dr. Tyler is recognized as the editor of the *William and Mary Quarterly* (from its inception in 1892 until 1919), then of *Tyler's Quarterly.* He was a prolific and scholarly writer of Virginia history and genealogy and has made a great contribution through this compilation, and his many other academic endeavors. The original publication date should be noted, and it should be understood that subsequent records and additional information may have come to light concerning some of the earlier biographies. It should also be noted that many of the biographical accounts cannot be found elsewhere. #5856. Genealogical Publishing Co, 1001 N Calvert St, Baltimore, MD 21202-3897.

Gilbert S. Bahn, Ph.D., *American Place Names of Long Ago.* 347 pp., alphabetic, cloth. (1898) repr. 1998. $35.00, plus $3.50 ship. The alphabetical listing by state and by town, or post office is excerpted and reprinted from George Cram, 1898, *Cram's Unrivaled Atlas of the World.* He had the benefit of working with the 1890 US Census. It is an excellent tool to locate communities of 100 years ago; many of these places no longer exist, or have changed names. This may be the only source of identification of a particular place mentioned in records of that time. In each instance the county location is given and the population; where the population is too small to have been noted the designation is an "X". #225. Genealogical Publishing Co, 1001 N Calvert St, Baltimore, MD 21202-3897.

James Rood Robertson, *Petitions of the Early Inhabitants of Kentucky.* 261 pp., index, cloth (1914) repr. 1998. $25.00, plus $3.50 ship. This is a collection of legislative petitions presented to the General Assembly of Virginia (between 1769 and 1792) by people living in Kentucky County when it was a part of the Commonwealth of Virginia. With the right of petition, varied causes may be presented: land ownership, organization of the militia, marriages, establishment of ferries, roads, and communities, and other matters relevant to the settlement of a frontier land. A wealth of information, historic, property ownership and genealogical may be obtained from these petitions. The names attached to the petitions are also of significance in determining who were neighbors and had similar concerns. #4975. Genealogical Publishing Co, 1001 N Calvert St, Baltimore, MD 21202.

CDs AVAILABLE: System requirements: must have a CD-ROM drive, and in order to read the CDs you must use either *Family Tree Maker* **version 3.02 or higher or the** *Family Archive Viewer***, version 3.02 or higher, free with the purchase of CDs.**

CD-ROM: *Family History; Virginia Genealogies #2, 1600s to 1800s. Family Archive Viewer* **free upon request (see above).** Presenting the genealogies of Virginia families from the *William and Mary Quarterly*; of the three periodicals which were originally devoted to Virginia genealogy and history this was the most scholarly. These were originally published in 5 volumes by the Genealogical Publishing Co. and contain every family history article published between 1892 and 1943 when genealogical contributions ceased. Also included is the single volume of *Virginia Gleanings*, by Lothrop Withington; abstracts of 17th and 18th century English wills and administrations relating to Virginians. In this modern age, this is the way to search for and retrieve information quickly. The images are digitally reproduced, so that the pages from the 5 volumes are as originally published, they just take up considerably less library space and are readily available. Although additional information has been found in recent years, these articles from the *W&M Q* have become the starting point of research in many family lines. $39.95, plus $3.50 ship. CD #7186. Genealogical Publishing Co, 1001 N Calvert St, Baltimore, MD 21202. 1-800-296-6687.

CD-ROM: *Family History; Virginia Genealogies #3, 1600s to 1800s. Family Archive Viewer* **free upon request (see above).** Presenting the genealogies of Virginia families from *Tyler's Quarterly Historical and Genealogical Magazine*, originally published by the Genealogical Publishing Co. in 4 volumes; includes some 350 family history articles published first between 1919 and 1952. Also on the same CD is the complete set of

Virginia Colonial Abstracts, originally 34 paperback volumes by Beverley Fleet, then consolidated into 3 volumes published by Genealogical Publishing Co. These primary source records from a number of tidewater Virginia counties, with birth, marriage, death records, wills, deeds, court orders, militia lists, etc. This is the way to search and retrieve information quickly. The images are digitally reproduced, so that the pages from all of the volumes are as originally published, they just take up considerably less library space and are readily available. Although additional information has been found in recent years, these articles from the works Tyler and Fleet have become the starting point of research in many family lines. $39.95, plus $3.50 ship. #7187. Genealogical Publishing Co, 1001 N Calvert St, Baltimore, MD 21202.

Note: Genealogical Publishing Co., additional books, add $1.25 ea. ship.

Jeanne Brooks Gart, CG, *The Families of Joseph and Charlotte (Shelton) Ayers, Knox County, Tennessee and Macon County, Missouri.* including **Ralph Shelton, Middlesex County, Virginia and Reuben M. Dunnington.** 187 pp., index, photographs, chart, cloth. 1997. $29.50, plus ship. This family history begins with the life of Joseph Ayers who was born in the mid-1750s and who married Chastity about 1780, probably in North Carolina. It is a well-documented account of his life and the lives of the subsequent four generations, through the children of Joseph and Charlotte Shelton Ayers. Ralph Shelton of Middlesex County, 1706 is the ancestor of Charlotte Shelton, with the author presenting the genealogical and social history of this family until the time of Charlotte Shelton. Reuben Dunnington of Mecklenburg County is of the maternal line of Charlotte, and this family is presented through three generations. Also included are the Marvel Moseley and William Daniel families. Mrs. Gart is an experienced genealogical researcher and the book is extensively documented. Her accounts provide excellent insight into the lives and migrations of these people. Newbury Street Press, 101 Newbury St, Boston, MA 02116-3007.

Brent H. Holcomb, *Petitions for Land From the South Caroline Council Journals, Volume IV: 1754-1756.* 324 pp., name and place indexes, maps, hard cover. $40.00, plus 3.00 ship, add. books, add $1.00 each to max. charge of $6.00. 1998. This volume has been transcribed with the same meticulous attention Brent Holcomb has given to earlier volumes. This is the fourth volume of the series of petitions for land as transcribed from the Council Journals. They provide the best source for learning of the early immigration and migration to South Carolina and of the early land owners. Included is information about earlier places of residence, slave holdings, estates and heirs, as well as descriptions of the petitioned land. Through these petitions the locations of land owned can thus be definitively identified. It is known that there were many early Virginians who migrated to South Carolina and these volumes provide excellent identification and verification for research to be pursued with later land records. See *TVF* **V6:58, vol.I, 1734/5-1748; V7:57, vol. II, 1748-1752 and vol. III, 1752-1753.** Order from Brent H. Holcomb, PO Box 21766, Columbia, SC 29221.

Herbert Ridgeway Collins, *Cemeteries of Caroline County, Virginia, Vol 3, Private Cemeteries*. vi, 232 pp., index, paper. 1998. $20.00, plus $2.50 ship. A continuation of the identification and recording of the cemeteries of Caroline County. In this volume, Mr. Collins has recorded 170 private cemeteries, three additional church cemeteries and some additions to the entries in volumes 1 and 2. He has also included some private cemeteries on the border of Caroline and Spotsylvania counties that are of interest to Caroline County residents. His outstanding knowledge of the people and places in Caroline County and his dedication to the preservation of its history make this a valuable and commendable work. Where so few county records have survived, this work is of even greater value. #T1527. Family Line Publications, 63 E Main St, Westminster, MD 21157.

TLC Genealogy, *Virginia in 1720: A Reconstructed Census*. 221 pp., index, 8½x11, spiral binding. 1998. $25.00 postpaid. This reconstructed census is based on primary record sources, that is, wills, tax or tithe lists, order book entries and deeds, etc. The source of the reference (refer to key in front of book) is given after the name. The surname listing is alphabetic, with variations of surnames listed, and given names for each surname found. It is as complete as is possible, given the fact that it is for the one year of 1720, and that there are many names lost to future generations through the destruction of many of the county records. It is, however a good starting point to finding an ancestor and identify his county of origin. There are all some 12,500 persons listed. TLC Genealogy, P O Box 403369, Miami Beach, FL 33140-1369.

ANNOUNCEMENTS:

William M. Kelso, Nicholas M. Luccketti, Beverly A. Straube, *Jamestown Rediscovery IV*. Association for the Preservation of Virginia Antiquities (APVA), Richmond. 1998. 75 pp., color illus., maps, coated glossy paper, soft cover. $7.95, plus $1.50 ship (& sales tax in VA). The first three volumes: *Rediscovery I, II, III* are also available at $6.95 each. Purchase from APVA, 204 W Franklin St, Richmond, VA 23220.

Golansville Cemetery Restoration Trust. Now that the survey has confirmed the presence of the cemetery a non-profit corporation can be formed and contributions received to restore the Friends Meeting House site. Those interested persons and descendants of the early Caroline Quakers (many of whom are buried in this cemetery), will want to contribute to this memorial to a stalwart people. See *TVF* 5:159-163, 221-226) Contributions may be made to: Golansville Cemetery Restoration Trust, ℅ Fay Parrish Wade, 8703 Ewes Ct, Richmond, VA 23235.

SEARCH:

HICKS, MARTIN. Richard Hicks, b c.1735, New Kent Co, in Rutherford Co, NC, Laurens Co, SC, d by 1812 Rutherford Co, NC; m Mary (?), known 2 children: dau,

Dicey and William. Other children? names? spouses? Info on w Mary? Shadrack Martin, New Kent Co, d 1803, Laurens Co, SC, m Jane (?). Seek info about Jane, parents and siblings. Shirley Wagstaff, P O Box 1559, Bandon, OR 97411.

JORDAN, ROE, SHAVER, VAUGHT. Henry Jordan, b 1803, Culpeper Co, m Jane Roe, dau Jacob Roe, Mason Co, KY, 1830. Henry Jordan d 1864, Mason Co, bur Orangeburg, KY. Seek parents and siblings of Henry. Adam Shaver, b 1790, Wythe Co, m Rosannah Vaught, dau Christley Vaught, 1811/12, Smythe Co; d 1872, Smythe Co. Seek parents & siblings of Adam Shaver. Will exchange info. Elizabeth Fogarty, 405 Vermont, McAllen, TX 78503.

CREWDSON. Seek exact dates & burial places for following Richmond Co Crewdson ancestors: George, b 1783; William, b 1762, d 1775. Crewdson wives: Milley Newman, b 1766, d 1793; Elenor Burbridge, d 1785. Linda Gardner, 2828 N 63rd St, Lincoln, NE 68507.

SACRA, BOHANNON. Isaac Sacra and bro, James (p) s of Robert to KY 1801. Isaac m Elizabeth George. Seek info about these as well as William Bohannon and s John, of Franklin Co, before 1801. All of these men were Rev War veterans. Jeff Scull, 104 Quincy Rd, Yorkville, IL 60560.

ROWLEY, WILLIAMS, SMITH. Richmond Co, John Rowley & wife Catherine Williams (dau of Hugh Williams), killed by Indians c.1699. How is s William Rowley related to Joseph Smith, m Kitty Anderson? Will of William Smith, 1723 names Williams. Jim Burgess, 37 S Udall, Mesa, AZ 85204.

BARTLETT, ADAMS. Hugh Bartlett, Person Co, NC, 1751, seek his whereabouts prior to that time. Gabriel (d 1750) & Priscilla Adams, Fairfax Co, was she a Pierson? Had s Simon, a Pierson name. Info will be appreciated. Catherine Bass, 12 Wactor St, Sumter, SC 29150.

BEAN, Richard, b 1893, Northumberland Co. Joined Genl. Harrison Army in Louisville, KY in 1812, War of 1812, KY. Seek info on parents & siblings. J. William Gorski, PO Box 182007, Shelby Twp, MI 48318.

DEAN, Reuben, b 1765 (where?), m Jenny Vawter, 1792 Caroline Co, in Spotsylvania Co 1806; d? Ch: Aylett, b 1794; John; Reuben; George, b 1806. Ch moved to AL then TX by 1850. Parents of Reuben? Barrie Dean Rosier, PO Box 105, Midway GA 31320.

INDEX

199

200

202

TIDEWATER VIRGINIA FAMILIES:
A Magazine of History and Genealogy

TABLE OF CONTENTS

Volume 7 Number 4   February/March 1999

From Virginia...............

TIME TO RENEW YOUR SUBSCRIPTION TO *TIDEWATER VIRGINIA FAMILIES: A Magazine of History and Genealogy*!!!
Subscriptions are now $25.00/YEAR, US;
Canada add $5.00, Overseas add $10.00 (for airmail)
A courtesy envelope has been included for your convenience.
Just enclose your check and mail!!!

PLEASE NOTE THE NEW SUBSCRIPTION RATE FOR
VOLUME 8 IS $25.00

Subscriptions to earlier volumes are still available and will remain $25.00 per volume, US; and $30.00 per volume, overseas. Volumes 1-6 are now available by volume and Volume 7 will be available after February 1999. Each volume is presented with perfect binding in heavy cover stock. These make a nice addition to your library, as well as an excellent resource for your research.   Also they shelve conveniently!
Order your complete set of *TIDEWATER VIRGINIA FAMILIES* now. Also give an outstanding gift to your local library of a complete set of *TIDEWATER VIRGINIA FAMILIES: A Magazine of History and Genealogy.*

Please note: Single copies available only for current volume at $8.00 each.

Subscribers to *TIDEWATER VIRGINIA FAMILIES: A Magazine of History and Genealogy* have had the benefit of the extensive research of LtCol James W. Doyle, Jr. for twenty-two consecutive issues of the magazine. His research, insight and ability to interpret and articulate his findings have provided a major contribution to our understanding of our early ancestors, and shed new light on the early settlers of Virginia and their many intermingled relationships. We all owe him a great debt of gratitude for his commitment and look forward to his next article in the first issue of Volume 8 of *TIDEWATER VIRGINIA FAMILIES.*

See the TVF Home Page for *TIDEWATER VIRGINIA FAMILIES: A Magazine of History and Genealogy* at **http://www.erols.com/tvf**. The Tables of Contents for Volumes 1-7 are included. Also refer your research friends to the home page so that they can subscribe with ease.   VLHD

John Burrows, 1608
James City County

Virginia Lee Hutcheson Davis

John Burrowes came to Virginia in October 1608 with the Second Supply, brought by Captain Newport to the unfortunate Jamestown settlers.[1] Captain Newport also brought to the colony, two women; the first in the colony. Mrs. Thomas Forrest[2], the wife of a settler and her maid, Ann Burras.[3] There is nothing to indicate that Ann and John were related, nor is there information that they were not.

Robert Gaile had financed the venture of John Burrows, and when he failed to receive a return upon his investment he petitioned the Virginia Company in London to require Burrows to give satisfaction.[4]

John Burrows remained in the colony and before 1623, married Bridget Buck, the daughter of the Reverend Richard Buck.[5] Bridget arrived in the colony with her father and mother to find the colony in desperate straits. Her father immediately took a position of leadership, and the colony would have relinquished the settlement without his encouragement and the arrival of a relief ship.

Richard Buck was assigned 750 acres at Archers Hope near Jamestowne. He remained the minister of James Cittie Parish, but evidently died before the census of 1623.[6] His daughter, Elizabeth appears to have remained in England[7] and his daughter, Bermuda had died before she reached Virginia. Bridget was the only child to make the complete voyage with her parents; however, subsequently there were four more children: Mara, Gercian (Gersham), Benoni ("son of my sorrow") and Peleg.[8]

In the muster of February 16, 1623, John Burrows and Mrs. Burrows were reported *living at James Cittye and with the corporacon thereof.* Listed separately under "Living", and thus indicating a separate listing, was Anthony Burrows, as an adult.[9]

In 1624 John and Bridget Burrows were living at his plantation, "Burrows Mount" (or Burrows Hill) on the south side of the James River in what became Surry County.[10] The plantation was in the tenure of John Smith and lay adjacent to land patented by Isabel Perry, the wife of William Perry. It was also adjacent to Pace's Pain,[11] just down river from Flower Dew Hundred and Brandon. Their lives were inextricably entwined with Bridget's family, as Mara Buck was counted with them in the muster of 1624.[12] John also had six of his men planted[13] with him, along with their arms and provisions.[14] There was no mention made of any children.

In 1626 John petitioned the Council for permission to *seat himself upon the neck of land near James Citty [Jamestowne] in order to care for the cattle due Mara Buck, his ward, daughter of Richard Buck*. Permission was granted and the Burrows thereafter were seated upon Buck lands.[15] John did not long survive, for he was fatally stabbed "in the belly below the navel", on 1 January 1627/28, by William Reade, a fourteen year-old laborer, who was convicted of manslaughter, but pled benefit of clergy (he could not be prosecuted). This incident took place at the house of Benjamin Jackson, at Blunt Point in Warwick.[16]

Bridget Burrows married, secondly, William Davis and then, John Bromfield. These marriages can be established through a land grant to John Bromfield, 15 December 1656, for 1200 acres at the head of Archer's Hope Creek in James City County.[17]

John and Bridget Burrows had no children by January 1624/25, as evidenced by the census of that year; they may have had a child later in 1625. By the time of John's death in 1628, it would seem that they would have had no more than three children.

No mention has been found of children of Bridget and her husband, John Burrows; which does not preclude the possibility of their having had children. There are no early records of James Citty and James City County extant. Any reference to the orphans of John Burrows, if there were any, would of necessity be found among other court or crown records and such information is difficult to extract.

There are, however, tantalizing references in the land patent records; Matthew Burrowes was claimed as a headright of William Davis in 1639 when he patented land on Archer's Hope Creek.[18] In 1656 Matthew was claimed as a headright of John Broomfield.[19]

Christopher Burrows patented several parcels of land in Lynhaven Parish in Lower Norfolk County between the years 1636 and 1651.[20] He claimed as headrights his brother, William and his sister, Ann. This in itself does not link Christopher with John and Bridget Burrows; however, a later entry in the land patent records names Benoni as the son of Christopher Burrows.[21] The entry describes land patented by Benoni as due him as heir to his deceased father, Christopher Burrows (1667 and 1671). Given the naming patterns of the colonial period, and the unusual nature of the name, one may speculate about the relationship. However, a definitive relationship to John Burrows has not been found.

An entry in the Lower Norfolk County records (1654) reveals the information that Christopher Burrows had other children; however, they are not named. Christopher died in 1652, leaving his children under age, the document stating that a specified amount of tobacco was to go to the six children of Christopher

208

Burrows, their brother's (Benoni) one-third being satisfied along with the land untouched.[22]

A second tantalizing series of entries in the records provides no additional answers. Anthony Burrowes held land in tenure on the east side of Blunt Point Creek adjacent to John Leyden (Laydon) in December of 1628.[23] It would seem that he was a contemporary of John Burrows and it is of interest that the latter died on Blunt Point that same year. It is also interesting that Anthony owned land adjoining that of John and Ann Burras Laydon at that time.

The next record that has been found concerning an Anthony Burroughs is found in the orphans court records of York County, dated September 25, 1655.[24] Land formerly conveyed by Mr. Jos. Croshaw to Anthony, Robert and Mary Burrowes, children of Robert and Grace Burrowes, shall be enjoyed equally between the said children. At the August 25th court in York County in 1662, Anthony Burroughs, an orphan, was judged to be twenty-one.[25] He was thus born in 1641 and his father had died before 1655 when the entry was made concerning the land. In 1659 Reynold Henley presented a list of a part of the estate of Anthony Burrows (orphan) to the court.[26]

No earlier information has been found concerning Robert Burrowes, no land patent or any court records to associate him with the earlier Anthony Burrowes; although, the naming patterns of the time would suggest a relationship. It is clear, however, that Robert Burrowes did not have a son, John living at the time of his death.

Anthony Burrows was living in St. Peter's Parish in May 1689, as he was included in the listing of processioners at that time.[27] John Burross was also living in St. Peter's Parish in May 1689 and was among those several landowners living in Pamunkey Neck.[28] The two men were not close neighbors.[29] At no time were the two men named together in the parish records, and the vestry minutes indicate that Anthony certainly needed the assistance of a family later in his life. From the extant records no relationship can be established between the two men.

The associations of time, places and persons certainly lead one to feel that there must have been family ties among John Burrows of "Burrows Hill" and Blunt Point, Ann Burras Laydon and Anthony Burrows of Blunt Point. The relationship of these early settlers to later Burruss settlers in the colony has not been found. A relationship of John Burross of St. Peter's Parish, Pamunkey Neck, with earlier Burrowes in the colony of Virginia has not been established. It can be discounted, in some instances, either by the fact that the records show that he was not the offspring of that Burrows, or the time constraints are such that the relationship could not have been that of father and son.

Anthony Burrows was stricken blind and he and his wife were "very ancient" in 1696[30] when Anthony petitioned the St. Peter's parish vestry for maintenance.

He said they were incapable of getting their living. The church wardens offered to keep Anthony and his wife, if he would convey his plantation, cattle, horses and hogs to the parish. The vestry agreed to allow them each 500 pounds of tobacco and cash for their maintenance during their natural lives or until Anthony may recover his eyesight.

For sixteen years, or until April 1712, the church wardens included the 1000 pounds of tobacco in their parish levy, due the persons who kept Anthony and his wife. They gave James Tate thirty-five pounds of tobacco for making clothes for Anthony. They allotted 1275 pounds of tobacco to Capt. John Lyddall for taking Anthony in his sloop to the springs in Maryland. Anthony died before April 22, 1712, when the church wardens of St. Paul's Parish ordered that the estate of Anthony Burrows, lately deceased, should be sold to the best advantage of the parish use.[31]

John Burross was living in Pamunkey Neck by 1686 and died there before 1705.[32] No documented relationship has been established between this John Burross and the earlier Burrows in the colony of Virginia. A further tantalizing use of the name Benoni, since it had the unusual translation of "child of sorrow", in the 1800s leads one to think again of the naming patterns. One wonders whether a Burruss connection to Benoni, the son of Christopher Burruss may have migrated to the frontier of what was then New Kent County. A Benoni Carleton was living in King and Queen County in the mid-1800s, and a Benoni Lipscomb was living in King William County in 1812.[33]

John Burrowes was living in the parish of St. James (James City County) when *an account of the land as it standeth in church books with the number of servants and Negroes, with the names of the owners thereof,* was made. It was taken by the church wardens on December 20, 1679. He was credited with ten acres of land and two Negroes.[34]

This John Burrowes may well have been the same John Burruss who was living in St. Peter's Parish, New Kent County in Pamunkey Neck by 1686.[35] He was seated on 590 acres of land that had been granted the Pamunkey Indians, and this land came under question by the Council in June 1699. In listing John's land holdings, the record showed he had been seated on the land for thirteen years.

The Queen (Anne) of the Pamunkey Indians had been able to negotiate a grant from the crown to secure land to her people. It was found that they had then leased some of the land to white settlers. It was the task of the committee to decide what disposition was to be made of this land since a part of the agreement was that the Indians would not lease the land. The settlers had ignored this agreement and continued to move north and west into Pamunkey Neck and the wilderness.

The solution reached by the committee was to allow the settlers to keep the land they had leased from the Indians for ninety-nine years. The land held by the Indians was adjudged to be sufficient for their habitation.[36] By this means the Pamunkey Indians lost part of the land that had been granted them, but also, by virtue of the foresight of Queen Anne, the widow of Totopotomoy, they were able to keep land that they hold to this day.

On May 4, 1689, the church wardens of St. Peter's Parish ordered the parish into precincts for processioning.[37] Each land owner was required to be present to walk the bounds of his land so that the boundary lines could be established and remembered in case of a land dispute. This was required every four years, and the younger men were expected to be in attendance and pay careful attention to the boundary marks so the information could be handed down from one generation to the next.

Among the persons ordered to procession and re-mark the bounds of each man's land were the inhabitants belonging to the parish in Pamunkey Neck: Susanna Page, Thomas Spencer, John Burros, Mrs. Gooch, William Turner, James Henderson and Colonel Johnson.[38] This was the only entry found in the processioning orders that included the name of John Burruss.

It would appear that John was living on the same land in 1699 at the time that the agreement was made with the Pamunkey Indians. On April 25, 1701, he patented an additional 439 acres in Pamunkey Neck in St. John's Parish.[39] While the patent identified the land as lying in King and Queen County, it was described as being on the west side of John's Creek[40], and this, with the other identification, would place it in King William County (formed in 1701 from King and Queen County). The land also lay adjacent to the land of the late William Woodward and on Mrs. Gouge's line. John claimed his right to the land for having imported nine persons: Cha. Baley, Eliza. Hughs, Eliza. Linsey, Elinor Mason, Mary Snideley, Marshall Core, Jane Collings, Diana Norfolk and Robert Brookes.

The father of John Burruss has not been identified, from any land records, consideration of the time frame, or from any associations of his in King William County. No record has been found of the wife of John Burruss. There were numerous land transactions among the Burruss brothers (sons of John) with no mention made of a widow's dower rights. It is believed that the wife of John Burruss had died earlier.

John Burruss deeded 100 acres of land, in St. John's Parish, in August 1702, to his son, John.[41] The land was described as the land on which he (the son) lived and lay adjacent to John Burruss (Sr.). Thomas Burruss deeded 100 acres of land on Jack's Creek adjoining Woodward, to Jacob Burruss on December 20, 1703.[42] Thomas, Jacob and Edmund, who were later identified in a land transaction in King William County, were also sons of John Burruss, Sr. In February 1705, Thomas Burruss of St. John's Parish, King William County deeded land to Jacob and Edmund Burruss of the same parish and county. it was described as a division made to them by his father, John Burruss, late of the same county and parish.[43] The deed of his son, Thomas Burruss was recorded in King William County on March 20, 1705.

The quit rent rolls for 1704 show that John Burruss and Thomas Burruss were each required to pay rent to the crown on sixty acres of land in King William County.[44] This was land that they had patented, as rent was required on all patented land. The quit rent rolls, in a number of counties are the only surviving records of the residents of the county and of land owned at that time. The acreage listed does not reflect the total land holdings, as land received by deed of gift or purchase was not included.

The land that John Burruss (Sr.) had patented had evidently been transferred to his sons by this time as there was no large amount of land on which a John Burruss was required to pay quit rent. Thus the sixty acres credited to Thomas Burruss and to John Burruss, each, would have been two of the sons of John Burruss (Sr.).

There were several land transactions among the Burruss men during the years 1702 to 1705. It appears that they were all brothers. Thomas Burruss deeded land (1705) to Jacob Burruss: *all the plantation whereon I now live* for a total of 100 acres on William Woodward's line and Jack's Creek.[45] He later (1707) deeded land to John Burruss (Jr.), *all the revision when it shall happen to come, by death of Charles Burruss, brother of John Burruss.*

All of the land transactions involved land on Jack Creek and much of the land was adjacent to William Woodward. The land of John Burruss, Sr. lay on Jack Creek adjacent to William Woodward and Nathaniel West.[46]

It would seem that John Burruss, Sr. had sons: John, Thomas, Jacob, Edmund and Charles. The order of their birth has been inferred from the dates of the land transactions, with Charles deeding land to John in January 1706. All of the sons must have been of age by this date. John, the father must have died after August 1702 (when he deeded land to his son, John), but prior to the listing of the quit rents in 1704.[47] He surely died before February 1705. It is likely that John had died by December 1703 when Thomas first deeded land to Jacob.[48]

A deed from William Burruss to Thomas Burruss for sixty-one acres of land on John's Creek was recorded on January 20, 1706.[49] Charles Burruss was a witness. The relationship of William to the brothers is not defined.

The records of King William County were burned in a courthouse fire. A dedicated clerk attempted to rescue the records and he was able to save a few scattered pages. Years later another dedicated clerk pieced these remaining burned pages together and had them bound. It is by sheer good fortune that one finds a record of an ancestor that has survived, and from which one can draw inferences. The deed of Thomas Burruss to his brothers, Jacob and Edmund, is one of those scraps of paper; the complete page was not salvaged, but enough has stood the ravages of time (and fire) to present an account, though brief, of the father's wishes.

The life of the son, John Burruss has not been followed, nor have the lives of Thomas and Edmund been followed in detail. Further information concerning them comes from an undocumented source and has not been confirmed. It is stated that Thomas married Mary and settled in Stafford County. He is said to have had children: Matthew, Charles, Thomas, Henry and Elizabeth.[50]

Edmund Burruss is said to have had sons, Thomas and Edmund. It is believed that these sons settled in Orange County and that it was the son, Thomas who married Frances Tandy.[51]

Charles Burruss was living in St. John's Parish, King William County in May 1745. He had an adult son, Samuel, by this date. Charles deeded 473 acres of land on Herring Creek in Caroline County to his son, Samuel Burruss of Drysdale Parish, King and Queen County, on May 7, 1745.[52] It was recorded in the Caroline County Court on the fourteenth of June that year. This was half of the land that Charles had bought from William Meriweather in 1744.

Samuel Burruss was the progenitor of the Burruss families who lived in the Reedy Creek area, and were the early neighbors of the Norments, Peatrosses and Brames. The sons of Samuel Burruss: Samuel, Jr., Jennings and Charles, continued to live in that area in the 1700s and mid-to-late-1800s. There are a number of Chancery Court suits in the Caroline County Circuit Court records that relate to these families. For those interested, many family relationships can be documented from these original court papers.[53] The life of the son, Jacob will be followed in the first issue of Volume 8 of *TVF*.

Notes

1. Virginia Meyer and John Frederick Dorman, *Adventurers of Purse and Person, 1607-1624/25*. 1956 (Richmond: Dietz, rev. 1989) 142-143. The name has been transcribed with this spelling. As with all names during the colonial period, there may have been many variations: Burrows, Burrowes, Burros, Burras, Burroughs. Burrus and Burris.
2. The grave and the remains of a woman were exhumed during the Jamestown Rediscovery archaeological work of 1997. A study made since, and based on the time of burial, it is believed that this was probably the grave of Mrs. Forrest, since it is known that Ann Burras was still living at a much later time. Dr. William Kelso, APVA Lecture Series, September 24, 1998, Jamestown, VA.
3. Virginius Dabney, *Virginia, The New Dominion*. (Garden City, NY: Doubleday, 1971). 13-14. Ann Burras' marriage to John Laydon, on Virginia soil, after six-weeks courtship, was the first in the Anglo-American colonies. Their daughter, Virginia was born the following year, also the first in the Anglo-American colonies.
4. Meyer and Dorman 143.

5. Dabney 140. Richard Buck was the son of Edmund Buck of Wymongham, County Norfolk and was admitted sizar at Cains College, Cambridge, 26 April 1600, aged eighteen. He was chaplain of the expedition led by Sir Thomas Gates with a fleet of seven ships and two pinnaces. He left England on the "Sea Adventure" in 1609.

6. Neither his nor his wife's name was mentioned, nor were they listed in the muster of 1624.

7. Dabney 142-143. Elizabeth Buck was later in the colony as the wife of Thomas Crump.

8. Dabney 141.

9. William Thomson Baker, Sr., in his book, *The Baker Family of England and of Central Virginia* stated that Anthony was a baby, and thus the son of John. This is an erroneous interpretation of the record. One can only draw conclusions based on the facts as given, and cannot "make up" desired relationships. Mr. Baker apparently did not have an understanding of the historical background of the times necessary to interpret correctly the records he searched; information seems to have been taken out of context and thus lacked accurate interpretation. He also did not appear to have a clear knowledge of the geography of the colony of Virginia. There are a number of flaws in his continued account of the early Burruss family.

10. Dabney 143.

11. Land Patent Book (LPB) 1 1:62.

12. Meyer and Dorman 33.

13. The term planted simply meant located or situated (settled), not planted in the sense of a planter cultivating land.

14. Meyer and Dorman 38.

15. Meyer and Dorman 143.

16. Meyer and Dorman 143.

17. LPB 4, 55 (81). James Citty was first the settlement at Jamestown and one of the original four plantations. It became one of the eight shires and encompassed land on both sides of the James River. It later became James City County on the north side of the James River and Surry County on the south side. This land was formerly granted William Davis 27 March 1643, *whoe dying intestate and no heir appearing*, since Bromfield had married Davis' widow.

18. LPB 1, 1: 661.

19. LPB 4 55.

20. LPB 1, 1: 341; 2: 628; LPB 2 164, 347.

21. LPB 6 379; LPB 7 676.

22. Lower Norfolk County Book D 96, April 18, 1654.

23. LPB 1, 1: 69.

24. York County Records (Deeds, Orders and Wills, Books 1-2) No.1 265.

25. Benjamin B. Weisiger, III, *York County Records, 1659-1662.* (Richmond: Privately printed, 1989) 140.

26. Weisiger 8.

27. C.G. Chamberlayne, *The Vestry Book and Register of St. Peter's Parish, New Kent and James City County, 1706-1786.* 1937 (Richmond: The Library Board, rep.1989) 21.

28. Chamberlayne, St. Peter's 22.

29. Chamberlayne, St. Peter's, xiii; C.G. Chamberlayne, *The Vestry Book of St. Paul's Parish, Hanover County, Virginia, 1706-1786.* 1940 (Richmond: The Library Board, rep. 1973) 8. Anthony Burrows lived in the part of St. Peter's Parish that later became St. Paul's Parish in Hanover County, while John Burrows lived in Pamunkey Neck in the area that became St. John's Parish in King William County.

30. Chamberlayne, St. Paul's 21, 51, 52, 54, 55, 60, 61, 63, 66, 67, 72, 84, 93, 105.

31. Chamberlayne, St. Paul's 13, 17, 20, 28, 29, 35, 42, 49, 54.

32. Louis des Cognets, *English Duplicates of Lost Virginia Records.* 1958 (Baltimore: Genealogical Publishing, rep. 1990). 60.

33. See TVF 5:49; 6:237.

34. John Camden Hotten, *The Original Lists of Persons of Quality, 1600-1700*. 1894 (Baltimore; Genealogical Publishing, rep. 1986) 500.

35. des Cognets 60.

36. des Cognets 57-58.

37. Chamberlayne 20, 22.

38. Chamberlayne 20, 22.

39. LPB 9 358.

40. It is believed that the subsequent use of Jack's Creek and John's Creek, apparently interchangeably, in the identification of the land of John Burruss all refer to the creek that is found on present day maps of King William County as Jack Creek.

41. King William County Record Book 1, 18.

42. Book 1, 155.

43. Book 1, 290-292.

44. des Cognets 60.

45. Book 1, 245.

46. Book 1, 18, 108, 155, 245, 290, 307, 311-313, 333-334, 340-341.

47. This inference is made based on the fact that John Burruss was not credited with the two large land patents he had made. The land passed to his sons from his estate.

48. Book 1, 155.

49. Book 1, 334.

50. Unpublished Mss. in hands of Henry W. Burruss, Crozet, VA (1990), by a great-great-grandson of Overton Burruss (not named).

51. Burruss Mss.

52. Caroline County Court Records, 1742-1864, Acc. No. 22656, The Virginia State Library Archives.

53. These may be found in Archival and Information Services, The Library of Virginia. Most of these papers relate to the descendants of Charles Burruss rather than those of Jacob Burruss, simply because of the time period they cover. The family of Jacob Burruss (III) was living in King William County during that time. It may also have been that the descendants of Jacob Burruss who lived in Caroline County did not have any estate matters that required litigation in the Chancery Court. See also William L. Hopkins, *Caroline County Court Records and Marriages, 1787-1810*. (Richmond: Privately printed, 1987).

The Boswell-Hockaday Family Connection
James City and New Kent Counties

Mary French Turner Boswell[1]

The Boswell Family

This pedigree history of one family line begins with Thomas Boswell, who first appeared in 1807 in James City County. He was listed on the personal property tax list with one tithable.[2] In 1804 and 1805, three young Boswell men: John, Thomas and William (they could have been brothers), appeared in New Kent County on the personal property tax list. John and William continued to be listed in New Kent County each year, and apparently lived out their lives there.[3] Thomas Boswell's name appeared for the last time in New Kent County in 1805 and in 1807 for the first time in James City County.

There are strong indications that these Boswell men could have been descended from the Gloucester County Boswells and descended from the first Thomas Boswell in Gloucester County. As possible verification involves the records of three burned record counties: Gloucester, New Kent and James City; a connected genealogy, unfortunately, has not been established.

Thomas Boswell was living in the Taskinas Creek area of James City County, near the York River and in 1810 married Elizabeth Richardson, widow of Stanhope Richardson (died 1804). Thomas Boswell was shown on the James City County Land Tax List in 1811 as taxed on the acreage that previously was in the name of Stanhope Richardson, and then in Elizabeth Richardson's name; 474¾ aces of land on Taskinas Creek.[4] Thereafter Thomas Boswell's name was found in the land tax records each year until his death in 1838; the only Boswell family listed in James City County. The land adjoined that of Allen Richardson.[5] Now the land of Allen Richardson can be identified as York River State Park.

The land tax record shows that Thomas Boswell's land was twelve miles northwest of the courthouse. He paid taxes on nine slaves and a gig valued at $80.00. On the 1830 census record Thomas Boswell was listed with a son (Thomas), born 1714, a young male child five to ten years of age (he may have been John, according to later census records) and two daughters (names unknown).[6]

In the 1837 land tax records, Thomas Boswell was taxed on the 474¾ acres and in addition, one tract of 575 acres with a note attached: *By deed from E. Taylor, devisee.* The land was described as seventeen miles northwest of the courthouse and bounded by land, among others, of John Goddins, Isaac Saunders and Jno. Slater.[7]

Thomas Boswell died before the compilation of the 1838 land tax list. That year his estate paid taxes on both tracts of land. In 1839 the estate paid taxes on the 474¾ acres on Taskinas Creek. His son, Thomas Boswell II was taxed on 287½ acres (one half of the 575 acre tract in the Diascund area of James City County). A note in the land tax record read, *By will of his father.* Elizabeth Boswell was also taxed on 287½ acres with a note attached to her listing, *Devised to her by will of her husband.* This is to say that the above information confirms the fact that Thomas Boswell did leave a will in James City County.[8]

In 1840 Thomas Boswell II paid taxes on his share of his father's land (575 acres) which was bounded by Mary Slater, John Goddins and Elizabeth Boswell.[9] On the 1840 census Thomas is shown to have married Frances Elizabeth Richardson (probably in 1838, as his eldest son, William Thomas Boswell, was born in 1839).[10] As shown on the census, his household consisted of his mother, Elizabeth, one younger brother and one younger sister; fourteen in all, with six in his family and eight slaves.[11]

Elizabeth Boswell died by 1842, at about sixty-seven years of age. On the 1842 land tax list, Thomas Boswell II paid taxes on the entire 575 acre tract. A notation stated: *Devised to Thomas Boswell under the will of his father at the death of Elizabeth Boswell.*[12] The 474¾ tract on Taskinas Creek belonging to Elizabeth Boswell became the property of her son, Stanhope Richardson, Jr. in 1843.[13]

The children of Thomas Boswell and Frances Elizabeth Richardson were: William Thomas Boswell, born 1839; Walter H. Boswell, born August 30, 1840, fell at the Battle of Malvern Hill, July 1, 1862 in the 22nd year of his age; and a daughter, Mary Ozella Boswell, born March 10, 1842.[14]

The Richardson Family

The land in the Taskinas Creek area of James City County, originally owned in the 1600s by Daniel Parke (who had gotten it from Bryan Smith) was inherited by his two daughters, Lucy, who married William Byrd, II, and Frances, who married John Custis. In the late eighteenth century *Taskinask Plantation*, which lay east of the creek, and acreage directly behind it belonged to the Richardson family.[15]

There were William Richardson, his sons, William, Jr. and Stanhope; also there were Edward and Dudley of unknown relationship.[16] Allen Richardson, who owned land east of Taskinas Creek, which consisted of about 1200 acres, was said to have inherited it in 1804 from John Richardson. Another reference indicated that he married Elizabeth Lewis, who inherited the land from her father, John Lewis. It is not known which is correct.[17]

The land of Stanhope Richardson, which by 1811, was owned by Thomas Boswell I, adjoined Allen Richardson's land on Taskinas Creek. In 1968 the Allen

Richardson's 1200 acres was part of the 3,000 acres of river front land, east of Taskinas Creek, acquired to create York River State Park.

The first Richardson to which this family can be traced is Edward Richardson (c.1760-1813), who married Mary Ann (-?-)(c.1770-1835). Each year in the James City County tax lists, beginning in 1788 Edward Richardson was taxed on 438¾ acres of land. His land joined that of Stanhope Richardson.[18] Edward died in 1813 and in 1816 his estate was divided, giving his widow her dower right and each child his or her share. This included his son, William R. Richardson.[19]

From the 1820 census it appears that William R. Richardson was the next generation in the Boswell-Richardson history.[20] He was listed each year, beginning in 1815, on the personal property lists, when in 1815 he paid taxes on one tithable, four slaves, two horses and one watch. Later he was listed with one gig valued at $50.00.[21]

The name of William's wife was Mary Richardson, born 12 June 1790; see W. T. Boswell Family Bible (WTBFB). They had a daughter, Frances Elizabeth Richardson, born January 6, 1815. Mary Richardson, as a widow before 1840, married Mr. Slater, probably John Slater. She lived out her life as Mary Slater, widow, in the home of her daughter, Frances Boswell, and died January 19, 1868 in the 78th year of her age (see WTBFB).

The Boswell Family

Thomas Boswell II was listed on the 1850 census as thirty-five years old, a farmer with real estate valued at $2,500.00. The remainder of his household was listed as follows: Frances E. Boswell, 34; William T. Boswell, 10; Walter Boswell, 9; Ozella Boswell, 7; and Mary Slater (his mother-in-law).[22] Thomas Boswell appeared on the James City County Personal Property Tax List for each year until his death. In 1852 his personal property listed for taxation was: one free male over sixteen; ten slaves; four horses; fifty cattle; one pleasure carriage, value $50; and one gig, value $10; one metallic clock; and household furniture at $175.00. He died sometime between April 1858 when he was listed in the tax records and April 1859, when his widow, Frances E. Boswell was found on the tax list. She was charged with two tithables, eight slaves, two horses and twenty-eight cattle.[23]

On the 1860 census, Frances E. Boswell was listed as forty-five years of age, engaged in the running of a farm with real estate valued at $5,000 and personal property valued at $67.50. Her household consisted of William T. Boswell, age twenty-one, a farmer; Walter H. Boswell, age nineteen and Mary Ozella Boswell, age eighteen. Her mother, Mary Slater, was also a part of her household.[24] On the 1870 census, at age fifty-five, Frances Boswell was living with her son, William Thomas Boswell. She died October 15, 1878 (see WTBFB). As has been stated

Walter Boswell died while serving in the Army of the Confederate States (see WTBFB).

Mary Ozella Boswell (nicknamed "Puss" by her family) married Samuel Edwards. Samuel and Mary Boswell Edwards had a daughter, Lula Edwards, who married Mr. Marcus Cotrell. They had two sons, Edwin and Samuel Cotrell. Edwin Cotrell married Jennie Woodward; they had two sons, Willis Cotrell and Joseph Maitland Cotrell, and two daughters. Edwin Cotrell died some years prior to 1965. Dr. Samuel Cotrell was still living in Richmond in 1965.[25]

William Thomas Boswell, the eldest of the children of Thomas and Frances Boswell (born 1839 and died January 28, 1874) married November 23, 1862 Judith Williams Hockaday (born November 12, 1836 and died March 20, 1817). Judith recorded the marriage as performed by the Reverend Dr. Barnes in Richmond during the Rebellion. Judith was the daughter of William Hockaday, Jr. and Eliza Ann Ratcliffe of New Kent County.

William Boswell served in the Confederate forces during the Civil Ware. He was a member of the Barhamsville Greys. He also served in a James City County Company. Quoting from a letter from his grandson, Edwin T. Chapman (February 14, 1961), he said *William Thomas Boswell was home on a sick furlough and when he got better he told his sister-in-law, Sally, that he would take the horses to water as soon as the scouts passed; so, he was on one horse and leading another when a black Yankee bushwacker rode up and ordered him to dismount. When he refused the man shot him in the side, pulled him off [his horse] and took both horses on to the Yankee scouts. The black man met Dr. Jones and told him to hurry on to that fellow Boswell who had been shot opposite his home. Grandpa crawled over the rail fence. Dr. Jones found him and treated him. He lived eleven years with an open wound and then died.* This tragic incident happened in 1863.

Following the Civil War farmers in the area where heavy fighting had taken place found life hard. William T. Boswell lost his home to fire two years after the war ended — only fifteen days after the birth of his son, J. Walter.[26]

On the 1870 census, William T. Boswell was listed as thirty-two years of age, a farmer; he owned real estate valued at $600.00 and personal property at $240.00. His household consisted of: Judith W. Boswell, 34; William T. Boswell, Jr., 6; Lucy H., 5; J. Walter, 3; Anna E, 2; Frances Boswell, 55 (his mother); George Green, a black male, 40, labourer; and Charles Greenhow, 12, a black male domestic servant.[27]

After the death of W.T. Boswell, on the 1875 tax list, his widow, Judith W. Boswell, residence Diascund Creek, was taxed with one horse, value $50.00, two cattle, six hogs, one carriage, value $25.00, five farming instruments, one clock and household furniture valued at $50.00.[28]

The appraisement of the estate of William T. Boswell, which included household furniture, farming equipment and livestock, was dated 6 July 1875, with A.P. Richardson as the administrator. *At a court held for James City County and City of Williamsburg at the courthouse thereof in the said city on Tuesday the 9th day of November 1875 an appraisement of the personal effects of William T. Boswell, dec'd was this day presented to court and ordered to be recorded. Teste C.C. Dixon, D.C.*[29]

The Hockaday Family

William Hockaday of Cornwall, England, came to the Virginia colony before July 30, 1636.[30] He was baptized 12 November 1610, the son of William Hockaday and Millosentia Hosken, whom he married in Blisland Parish, Cornwall, 26 January 1604/5.[31] He claimed as headrights a number of settlers to the colony, for which he received numerous land patents in York County (later New Kent County). One of the patents, dated 1653, for 1,000 acres described the location as near the source of Ware Creek.[32] One of his descendants, William Hockaday, born 1804, married Eliza Ann Ratcliffe and was living in the nineteenth century in New Kent County on land at the source of Ware Creek.[33]

The first William Hockaday was active in the affairs of York County, then in Blisland Parish, New Kent County. He served in the House of Burgesses from 1652 to 1658. A land patent to John Mohun in October 1672, mentions land in New Kent County of Lieutenant Colonel Hockaday *now belonging to his son, John Hockaday*.[34] John Hockaday's name appeared as one of the twelve jurors elected regarding the building of the Capital City of Williamsburg by an Act of the General Assembly at James City (8 September 1699).[35] On the 1704 Quit Rent Roll of New Kent County, the only Hockaday on this list was William Hockaday credited with 300 acres.[36] It would seem that this was probably a grandson of the first William Hockaday.

Next noted is a William Hockaday in 1734 in the *Vestry Book of Blisland Parish*. Blisland Parish covered the eastern part of New Kent and part of James City counties. The extant *Vestry Book of Blisland Parish* dates from 1721-1786 and is the main source of the history of this family, as the Hockaday family was prominent in the parish through the whole period.[37]

The first generation to which this Hockaday history can be traced with official documents is this William Hockaday. These documents concern his eldest son, James, as will be explained later. William Hockaday first appeared as a member of the vestry *at ye Uper Church 17th day of October 1734*. At that meeting it was agreed to build a Glebe on the Glebe land. In June 1736 William Hockaday was mentioned in the parish vestry book as both a vestryman and a church warden. In 1744 he was listed as sheriff and appointed collector of the church levy for the parish. In 1745 as church warden of the Upper Church he was

220

to oversee the building of a vestry house.

He held the rank of captain in the militia. Captain William Hockaday served in the House of Burgesses from New Kent in Williamsburg at the colonial capital in 1748-49. He was a member of the vestry when major changes were made to the Upper (Warraneye) Church in 1755. His will was proved 15 September 1760, with Rebecca Hockaday, Dudley Williams and James Hockaday named as executors.[38]

William Hockaday and his wife, Rebecca Armistead(?) had these sons: Captain James, the eldest; Captain John; Lieutenant Philip, killed in the Battle of Brandywine on 17 September 1777; and probably Edmund. Edmund, born 1750 and married to Martha Otey in New Kent County, removed to Kentucky in 1788 and died there in 1807. The Hockaday Cemetery is in Becknerville, Clark County, Kentucky.[39]

James Hockaday (1732-May 10, 1787), the eldest son, according to later records on the settling of the estate of Philip Hockaday, became a vestryman of Blisland Parish in 1763. The land tax records indicated that he owned 300½ acres of land and his personal property tax records showed that he owned fourteen slaves, six horses and fifteen cattle. He and his wife, Mary had a son, William; both he and his son were recognized for service in the American Revolution. James Hockaday furnished supplies to the Continental Army and his son, William was a soldier.[40]

The following data on this family, and from which documented proof for three generations came, are from the John K. Martin Papers.[41] Martin was an attorney in Richmond who, in the nineteenth century, assisted heirs of Revolutionary War Soldiers and sailors establish their claims for bounty land. The brothers, Lieutenants John and Philip, entered the Continental Army in March 1776 and marched north. John was promoted to captain on the Continental Line. Philip fell at the Battle of Brandywine the 17th of September 1777. His records show he had served one year and seven months before his death. Captain John was at the Battle of Yorktown and served to the end of the war. He later was promoted to colonel in the New Kent militia. He left a will, probated 11 July 1799 in James City County, a copy of which was included in the Martin Papers.

One document in the Martin Papers reads: *At a County Court held for the County of James City on Monday the 14th day of May 1838...An attorney presented names of heirs of Lt. Philip Hockaday: James Hockaday, the eldest brother and heir at law died intestate...he had an eldest son, William who became his heir at law of any real estate and who also died intestate...then was listed the children of William who were the legal heirs [which included a son, William].* The document, establishing three generations was ordered to be certified in the James City County Clerk's Office, Warrant No. 2217, allowed the heirs 200 acres of bounty land.

William Hockaday, son of James (born 25 October 1762 and died 1824), married Elizabeth Bradenham on 29 April 1789. She was born 18 April 1771 and died before 1824, the daughter of John and Mary Bradenham of New Kent County. Their children: John Hockaday married Sarah Curle; Abner William Hockaday married Sarah Goddin; William Thomas Hockaday married Eliza Ann Ratcliffe; Cynthia Hockaday married John Williams; Mary Hockaday married John Jones and Susan B. Tyree (a widow); and James Hockaday.

William Thomas Hockaday (born 22 February 1804 and died 11 February 1850, married Eliza Ann Ratcliffe on 20 November 1835. She was born 19 January 1817 and died 24 May 1890, the daughter of John and Judith Ratcliffe of New Kent County. Their children: Judith Williams Hockaday (born November 12, 1836, died March 20, 1917) married November 23, 1862, William T. Boswell; John Ratcliffe Hockaday (born March 18, 1839, died November 28, 1916) married Bettie Gregory (Weisiger) February 20, 1868; Sarah Clarke Hockaday (born May 22, 1840, died February 2, 1914) married January 25, 1866, R. Harry Woodward; and Eliza Ann Hockaday (born February 3, 1848, died after 1921), married February 12, 1871, the Reverend William H. Barnes.[42] This family lived on a Hockaday farm that was at the source of Ware Creek. The Hockaday cemetery was in sight of the ravine at the source of the creek.

There was a marriage between the John Ratcliffe Hockaday family and the Boswell family (see Boswell family). John Ratcliffe Hockaday was born in New Kent County but moved to Richmond at an early age. He served in the Confederate Army during the Civil War. The following account of his part in the war was given by him to his daughter, Louise Hockaday Boswell: *Enlisted May 1861 in the Barhamsville Greys, later known as Company B, 53rd Virginia Regiment, Armistead's Brigade of Pickett's Division. Fought in the Seven Days Battle around Richmond, he sustained a severe wound at the Battle of Malvern Hill. He saw hot action at Manassas, Fredericksburg, Harpers Ferry and was in Pickett's charge at Gettysburg. Here he effected an escape with only twelve remaining men of his company.*

Transferred to the Confederate navy he served aboard the ironclad "Raleigh" on Cape Fear River until she was sunk in action off Fort Fisher. Joining the flagship "Yadkin", he served aboard her until transferred to navy yard duty at Wilmington, North Carolina. Taken prisoner February 22, 1865, he was assigned the duty of constructing coffins for dead Yankees. He escaped in June by joining in a company of Massachusetts soldiers who were being mustered out to get home. He left them at Danville and made his was to Richmond as best he could, finally arriving at his old home in New Kent in early July 1865.

After the war John Ratcliffe Hockaday married Bettie Gregory of *Rockwood,*

Chesterfield County, the daughter of the Reverend James Gregory and a niece of Judge James Marcus Gregory. They made their home in Richmond and had a family of eight girls and one son. In 1883 the family moved to Roanoke where he formed the Pioneer Real Estate Agency. They remained in Roanoke until 1893 when they returned to Richmond and lived at 320 South Fourth Street. They lived out their lives in Richmond and were buried in Hollywood Cemetery.

The Bradenham Family

The name Bradenham may have originated in Norfolk, England. There was (in 1538) a West Bradenham Parish and (in 1695) an East Bradenham Parish — two other parishes carried marriage records, in the sixteenth and seventeenth centuries of persons of that surname.

The first of the name in Virginia was Robert Bradenham, who arrived from England around 1700. There is a land grant dated 1711 which reads as follows: *Robert Bradeham, son of Robert Bradenham, deceased, late of New Kent County...76 acres... `new land' in Blisland Parish in said county..28 April 1711. Beginning at a branch dividing this from lands now or late of Capt. Hoccady and said deceased Bradenham's other development where he lived...for importation of 2 persons: Robert Bradenham and John Scott.*[43]

Robert Bradenham, Jr. had a son (or grandson) John Bradenham; the name appears in the *Vestry Book of Blisland Parish*, in an entry for 3 October 1772.[44] John Bradenham served in the American Revolution and also furnished supplies for the army in the form of beef and corn.[45]

After the Revolution ended John Bradenham was available for service, *Pursuant to the Act of Assembly...the Field Officers of the County of New Kent at the Courthouse on Friday, the 9th day of August 1782...to list men for active duty.* On this list was John Bradenham, also four Hockaday men: Edmund, William, James and John.[46]

As recorded in the New Kent Personal Property Tax Lists, beginning in 1791, until the death of John Bradenham, he paid taxes on eight slaves and three horses. John Bradenham made a will in New Kent County, dated 30 August 1795, and probated 8 October 1795, in which he named his wife, Mary and the following legatees: son, Robert; daughter, Elizabeth Hockaday; daughter, Susanna Harmon; daughter, Sally Sale; grandson, John Sandford Allen; son-in-law, James Chandler; and grandson Robert Bradenham Chandler.[47]

Elizabeth Bradenham (born 18 April 1771), daughter of John and Mary Bradenham, married on 21 April 1789 in Lynchburg, William Hockaday (28 October 1762-1824), the son of James and Mary Hockaday of New Kent County.[48]

To be continued with Ratcliffe Family

The Boswell-Hockaday Family Bible
James City County, 1814-1917

The Family Bible of William Thomas Boswell and Judith W. Hockaday Boswell of James City and New Kent counties. This Bible was probably purchased by his wife, Judith, and family data recorded by her. However, found throughout the Bible were small loose pages, written on both sides (due to the scarcity of paper), lightly pasted across the top, containing family information, possibly written prior to acquiring the Bible.

Marriages

William Thomas Boswell, son of Thomas Boswell and Frances Richardson his wife to Judith W. Hockaday, daughter of William Hockaday and Eliza Ratcliffe, were married November 23rd 1862 in Richmond during the Rebellion by the Reverend Dr. Barnes.

Edwin C. Chapman and Ann E. Boswell, daughter of Wm T. Boswell & Judith his wife were married February 16th 1887 by Mr. John A. Richardson in my House.

James T. Farthing & Lucy H. Boswell were married December 19th 1888 at Barhamsville Church by Wm H. Barnes, D.D.

Robert L. Boswell & Viola H. Drake were married June 1st 1904.

J. Walter Boswell & Lilly C. Hockaday were married August 8th 1898.

Births

Wm T. Boswell, son of W.T. & Judith his wife was born May 23 1864.

Lucy Hockaday Boswell, daughter of W.T. Boswell & Judith his wife was born August 17th 1865 Died May 5, 1920.

John Walter Boswell, son of the Above was born March 20th 1867.

Ann Elizabeth Boswell, daughter of Wm Thomas & Judith his wife was born Sept the 6th 1868. Died Dec. 18, 1924.

Laura Virginia, daughter of the same was born April the 12th 1871.

Robert Lee Boswell, son of Wm T. Boswell & Judith his wife was born September the 6th 1872.

My Grandchildren

Richard Bernice, son of Edwin Chapman & Annie E. his wife was born July 7th 1894. Died Mch 29th 1919.

Annie Bette Farthing, daughter of James Farthing & Lucy H. his wife was born February 17th 1895.

Marrion D. Chapman was born February 26th 1895.

Annie Lucy, daughter of the above was born September 30th 1903.

Edwill [sic] A. Chapman, son of Ann E. Boswell & Edwill [sic] C. Chapman his wife was born January the 14th 1888.

Robert A. Chapman, my second Grandson, was [born] August 20th 1889.

Araminta Pearl, *daughter of James T. Farthing & Lucy his wife was born April 21st 1890, my first Grand daughter.*

Walter G. Chapman, *son of E.C. Chapman & Annie his wife was born August 13, 1891.*

Ashby Ratcliffe, *son of J.T. Farthing & Lucy H. his wife was born April 8, 1892.*

Judith Slater Boswell, *daughter of Robert Lee Boswell & Viola his wife was born March 15th 1905 — the name of this my place "Fairfield", N K County Va being her birthplace.*

Ellanora Mitchell *was born August 12th 1877, daughter of Jeter G. Mitchell and Mary C. Dunsford his wife & left in my charge at his Death.*

Deaths

William Thomas Boswell, *Father of the within family departed this life January the 28th, 1874 in the 36th year of his age.*

Laura V. Boswell, *daughter of Wm T. Boswell & Judith his wife Departed this life September 26th 1877 in the 7th year of her age.*

Wm Thomas Boswell, *eldest son of Wm T. & Judith his wife died October the 6th 1877 in the 14th year of his age.*

(Both of these were bright & promising children they died in ten days of each other & were buried in the family burying ground on the Boswell farm)

Mary O. Edwards, *sister of Wm T. Boswell, Departed this life February 28th, 1892 near 50th year of her age.*

Lilly C. Boswell, *wife of J. Walter Boswell, died May 17th 1905.*

Walter H. Boswell, *Brother of Wm T Boswell, fell at the Battle of Malvern Hill July 1st 1862 in the 22nd year of his age.*

Frances E. Boswell, *Mother of Wm T. Boswell, Senior, & Walter H. Boswell, died October 15th, 1878 in the 64th year of her age.*

Eliza A. Hockaday, *Mother of Judith W. Boswell, died here at my house May 24th 1890 — in her 74th year. Was buried in the old family burial place by my Father's side on the Hockaday Homestead.*

Loose Pages in the Boswell-Hockaday Bible

After the death of William Thomas Boswell in 1874, on his 575 acre farm in the western part of James City County, Judith Hockaday Boswell, his wife disposed of the farm and moved her family to an 84 acre farm in New Kent County (part of her family Hockaday homestead) and there raised her children. Her home and the Hockaday burying ground were in sight of the source of Ware Creek.

William Hockaday, son of William Hockaday & Elizabeth Bradenham his wife was born February 22, 1804.

Eliza A. Hockaday, wife of William Hockaday & daughter of John Ratcliffe & Judith B. his wife was born January 19, 1817.

Judith W. Hockaday, daughter of William Hockaday & Eliza Ann his wife was born November 12, 1836.

Frances E. Boswell, wife of Thomas Boswell & daughter of William T. [or L.] Richardson & Mary his wife was born January 6th, 1815.

Thomas Boswell, son of Thomas Boswell and Elizabeth his wife [rest of the page torn off. Elizabeth Richardson, widow of Stanhope Richardson, MFTB].

Mary wife of William Richardson was born the 12th of June 1790 and departed this life January 19th 1868 in the 78th year of her age.

Mary Slaughter [torn], mother of Frances E. Boswell was born June 12th, 1790 & Departed this life Jan. 19th 1868 in the 78th year of her age. [A later census record shows her name as Mary Slater MFTB].

Walter H. Boswell, son of Thomas Boswell & Frances his wife was born August 30, 1840 and fell at the Battle of Malvern Hill July 1st 1862 in the 22nd year of his age.

Mary O. Boswell, daughter of Thomas Boswell and Frances his wife was born March 10th 1842.

Sallie E. Hockaday, daughter of William & Eliza Ann his wife was born Mar. 22 1841.

Bettie A. Hockaday, daughter of William & Eliza Hockaday born Feb. 3rd 1848.

R.H.[Harry] Woodward was married to S.[Sarah] C.[Clark] Hockaday the 25th day of January 1866.

Marianna Woodward, daughter of R.H. & S.C. Woodward, was born the 19th April 1867 and Departed this life the 7th of Sept 1868.

George C. Woodward, son of R.H. & S.C. Woodward, was born the 24th of January 1870.

Bettie L. Woodward, daughter of R.H. & S.C. Woodward was born the 23rd of May 1872 and Departed this life the 25th of September 1872.

William A. Woodward, son of R.H. & S.C. Woodward was born the 20th of December 1874 and Departed this life the 18th of August 1875.

Mary Eliza Woodward was born January 10th, 1877.

* * * * *

Judith W. Boswell, widow of the late William Thomas Boswell and daughter of William and Eliza A. Hockaday and mother of J.W. Boswell of Roanoke, Va — born November 12th 1836, died March 20th 1917, aged 80 years 4 months and 8 days — buried in the Hockaday burying ground in New Kent County, Va.

* * * * *

In the handwriting of Judith Boswell, on the back of the title page of Bible:
Claudia Parks (Coloured) born on my place April 4th 1876 and named by me.
Robert James, son of my servant Pocahontas Johnson was born May, 1879.

226

Notes

1. Mary French Turner Boswell has been involved in well-researched family history for some thirty years, and has generously shared her work for publication in *Tidewater Virginia Families*. As is evident, she has employed a variety of original records and respected published sources. Mary French Boswell (Mrs. John Boswell), 3206 Ashby St SW, Roanoke, VA 24015 has in her possession the William Thomas Boswell Family Bible (WTBFB). Her husband, John Boswell was the son of J. Walter Boswell.

2. James City County Personal Property Tax List (PPTL), 1807.

3. New Kent County Personal Property Tax Lists, *passim*.

4. James City County Land Tax List (LTL), 1811.

5. Ibid. 1811-1838.

6. US Census 1830, James City County.

7. James City LTL, 1837.

8. Ibid. 1838-39.

9. Ibid. 1840.

10. *"History of Virginia"*, *American Historical Society*. 6(1924): 310.

11. US Census 1840, James City County.

12. James City LTL 1842.

13. Ibid. 1843.

14. W.T. Boswell Family Bible (WTBFB).

15. Martha W. McCartney, *James City County: Keystone of the Commonwealth*. (Virginia Beach: Donning Company, 1997) 144, 262.

16. James City County LTL, *passim*.

17. McCartney 262.

18. James City County LTL 1788.

19. Ibid. 1816.

20. US Census, James City County.

21. James City County PPTL 1815.

22. US Census 1850, James City County.

23. James City PPTL 1852, 1858, 1859.

24. US Census, 1860, James City County.

25. Information supplied by a niece, Pearl Farthing Harris, and a nephew, Edwin T. Chapman from Boswell Family Records.

26. Boswell Family Records.

27. US Census 1870, James City County.

28. James City County PPTL, 1875.

29. James City County Will Book 1 291.

30. See also LtCol James W. Doyle, Jr., *"The Hockadays Before Blisland"*, *Tidewater Virginia Families: A Magazine of History and Genealogy*. 2(1993): 136-142; York County Deeds, Wills and Orders No. 1 (1636-1657) 35.

31. Blisland Parish Registers, Library, Society of Genealogists, London, LDS Family History Library.

32. Land Patent Book 3 89.

33. Hockaday Family Records.

34. Land Patent Book 6 440.

35. Louis des Cognets, *English Duplicates of Lost Virginia Records*. 1958 (Baltimore: Genealogical Publishing, rep. 1990). 247.

36. Ibid. 166.

37. C.G. Chamberlayne, *The Vestry Book of Blisland (Blissland) Parish, New Kent and James City Counties, Virginia, 1721-1786*. 1935 (Richmond: Virginia State Library, rep. 1979). *passim*.

38. York County Judicial Orders 3 183, 194, 197.

39. William Norris, *The Hockaday Family and Allied Families.* (New York, 1977).

40. DAR Patriot Index, Centennial Edition, Part II, 1990 1444.

41. John K. Martin Papers, Archives and Information Services, Library of Virginia.

42. WTBFB; Ratcliffe Family Bible.

43. Land Patent Book 10 16.

44. Blisland Vestry Book 191.

45. John H. Gwathmey, *Historical Register of Virginians in the Revolution, Soldiers, Sailors, Marines, 1775-1783.* 1938 (Baltimore: Genealogical Publishing, 1996) 86; New Kent County Court Booklet, 15 Mar 1782, 9, Public Service Claims File, Archives and Information Services, Library of Virginia.

46. *Tyler's Quarterly.* 10 177.

47. Hockaday Family Records.

48. Hockaday Family Bible.

Residence at Boswells, James City County, Destroyed by fire, 1867

Untangling Some Obadiah and Luke Smiths

By Betty M. Harris[1]

Legend: Roman numerals are used to identify different persons with the same name. The use of Roman numerals does not necessarily imply successive generations. A (?) after a name indicates that it is not certain to which Smith the entry refers. A (?) after a Roman numeral indicates uncertainty as to the particular Smith references. A (?) before a name indicates that it is not certain that the name is the correct identification of that person. Some data are from primary sources and some from family records.

*About 1637-Jacob Smith I paid an English merchant 10 pounds to transport him and his son to Virginia. *If son is not shipped, only 6 pounds is to be paid and the remainder spent on apprenticing the son.*[2]

*Feb 1638-William Daft (?Jr.), wheelwright and inhabitant of Easton, England and Joane Parker, (?spinster, daughter) of Lawrance Parker of Easton, chandler, were married.[3]

*1 May 1638-Edward Oliver received 500 acres for importation of 10 persons including John Smith(?).[4]

*1 Dec 1643-Jacob Smith I bought 200 acres in Diggs Hundred west on Turkey Island Creek in Charles City Co.[5]

*26 Sep 1648-Cuthbert Harbert married Joan Daft in Oakham Parish, County. Rutland, England.[6]

*4 Dec 1649-Samuel Herbert and 17 May 1652-Luke Herbert were born in Monks Kirby Parish, Warwickshire, England to Cuthbert Herbert and wife, Joane.[7]

*25 Feb 1653-Firdinando Austin received 1200 acres in Charles City Co. for importing 24 persons including John Smith(?) and Edward Smith.[8]

*25 Nov 1662-Mrs Smith, wife of John I near Turkey Island, said Mr. Thomas Cocke's wife was *shrewd and misfed servants.*[9]

*1665-at Charles City County Court, John(?) and Richard Smith deposed: John Smith(?) was 28 years of age; Richard was 31.[10]

*1665-Howell Pryse granted 750 acres for importation of several including John Smith(?) in Charles City County.[11]

*24 Oct 1673-Thomas Harris of Turkey Island, Henrico County sold to John Smith(?) of Charles City County an Indian boy.[12]

*11 May 1675-Mr John Smith I received 636 acres in Charles City County on north side of James River for transporting 13 persons.[13]

*14 Sep 1677-Ed Hill, plaintiff, against John Smith I, shoemaker, and Henry May; referred to next court.[14]

*4 Feb 1677/78-John Smith I deeded land, except for tan pits and tan yard, in Henrico County to R. Bolling to pay for debts.[15]

*15 Aug 1678-at court John Smith(?) says he married the widow, Sarah, administrator of Nicholas Gattley's estate; court discharges will.[16]

*20 Dec 1678-Luke Herbert's will probated in Consistory Court of Peterborough, Northamptonshire, England-written 12 Dec 1678; mentions brother-in-law John Smith I and his wife, Luke's sister, Hannah Daft. They are *to receive 80 pounds from his estate out of 300 pounds left Luke by his uncle, Luke Parker, when they come over and ask for it.*[17]

*1680-Hannah Smith, wife of John Smith I of Charles City County, appeared in Henrico Court stating *she is age 36 and the daughter of William Daft, deceased, who lived in Great Eson in Rutland, a wheelwright; and sister on her Mother's side to Luke Herbert who was born in Monks Kirby Parish, Warwickshire, who died in Peterborough Minster.* Mary Leed and James Horton deposed that what Hannah said is true.[18]

*28 Sep 1681-Mr John Smith(?) received 306 acres Charles City, Bristol Parish for importing 6 persons.[19]

*28 Feb 1684/5-William Cocke I sold 59 acres on Turkey Creek Island, next to brother, John. Wife Jane relinquished dower 1 Apr 1685.[20]

*1684-John Smith(?) emigrated to Virginia from *Haraby in The County of Leicest*, England.[21]

*1 Apr 1685-John Smith(?) is deceased.[22]

*3 Feb 1687-Suit commenced by William Morris as marrying Sarah, the adm'x. of John Smith(?), dec'd in Charles City County.[23]

*16 Jun 1691-William Cocke I married Sarah Dennis.[24]

*28 Apr 1691-John Smith I, son and heir of Jacob Smith I, received 200 acres in Diggs Hundred, Charles City County on Turkey Island Creek granted Joseph Royall 4 May 1638; sold to Edward Martin 22 May 1643 who sold it to Jacob Smith 1 Dec 1643.[25]

*3 Jun 1692-at Westover Court, Capt. Daniel Lewellin to name and swear appraisers for estate of John Smith I.[26]

*3 Aug 1692-Obadiah Smith I and Mary Smith I, son and daughter of John Smith I, late deceased; William Harding and Henry Brazell, sureties, gave 48,000 pounds tobacco to James Biss for the appointment of executors of will of John Smith I dated 27 Aug 1689; probated 3 Jun last past. (1692).[27]

*15 Sep 1692-at Westover Court These persons: *John Turner, John Rix, of Westover Parish, Obadiah Smith [I], and Christopher Hudson have appeared with their orphans and are continued in their care.*[28]

*1 Jan/Feb 1693/4-William Cocke I's will, written 13 Oct 1693, was probated; mentioned wife, Sarah; daughters, Mary and Elizabeth; and son,

William II; *daughters to live with stepmother or his mother, Mrs. Mary Clarke or his brother, Richard Cocke, til of age or married.*[29]

*1 Oct 1694-Sarah Cocke told Henrico Court she is selling William Cocke I's estate at his dwelling house.[30]

*1 Jun 1695-Mrs Sarah Cocke, relict, gave inventory of William Cocke I's estate.[31]

*26 June 1695-Mary Smith(?) married Peter Harris.[32]

*1 Feb 1697-Obadiah Smith I witnessed deed in Henrico Co; signed OS[33]

*1704-Obadiah Smith I had 200 acres Henrico County and 100 acres in Charles City County and lived in Charles City County.[34]

*6 Apr 1705-Obadiah Smith I and wife Mary Cocke of Henrico County and Elizabeth Cocke and husband, Lancelot Woodward of James City County sold a plantation inherited from father, William Cocke I, presented 1708. Also the wives got another plantation from John Flowers of James City County, their uncle on their mother's side, on Turkey Island Creek in Henrico County next to Pleasant's Mill — 254 acres.[35]

*2 Aug 1708-Luke Smith I witnessed document in Henrico County.[36]

*c.1712-Obadiah Woodson I, son of Richard Woodson I, (third son of Robert) and Ann (?Smith I) was born. (estimation from various genealogies. Since his uncle left Obadiah land in his will of 1716, Obadiah was born before that date.)[37]

*2 Jun 1712-Gilly Gromarrin I deeded to *son-in-law Luke Smith I and my daughter Arabella,* land on south side of Chickahominy Swamp of 439 acres in Henrico County; wife, Susanna, relinquished dower rights.[38]

*5 Nov 1716-Gillee Gromarrin I's will was probated in Henrico County; written 16 Oct 1716; mentions sons: Francis, Wiltshire I, and Gillee II; and daughters; Arabella and Anne. Son-in-law Luke Smith I appointed executor.[39]

*7 Jan 1716/7-Obadiah Smith I bought for 200 pounds 300 acres on north side James River and south side Chickahominy Swamp *where Obadiah Smith now lives*; also for 10,000 pounds tobacco, 600 acres near Cornelius Creek.[40]

*May 1720-Obadiah Smith I petitioned Henrico Court for one acre of land for a water gristmill on Pickanockey Cr. Received it by Dec 1720.[41]

*1 Aug 1734-Luke Smith I received grant of 300 acres on east side of branch of Shacoe (Shockoe) Creek adj. to Gilly Gromarrin II and Obadiah Smith.[42]

*2 Sep 1734-Obadiah Smith I sold for 80 pounds land on north side of James River in Henrico County near Turkey Island Creek which was given by William Cocke I in his will, to his daughters, Mary and Elizabeth, recorded Oct 1696 (restatement of 1708 deed).

*1735-The results of the Henrico Parish processioning show that the lands of Obadiah Smith I, *himself present,* Mary Cannon, Gilly Grew Marren II, and

Luke Smith I (in that order) were presented to county by March 1736; owners were noted present. The processioning was for lands between Chickahominy Swamp and Brook Road.[43]

    *16 Mar 1735-Michael Holland sold to Luke Smith (?I) 175 acres on Tuckahoe Creek in Goochland County.[44]

    *c.1739-Luke Smith II married Judith Ferris (1715-1811). (IGI has marriage listed in 1729 as well as 1739. Another source says they had a daughter, Phoebe, born about 1760.[45])

    *1740-Luke Smith (?I) listed in Henrico County and Obadiah Smith (?III) in Goochland County.[46]

    *30 Jul 1742-Luke Smith (?I) bought 400 acres in Brunswick County, on north side of Staunton River, north side of Turnip Creek.[47]

    *Feb 1742/3-in Henrico Court, Luke Smith I sold land he patented 1732 to Samuel Tscheffely. Arabella, his wife, relinquished dower rights. Land bordered Shockoe Creek, Capt. J. Cocke, Gilly Gromarrin II, Fr. Chumbley, Obadiah Smith I, Widow Cannon and Col. Wm. Byrd.[48]

    *before 23 Aug 1744-Obadiah Smith III, son of Luke I, married Mary Burks, daughter of Samuel, in Virginia.[49]

    * 23 Aug 1744- Luke Smith IV, son of Obadiah III and Mary Burks Smith, was christened in Goochland County.[50]

    *18 Sep 1744-Arabella Smith relinquished her dower rights to 175 acres of land on Tuckahoe Creek in Goochland County Luke Smith I deeded *for love and natural affection* to Obadiah III and Mary Smith.[51]

    *4 May 1745-Obadiah Smith IX born to Jacob II and Ann Smith.[52]

    *17 Oct 1745-Luke Smith I advertised in *Virginia Gazette,* 439 acres for sale, 4 miles *from James River Falls, 2 plantations with very good buildings, plantations in good repair. Owner living on premises* (in Henrico County).

    *June 1746-Obadiah Smith I's will probated, written 29 Oct 1744, Henrico County; inventory recorded Feb. 1746/7; 137 pounds; mentions children: John II, Obadiah II, Jacob II, Luke II, William I, Elizabeth Ellis, Mary II and Ann II, and wife, Mary. Son Luke II received slaves, Valentine and Sampson.[53]

    *1746-Luke Smith (?)I was a processioner from mouth of Grassy Creek to mouth of Hico River in Cumberland Parish, Lunenburg County.[54]

    *13 Jun 1747-recorded on 1 Feb 1747/48, Luke Smith Sr./I of Lunenburg County gave to son Luke Smith (Jr/III) and wife Martha, *for love and affection,* 250 acres on south side of Dan River bounded by Bird's back line, Tenahominy (Aaron's) Creek and mouth of Dan River.[55]

    *27 Oct 1747-Luke Smith(?)I sold land totaling 400 acres on north side of Turnip Creek to John East, Thomas Pharis and Matox Mayse.[56]

    *19 Nov 1747-Luke Smith I entered 3200 acres with sons, Obadiah III, ,

Charles, Luke (Jr/III), and Zachariah in Lunenburg County.[57]

*16 Dec 1747-Luke Smith (II), son of Obadiah I, bought 400 acres at the Lick on Allens Cr, just below Bannister path in Pittsylvania County.[58]

*13 Jun 1748-Peartree Smith christened; son of Obadiah III and Mary Burke Smith in Goochland County.[59]

*Nov 1749-Obadiah Smith III sold 170 acres of land on fork of Tuckahoe Creek in Goochland County; recorded 20 Mar 1749/50; Mary, his wife, relinquished dower rights.[60]

*1749-Luke Smith(?) was a vestryman in Cumberland Parish and on list of tithes in 1748-49-50 from Cub Creek to Falling River.[61]

*1751-Luke Smith II was a processioner in Cumberland County from mouth of Allens Creek to Mayo Ford up from head of Bannister to Pig River. Also a Luke Smith(?) was a processioner from Grassy Creek to county line, Roanoke River, Dan River and Hico River.[62]

*30 Jan 1754-Luke Smith II bought 600 acres on branches of Allens Creek in what is now Pittsylvania.[63]

*1 Apr 1754-Mary Cocke Smith's will probated; written 3 Jun 1753; mentions John II, William I, Obadiah II, Jacob II, Luke II, Elizabeth Ellis, Ann II, Mary II, granddaughter Mary III (who was daughter of Mary Smith II), and William Smith (no known relation).[64]

*7 May 1755-Obadiah Smith IV, son of Obadiah III and Mary Burke Smith, christened St. James Church, Northam Parish, Goochland County.[65]

*30 Oct 1755-Obadiah Smith III of Henrico sold to Charles Smith of Halifax County 80 acres on south side of Hico River; recorded 20 May 1756 with Luke Smith (Jr/III), Smith, Zachariah Smith and Ralph Griffin witnesses.[66]

*16 Aug 1756-Land patent granted to Luke Smith II of 1032 acres in Lunenburg County, both sides of Allens Creek on the Bannister River by the mountain, adjacent Charles Anderson.[67]

*6 Sept 1757-Luke Smith I sold in Halifax County for 100 pounds 356 acres to Charles Smith of Halifax County on south side of Dan River; recorded 19 May 1757 in presence of Smith, Luke Smith Jr. (III) and Ralph Griffin.[68]

*15 Sep 1757-Luke Smith (Jr/III)'s will probated in Halifax County but written 20 Oct 1750 in Cumberland Parish, Lunenburg County, mentions wife Martha; sister Arabella Marrow's 3 children: Esther, Daniel and Arabella; brother Obadiah III.[69]

*15 Mar 1758-Luke Smith I's will probated; written 28 Dec 1757, in Halifax County mentions children: Obadiah III, Charles, Ursala, Arabella, Susannah, Zachariah and Hannah; grandchildren: Samuel Smith, John Pryor Smith, Daniel Morrow, and daughter of Charles Smith. Smith received land where father lives.[70]

*20 Jul 1758-Inventory of Charles Smith estate returned in Halifax County Court.[71]

*18 Oct 1758-Luke Smith II and wife Judith of North Carolina, sold to John East 200 acres on branch of Allens Creek next to Anderson; also to Joseph Ferris-632 acres; to Jacob Ferris-100 acres; to James Ferris-100 acres; all on Allens Creek all adjacent to each other.[72]

*17 Aug 1759-Land in Antrim Parish, Halifax County from mouth of Difficult Creek to Staunton River to confluence of the two rivers and up the Dan River to mouth of Bannister River to ford of Steward's Ferry to Difficult Creek was processioned. Smith was one of the processioners and owned land in the area.[73]

*1760-Luke Smith II listed with land in Halifax County; Obadiah Smith(?) in Henrico, Lunenburg and Chesterfield counties.[74]

*Mar 1760-Antrim Parish processioners; James Ferris, Joseph Ferris and William Laws processioned lands on Bannister River to the mountains, of Luke Smith II, Joseph Ferris, James Ferris, Joseph Mayo, William Lightfoot, John East Jr. and John East.[75]

*1 Mar 1763-Obadiah Smith V born in Powhatan County, Va. (see 1832 pension record).[76]

*Oct 1765-Henrico Court-Obadiah Smith II's will presented by Jacob Smith II (brother); sons: William II, Samuel, John IV, daughter Martha who was married to Giles Carter. William Smith II appointed executor.[77]

*23 Aug 1767-Obadiah Smith VIII born to William Smith and Mary Smith II, daughter of Obadiah I.[78]

*1 Jul 1768- Smith of Mecklenburg County sold 200 acres of land on Dan River in Halifax County, that he inherited from father, Luke I, by will.[79]

*c.1775-Obadiah Smith VII born to Peartree and Isabella Hopkins Smith.[80]

*30 Aug 1775-Betsey christened; 20 Dec 1776. Sally christened; daughters of Obadiah Smith VI and Lucy Poor[81]

*1776-Captain Luke B. Smith V (professor at Prince Edward Academy/Hampden-Sidney College) led out a Company of Students; served 6 weeks at Williamsburg.[82]

*18 Feb 1777-Obadiah Smith III died.[83]

*25 Feb 1777-letter to Lt. William Smith III addressed to Paymaster 5th Virginia Regiment in New Jersey informing him of death of father and to inform brother, Lt. Obadiah IV.[84]

*2 May 1777-in Chesterfield County, Obadiah Smith III's will probated; sons; Peartree, land in Mecklenburg County; Obadiah IV, land in Chesterfield County & North Carolina; William III, land in Halifax County; daughters: Lucy and Elizabeth; and Edith Christmas mentioned.[85]

Written interview of Mary Watts Pitts, following (Roman numerals added):

*1778-Obadiah Smith IV married Lucy Harris. Granddaughter Mary Watts Pitts said they married while he was on furlough from Army service.[86]

*1778-Captain Luke Smith VI's volunteer student company was again in service for six weeks at Petersburg.[87]

*12 Apr 1779-will probated; written 7 Nov 1778, of Peartree Smith of Mecklenburg County, wife Isabella, daughters, Nancy and Elizabeth, son Obadiah VII mentioned. Peartree had land in Halifax County on Aaron's Creek. Obadiah VII was underage..[88]

*9 Jun 1781-Mary Burke Smith born to Obadiah IV and Lucy Harris Smith.[89]

*22 Aug 1782-Obadiah Smith VIII died.[90]

*c.1788-Obadiah Smith XI born to William Smith III and Elizabeth Mayo.[91]

*7 Feb 1791-will of Jacob Smith probated; written 16 Jan 1790; mentioned wife Ann and children: Jesse, Obadiah IX, Mary Ann Hentley, Susannah Ellis and Jacob III.[92]

*10 May 1792-Obadiah Smith X born to Obadiah Smith IX and Elizabeth Povall Burton.[93]

*5 Aug 1794-Obadiah Smith IX died.[94]

*22 May 1798-Obadiah Smith VII married Tabitha Osborne Wilson in Antrim Parish, Mecklenburg County.[95].

*13 Oct 1800-Obadiah Smith VII of Mecklenburg County sold to Shadrack Overby of Halifax, land lying on Aron's Creek which was inherited from Obadiah VII's father's.[96]

*12 Feb 1801-Will of William Smith III probated, written 20 Oct 1800 in Chesterfield County; 8 children mentioned with one being Obadiah Smith XI.[97]

*22 Dec 1803-Mary Burke Smith, daughter of Obadiah IV, married William Watts.[98]

*3 Feb 1808-obituary, Obadiah Smith IV died age 53 on 3rd at his seat in Chesterfield County.[99]

*1829-Obadiah Smith VII died.[100].

*1832-Obadiah Smith V applied for American Revolution Pension; born 1 Mar 1763 in Powhatan County; moved at age 4 to grandfather's home in Buckingham County; resided in Jefferson County, Tennessee in 1832.[101]

Some Conclusions

Obadiah Smith I and Luke Smith I are recorded as living next to each other in both 1712 and 1735 in Henrico County on the south side of Chickahominy River. Gilly Gromarrin I, Luke's father-in-law, also lived near them. This is in the area of *Pickanocky Plantation*, where Obadiah wanted to construct a mill on Pickanocky Creek in 1720. There is a Gillys Creek also in the area; near the Richmond airport.

1-About John Smith I (b. before 1637 in England-d. 1692 in Virginia)

John Smith I was the son of Jacob Smith I, who died in Charles City County before 1691, and lived in Diggs Hundred on Turkey Island Creek in Charles City County. He is the most likely candidate for John Smith, shoemaker, who might have owned the tan yards in Henrico County which were on the other side of Turkey Island Creek. He is most probably the husband of Hannah Daft, who lived in Charles City County, but appeared in the Henrico County Court.

2-About Obadiah Smith I (about 1672-1746)

This man was the son of John Smith I and grandson of Jacob Smith I. He was over 17 in 1689 when named executor of his father's will. Therefore he was born by 1672. All three of these men owned land in Diggs Hundred, north of the James River on Turkey Island Creek. He married Mary Cocke after 1693 and before 1705 as she was not married when her father, William Cocke I, wrote his will. They may have been married by 1695 when her stepmother sold her husband's estate. Thus one might assume that Obadiah I had no children born before 1696. In 1705 he sold the land in Henrico County that his wife inherited from her father. Obadiah I had a son, Jacob II, who had a son named Obadiah IX, while his sons, John II, Luke II and Obadiah II did not name any sons, Obadiah or Luke, and such information about his son, William I, is lacking. One of his daughters, Mary, married William Smith (no known relation) and had a son, Obadiah VIII.

William Cocke, Sr. (I) (1657-1693), married Jane (?)Flowers before 1685. Since John Flowers left land to his nieces, Mary and Elizabeth Cocke, Jane's maiden name was probably Flowers. Jane Flowers Cocke died between 1685 and 1691 as William Cocke I married Sarah Dennis in 1691.

3-About Obadiah Smith II (c.1700-1765)

He was the son of Obadiah I and is mentioned in Obadiah I's will. His sons were named William II, Samuel, and John III.

4-About Obadiah Smith III (c.1715-1777)

This man was the son of Luke I. He married Mary Burke by 1744 and had several children including Luke IV born in 1744, Peartree in 1748, William III in 1752, Obadiah IV in 1755, Charles in 1758 and Joseph in 1761. Obadiah III owned land in several places; but lived in Goochland County where most of his children were christened by the Reverend William Douglas. He died in Chesterfield County. Peartree and William III named a son, Obadiah (VII and XI, respectively). Obadiah IV and Charles II did not, and it is not known whether Luke IV or Joseph named sons Obadiah.

5-About Lt. Obadiah Smith IV (1755-1808) and Obadiah Smith VI (alive in 1775)

Since the maiden name of Obadiah IV's mother was Mary Burke and he named a daughter Mary Burke Smith, one can reasonably assume that he is the son of Obadiah III. Obadiah IV was born to Obadiah III in 1755 in Goochland; married in 1778 Lucy Harris; and died in 1808 in Chesterfield County. He had no sons named Obadiah or Luke. His granddaughter, Mary Watts Pitts listed as siblings of her mother: John IV, Peter Field and Jordan. No mention is made by Mrs. Pitts of aunts named Betsy or Sally, who were daughters of Obadiah VI and Lucy Poor. There is no proof yet that Lucy Poor died before 1778 and that these two men were the same person as several genealogists have stated.

6-About Obadiah V (1763-after 1832)

This man testified in his pension application as to being born in Powhatan (then Cumberland County) in 1763, living with his grandfather in 1767 in Buckingham County, and residing in Jefferson County, Tennessee in 1832. So far no records have been found as to his ancestry.

7-About Obadiah Smith VII (say 1775-1829)

Obadiah Smith VII of Mecklenburg County was named in a deed of land on Aarons Creek. His father was Peartree Smith who owned the land before him. He married Tabitha Wilson 22 May 1798 in Mecklenburg County. He died in Henderson, Kentucky.

8-About Obadiah Smith VIII (1767–1782)

He was son of William Smith, son of Robert and Ann Sterling Smith of Gloucester County and Mary Smith II. They lived in Powhatan County. She was the daughter of Obadiah I and Mary Cocke Smith.

9-About Obadiah Smith IX (1745-1794)

Ann and Jacob Smith II, son of Obadiah I and Mary Cocke Smith, were the parents of Obadiah IX. His wife was Betsy Povall Burton. They were married before 1774 when their first child was born.

10-About Obadiah Smith X (1792-?)

He is the son of Obadiah Smith IX and Betsy Povall Burton.

11-About Obadiah Smith XI (say 1788-aft 1800)

His parents were William III and Elizabeth Mayo Smith.

12-About Luke Smith I (about 1682-1758)

This man was married by 1712 when he and his wife, Arabella Gromarrin, received land in Henrico from her father. Luke I would have been 16 or younger to have been Obadiah I's son and to be married by 1712. Also the 1747 deed to Luke Smith II reads he was the son of Obadiah. Thus it is more likely that Luke I was the brother of Obadiah I, or no relation at all.

Luke Smith I moved from Henrico County to Lunenburg County about 1746. Part of Lunenburg County became Halifax County in 1752, where his will was probated in 1758. His children, except for Obadiah III, were probably living on land he purchased in Lunenburg County in 1747. Luke Smith I lived in the area of Difficult Creek, Halifax County, where he left land to his son, , where *I now live*. Luke I had sons named Obadiah III, Luke III, Charles I, and Zachariah. His daughters were: Ursalla. Arabella, Hannah and Susanna.

12-About Luke Smith II (about 1710-about 1780)

Luke Smith II married Judith Ferris before 1739. He died in Union County, South Carolina after 1770 and before 1783 when his widow remarried. Judith was born in 1715, if her obituary is correct. This means she was still having children at age 47 if her last child was born about 1762. Luke Smith II owned land his father, Obadiah Smith I, deeded to him in 1747 on Allen's Creek where it flows into Bannister River.

Luke II was taxed for this land in 1759 and thus was still alive when we know Luke Smith I and Luke Smith III had died. Luke Smith II is surely the son of Obadiah Smith I, as no other mature Luke Smiths have been found in the 1750s. The known children of Luke II are: Edith married Nehemiah Howard; Sarah married Thomas Greer; Martha (d. 1840) married William Jackson; Archer; and Phoebe (d 1825) married (1) Hosea Holcombe and (2) William Wilbanks.[102]

13-About Luke Smith III (about 1716-1757)

By deed of 1747, Luke Smith III is shown to be son of Luke I. Luke III was married to Martha (-?-) by 1750. No children were mentioned in his will, but he could have had some born between 1750 when his will was written and 1757 when his will was probated. However, his father Luke I, did not mention Luke III or his children in his will of 1758. Luke Smith III lived south of the Dan River on Aarons Creek and died in 1757.

14-About Luke Smith IV (1744-?)); Captain Luke Smith VI (living 1778)

When Obadiah Smith III's will was written, there was no mention of his son, Luke IV, who was born in 1744, and who may have died before 1777. These two Lukes may be the same person, but Captain Luke Smith VI was still alive after Obadiah III died.

15-About Ann Smith I (c.1680-after 1724) and Mary Smith I (c.1670-?)

Some genealogists state that the wife of Richard Woodson II was Ann Smith I, the daughter of Obadiah I and Mary Cocke Smith. This must not be correct as they were both having children in the same time frame. There is the possibility she was the underage sister of Obadiah I mentioned in John I's administration in 1692. She was referred to as "orphan" in the administration of the estate. She named a son, Obadiah Woodson I — not a common name in Virginia. This is the only evidence found by this researcher to surmise that Mrs. Ann Woodson was formerly Ann Smith I. Obadiah Smith I and his sister, Mary I were guardians of orphan/s of John Smith I — could they have been Ann I and Luke I? Mary Smith I may have been the wife of Peter Harris.

16-About Hannah Daft (1644 in England-after 1680 & before 1689)

Hannah Daft's mother's name was Joan Parker, probably the Joan born in 1612 in Great Easton Parish, daughter of Lawrence. She married in 1638 William Daft, who died before 1647; and then she married Cuthbert Herbert in 1647. Hannah had a valid reason to name a son Luke. Her children were probably born before 1689 when she would have been 45.

Hannah Daft was married before 1678 when Luke Herbert wrote his will. If she was the wife of John Smith who appeared in court in 1662, she would have been 18, but her children seemed to have been born nearer 1670 and after. John Smith I had 2 children over age of 17 in 1689, Obadiah I and Mary I; and child/children under 17 in 1692, possibly Luke I and Ann I, if one concludes the orphans of whom Obadiah I was guardian were his siblings. Hannah, the mother, was not appointed a guardian of her under-age children born after 1675 and before 1692.

The fact that Hannah Daft had a half-brother named Luke, who left her a money legacy, that both Obadiah Smith I and Luke Smith I of Henrico County had sons named Obadiah and Luke, and the close proximity of the plantations of both Obadiah I and Luke I provides evidence that they were related. Hannah Daft Smith does not seem to have been alive in 1692, or to have moved, perhaps back to England to claim her legacy. She was not mentioned in the administration of the estate of John Smith I although there were under-age children; or she was not the wife of this John Smith.

The Questions Remain:
Was Luke Smith I the son or the brother of Obadiah Smith I?
Surely not his son; most likely his brother
Was Luke Smith I the son of Hannah Daft Smith?
Probably; as was Obadiah Smith I
Was Ann Smith the maiden name of Ann, the wife of Richard Woodson II?
Was she a daughter of Hannah and John Smith? Possibly
Who was Luke Smith II who married Judith Ferris?
Most certainly the son of Obadiah Smith I as shown in the deed of 1747 of his father, Obadiah I
Are all of these Smiths related?
Probably, but more research is needed.

Notes

1. Mrs. Betty M. Harris, 3601 L St., Lincoln, NE 68510-3361. harris@inebraska.com. She has additional information about the Smith descendants.
2. George F.T. Sherwood, *American Colonists in English Records 1625-49,* (London: G. Sherwood, 1932/3) 7.
2. *Great Easton Parish Records, Leicestershire,* 1638. Latter Day Saints Family History Center) (FHC) Film #0592703; n.p.; International Genealogical Index (IGI).
4. Louise Foley, *Early Virginia Families Along the James River,* vol 2. (Richmond: privately printed (p.p.), 1978) 10.

5. Nell Marion Nugent, *Cavaliers and Pioneers*, vol 1. (Richmond: Virginia State Library (LVA), 1934) 364. Diggs Hundred is in Charles City County with Turkey Island Creek being the dividing line with Henrico County.

6. *England*, IGI, FHC. Widow of William.

7. *Monks Kirby Parish Records, Warwickshire, 1656* n.p.; FHC #0557302.

8. Foley 26.

9. Beverly Fleet, Deposition of Edmund Davy, Charles City Co. Court Orders, 1661-1664 357, *Virginia Colonial Abstracts*, vol 12. (Richmond: privately printed, 1941) 37.

10. Fleet, Charles City County Court Orders, 1664-1665, fragments 1650-1696, VCA, vol 13 54. Therefore John was born 1637.

11. Ibid.

12. *Henrico County Deeds* 135; FHC Film #0031769.

13. Foley 46.

14. Margaret Ayers, *Charles City County, Virginia Court Order Book, 1676-79.* (Memphis: 1968) 79. A John Smith lived in Charles City County and was a shoemaker and a member of the Cordwainers Guild.

15. Ibid. 83.

16. Ibid. 106. This is John Smith of Bristol Parish, who married a Sarah, and who died in 1685. Bristol Parish is on the south side of the James River.

17. *Northamptonshire Will Book O* 149; FHC #0174855.

18. *Henrico County Deeds Book 1* 152; FHC #0031769.

19. Foley 50.

20. *Henrico County Deeds Book 1* n.p.; FHC #0031769.

21. Rev. L.W. Burton, ed. and comp. J. Staunton Moore, *Annals and History of Henrico Parish.* (Richmond: St. John's Church, 1904) 182.

22. Foley 58. See also 1678 entry.

23. Benjamin B. Weisiger, III, *Charles City County, Virginia Court Orders 1687-1695.* (Richmond: privately printed, 1980) 100.

24. James C. Southall, "Richard Cocke of Bremo", *Virginia Magazine of History and Biography.* 4(1898): 9.

25. Foley 67.

26. Weisiger, *Charles City Co. COB.* 126.

27. Ibid. 406, 130.

28. Ibid. 416, 134.

29. *Henrico County Deeds and Wills* n.p.; FHC #0031770.

30. Ibid.

31. Ibid.

32. Burton 226.

33. Weisiger, *Henrico County Deeds, 1677-1705,* (Richmond: privately printed, 1985) 58.

34. Howard Oliver, *The 1704 Virginia Quit Rent Rolls.* (Riverside: privately printed, 1993) 82.

35. Weisiger, *Henrico County Deeds, 1706-1737.* (Richmond: privately printed, 1985) 127.

36. Ibid. 107; Lecture *Age Categories and Legal Ages*, Eric G. Grundset, Fairfax, VA, 1997, stating that males 14 and over could be witnesses.

37. Virginia L.H. Davis, *Tidewater Virginia Families.* (Baltimore: Genealogical Publishing Co., 1989) 404.

38. *Henrico County Deeds and Wills, 1694-1739* 113; FHC #0031770.

39. Ibid. 119.

40. Weisiger, *Henrico County Deeds 1706-1737.*(Richmond: privately printed, 1985) 134, 54.

41. Weisiger, *Henrico County Court Order Book, 1719-1724*, (Richmond: privately printed, c.1985). 25,168; FHC #1697555 10. *Pickinocky Plantation* is in the Richmond Quad on the east side of Bridge Road along the bluffs of the Chickahominy River. 43-169; Jeffery Marshall Odell, *Inventory of Early American Architecture and Historic Sites, County of Henrico, Virginia.* (Richmond: Henrico County, 1976) 250.

42. *Henrico County Deeds and Wills Book 15* 239; FHC #0031770.

43. R.A. Brock, *The Vestry Book of Henrico Parish, Virginia, 1730-1773.* (Bowie, MD: Heritage, 1991). 26.

44. Linda Cheek,"Goochland Wills & Deeds 1742-49" 173, *Ancestors and Descendants of Smiths.* (Easley, SC: 1988). 288.

45. Brent Holcomb, *Greer and Related Families.* (Columbia, SC.: B. H. Holcomb, c.1987) 84. Judith died March 1811 in Union District, SC. in her 96th year-*The Republican & Savannah, GA. Evening Ledger*, Issue 3, Dec. 1811. If Judith was 95 at death she would have been born in 1716 and not married much before 1735.

46. *Virginia in 1740-A Reconstructed Census.* (Miami Beach: TLC, 1992) 255.

47. Dennis Hudgins, ed. *Cavaliers and Pioneers, 1741-1749*, vol 5. (Richmond: Virginia Genealogical Society, 1994) 27.

48. Weisiger, *Henrico County Deeds 1737-50,* Part 2. (Richmond: privately printed, c.1985). 206.

49. William Douglas, *Douglas Register.* (Richmond: J.W. Ferguson & Sons, 1928) 296.

50. Ibid.

51. *Goochland County Deeds Book 4, 1728-1859.* 413; FHC #0031654.

52. Leonie D. Cocke and Virginia W. Cocke, "Smith Family Bible", *Cockes and Cousins*, preliminary draft, 1967. n.p.

53. Weisiger, *Colonial Wills of Henrico County, Virginia, 1737-1781*, Part 2. (Richmond: privately printed, 1976-1977). 24.

54. L.C. Bell, *Cumberland Parish Records, 1746-1816.* (Richmond: William Byrd Press, Inc. c.1930) 326.

55. *Lunenberg County Deeds 1* 283; FHC #0032388. Aaron's Creek is the dividing line between Halifax and Mecklenburg counties.

56. Ibid. 1:288.

57. Ibid. 2: 389. Luke Smith made purchases in Lunenberg, Halifax and Pittsylvania counties during the next 10 years. There may have been more than one Luke Smith making these purchases. One was on Allens Creek; other purchases were made on land between the Dan and Roanoke rivers. There are two Allens Creeks in that area; one in present day Mecklenburg, and one in Pittsylvania. The one in Mecklenburg flows into the Roanoke River near Elm Hill. The one in Pittsylvania flows into the Bannister River near the Halifax County border.

58. Cheek 288.

59. Douglas 296. Peartree married Isabella Hopkins, daughter of Dr. Arthur Hopkins and Elizabeth Petters/Pettus in Mecklenburg County. FHC Family G Sheet.

60. *Goochland County Deed Book 6* 39; FHC #0031654.

61. *Cumberland Parish Records* 282.

62. Ibid. 340.

63. Cheek 288.

64. Weisiger, *Colonial Wills of Henrico County, Part 2.* 51.

65. Douglas 296.

66. *Halifax County Deed Book 1* 164; FHC #0031881.

67. Dennis Hudgins, ed, *Cavaliers and Pioneers, 1749-1762*, vol 6. (Richmond: Virginia Genealogical Society, 1998). 193

68. *Halifax County Deeds Book 1* 253.

69. *Halifax County Will Book O, 1752-1773.* 37; FHC #0031862.

70. Ibid. 43.

71. Ibid. 49.

72. *Halifax County Deed Book 2* 34; FHC #0031881.

73. *Antrim Parish Records* 57; FHC #0030163.

74. *Virginia in 1760: A Reconstructed Census.* (Miami Beach: TLC Genealogy, 1996). 313.

75. *Antrim Parish Records* 76.

76. *Pension Records of American Revolution, Se-So.* FHC #0882888. Then Cumberland County.

77. Cheek 216.

78. Cocke and Cocke, *Cockes and Cousins.* (Ann Arbor, MI: Edwards Bros., 1967) 10.

79. Cheek 225.

80. Cocke and Cocke n.p.

81. Douglas 237.

82. J.T. McAllister, *Virginia Militia in the Revolutionary War,* vol 1. (Hot Springs, VA: McAllister Publishing Co., 1913) 40.

83. Cocke and Cocke 10B.

84. James C. Southall, "Genealogy of the Cocke Family in Virginia", *Genealogies of Virginia Families Cl-Fi,* vol 2 (VMHB) 176; CD162 (Broderbund, 1998).

85. *Chesterfield County Will Book 3* 100.

86. Watts family files; copy at Virginia State Library; DAR #57077.

87. McAllister, vol. 2 156.

88. Cheek 222; *Mecklenburg County Will Book 1* 294.

89. Watts Family Files.

90. Cocke and Cocke 10.

91. Ibid. 40B.

92. Cocke and Cocke n.p.; *Henrico County Will Book 1, 1787-1802.*

93. North America IGI.

94. Cocke and Cocke n.p.

95. "Mecklenburg County, Virginia", *Marriage Records, Southern States,* 1: 56; CD 004 (Automated Archives, Inc., 1994).

96. *Halifax County Deed Book 18* 522; FHC #0031881.

97. Cocke and Cocke 40B.

98. Cheek 73.

99. *Richmond Argus* 3 Feb 1808 p3, "Obituaries from Richmond Virginia Newspapers", *Virginia Vital Records,* CD 174 (Broderbund, 1998).

100. Cocke and Cocke 10.

101. *Index of Revolutionary War Pension Applications,* (specially paged supplement) S3938. National Society of Genealogy Quarterly, 47(1959): 1029.

102. Holcomb 81. Without the research supplied by several Smith descendants, this compilation could not have been written. My grateful thanks to all, including Peggy Chapman, Paul Gilbert, Bob Durham, and Camp Gilliam.

List of Clerks Fees, 1766
Northumberland County

Editor's note: Following is an alphabetical listing of the individuals of Northumberland County, who transacted business with the court and the fees, in pounds of tobacco owed to the clerk of the court for services rendered. This provides not only the identification of many of the residents of the county in 1766, but also the extent of their business with the court. The notations after the names are not explained.   Transcribed by VLHD.

A

Thos Ashburne		14
William Ashburne		90
John Adams		14
Rawleigh Alexander		126
William Aire		96
John Alloway	R	45
John Adkins		108
Jesse Alexander		100
Wm Algood	R	183
John Ashburne		48
Thomas Allen		32
Geo. Anderson		32
John Alexander		72

B

M. Beckwith	A	19
Isaac Baysie		86
John Baysie		59
David Boyd	✓	1061
George Bearcroft		152
Joseph Ball		815
George Ball		263
James Ball Junr		45
Neddy Barnes		30
George Boswell		45
Jn° Blackwell		143
Betty H. Booth		41
Wm Blackerby		50
John Beam		45

Saml Blackwell		53
James Ball	1	142
Smith Barret		9
William Barber	R	99
Charles Barret		63
William Ball		96
Judith Blundall		50
Leanna Badger		50
William Bailey		283
Hugh Brent	1	276
Wm Bussell		68
Royston Betts		261
John Barr		239
Henry Bagguss		100
Charles Bill		90
Giles Bagguss		86
Job Braughton		44
John Berry		36
John Byrn		87
Elisha Betts		145
Joseph Bentley		14
Richd Ball		117
Major Bicerdick		44
John Baylis		60
Phillip Bussell		82
John Blincoe		82
Blackwell's Est		72
Benjn & Jn° Brown		68

C

Jesse Copedge		324
Thomas Cottere[?ll blot]		90
John Cox		59
Mary Curtiss		90
Spencer Corbell		120
John Crawley		78
Robert Clarke		48
Cralle & Lee		41
James Craine		574
Charles Copedge		306
John Clarke		168
George Clarke R		88
John Coles		42
John Cralle Jun[r]		144
Kenner Cralle		202
Stephen Chilton		469
Wilson M. Cary	✓	99
Rob[t] Carter Esq	W	9
Richard Creek A		41
James Gaine		9
Collin Campbell		80
Peme Claughton		126
John Corbell		36
Wil[m] Cadzake[?]		9
William Cop [?Cap]		172
George Curtiss		41

D

Daughity & Wornam		90
Travers Downman		156
W[m] Dameron Sen[r]		23
William Dew	R	76
Tho[s] Downing		154
James Daughity		143
W[m] Davenport		120
John Dameron		21
W[m] Dameron	W	50
Sam[l] Downing		95
George Dameron		107

John Denny		71
Moses Dunaway	✓	281
Barth[w] Dameron		351
Joseph Dameron		100
Richard Denny		196
Rob[t] Downman	R	32
William Doghead [Doggett?]		39
Cornelius Deforrest U		27
Joseph Dunaway		81
Thomas Dameron		36
Aron Dameron		50

E

Elias Edmonds		190
Hancock Eustace		36
Sam[l] Eskridge	✓	511
Cuth[b] Ellistone [Cuthbert]		77
Will. Eskridge	✓	86
Will. Edwards		158
John Edmonds		130
Cravin Everitt		135
Cath. Elds		45
John Eustace		68
Zackariah Efford		90
John Efford		54
Tho[s] Edwards Clk		36
Robert Edmonds		82

F

John Fouchee			355
Charles Fallen			140
David Fluker			21
John Fulks			90
Vauchel Faudree	1		96
Will. Fallen Jun[r]			90
Will. Flood	✓	W	86
George France			127
Fauntleroys Est	A		104
Nich[s] Flood	✓	A	270
Thomas Figgot			14

John Finnan	✓		28
Judith Fauntleroy			315
Griffin Fauntleroy			45
Mary Foushee			225

G

David Galloway	✓		8705
James Gordan	✓	1	402
Gaskins & Webb			126
Easter Gill			459
Thomas Gaskins			288
Betty Gill			261
Ellis Gill			132
Parish Garner			198
James Gibson	Nfk		99
Wm Glascock	A		238
W^m & Thos Glascock	A		21
Samuel Gates			32
Isaac Gaskins			36
Eliz^a Garlington			63
George Glascock	A		59
Francis Garner	C		27
Benjn Grayson			32

H

Hunter & Cox			1684
Charles Hill			36
Ellis Harcum			202
Judith Haynie			14
John Heath	✓		1033
Mungo Harvey	✓	1	1694
John Hurst			257
John Hunton			126
Onp^s Harvey [Onesepherus]			229
Will. Harcum			90
Hopkins Harding			18
George Hunt			90
Peter Haynie			158
Joseph Harcum			14
Harding's Exers			567
Harison W^m &c	W		241

Henry Hurst &c			168
James Hudnall			109
Wm Hutchings		1	107
Thos Hudnall			390
Anne Haynie			118
Spencer Hurst			87
Isaac Haynie			287
Elisha Harcum			29
John Hill		1	14
John Hornsby			41
Joseph Hurst			104
Thos Hughlett			50
Sinah Hudnall			45
Heze. Haynie			39
Jno Humphries			86
Jno Hutchings			131
Hump. Hurst			98
Richd Hudnall			44
Mark Harding			120
Will. Haynie			32
George Headen			32
George Hill			32
Saml Hughlett			36
John Haynie			82
James Hunter			117

I [&J]

George Ingram			55
Jamison & Edwards			21
Wattu Jamison			125
John Irons			135
Neil Jamison	✓ Nfk		99
Wm Johnstone	C		68

K

Judith Kenner		1	1680
Hugh Kerr			99
Newton Keene			349
Richd Kenner	Nfk		21
John Knight			100
Francis Kenner			247

245

Mary Kesterson		81
Winder Kenner		827
Edward Kerr		112
Wm Kent &c		36

L

Sarah Lowery		147
James Lamkin		76
Lewis Lamkin		641
Moses Lunsford		23
Richard Lunsford		108
John Leland	Clk	180
Dav^d Lattimore		165
Leanna Lattimore		59
David Lewis		259
Joseph Lunsford		90
Thomas Loney		53
George Lunsford		27
Rodham Lunsford		46
John Lewis		9
Will. Lattimore		306
John Lovelace	R	121
Isaac Lunsford		66
Lampkin & Keene		32
Allen Lancaster		96
Mary Mag. Lewis		118

M

John Mott			41
McKittrick &Co	✓		1064
Wm Miskell	R		346
Richd Maurison			15
Anne Mott			26
John Mayo			126
Joseph McAdam			180
George Mister &Co	✓	Nfk	99
Arch^d McCall	✓	E	68
Saml Mahanes			27
Allen Munn			32
Jere. Middleton			9
Thos Mahanes			32

John Meath		147
Danl Miskell		82
John McCall	✓	68
Moses Mathews		44

N

Charles Nelms		36
Willoby Newton	W	21
Ben. Northern	C	131
Nutts Exors		81
Thomas Nunum		53
Richard Nutt		53
Rodham Neale		67
Robt Nickelson	Wbg	99
Daniel Neale		144
Richd Neale	A	63
Thos Newman	A	49
John Newton	W	45
Mathew Neale		346

O

Will. Okland		71
Lindsy Opie &c		140
Wm Oldham	R	5
Leroy Oldham		39

P

George Payne			99
Will. Parrott			144
Elijah Percifull			171
William Parker			86
Richd Pope			45
John Plummer	R		23
George Phillips			5
Robert Potts			60
Toulson Parker			14
Joseph Power			53
William Pullen			186
Pomeroys &Co ✓		8	99
Spencer Pickrell			42
Jesse Pitman			72
Math. Patridge W			145

Name			Value
Robt Pinchard	1		71
Thos Pinchard	1		50
William Powell	1		141
Saml Patridge			27
R			
William Roane ✓		E	300
Jesse Reid			41
Richd Ritchie	✓	f	303
Hannah Rogers			36
Vincent Rust	H		32
John Rogers			366
Robucks Est			139
Ja^s Ritchie &Co	E		227
Jennings Rooker			48
Anth^y Routt			14
Mary Roberts			164
George Rice			44
S			
Robert Short			656
Straughans Exors			169
Saml Smith			63
Moses Sutton			27
Martin Shearman j^r			43
William Smith	R		123
John Suggitt	R		177
James Sims			77
Thos Simpson ✓	W		663
Span's Exor			9
Anth^y Stewart	W		113
George Smithers			144
Gabriel Smithers	R		612
James Sebree			23
Will Swift			41
Joseph Spriggs			32
Jn° Smith, Curch[?]			54
John Sydnor	A		405
Thos Shearman	1		72
Will. Sebree			41
Jn° Smith Jun. ✓			36

Name			Value
Jas. Singleton	R		32
Mathias Self			27
Robt Sibbalds			5
Mich Surlock			77
T			
William Taite			669
Spencer Thomas			21
John Tayloe Esq	R		208
Robert Thomas			135
John Tarpley	✓	R	467
Henry Tapscot 1			296
Eliz^a Tourelson			32
Manly Taylor			14
Presly Thornton Esq			77
Will Trussell			163
John Tippe			71
Jarvis Thrift	R		98
Mich^l Taylor			75
Joseph Taylor			53
Will. Thomas			126
Jam^s Templeman			78
George Turner			5
Saml Tillery	✓		27
Joshua Townsend			5
Will. Townsend			55
Edward Tycer			127
Thornton & Ball			61
Thos Thompson	✓		50
V			
Ben. Vanlandingham			82
W			
Robert Woddrop	✓		2610
John Williams			393
Webb's Exors			36
Hugh Watson			179
Giles Webb			152
Sam Williams	R		87
John Webb	E		153
John Wise	R		73

John Webb	W	90	Nat. Wilson			11-
John Webb		45	Thos Waddy			13-
John Walker Junr		53	Richd Walker j^r			4-
[edge of page cut off from here]			Joseph Walker			5-
Joseph Wildey		3-	John Webb j^r			-
Joseph Webb		1-	John Wilson			3-
Thomas Williams		9-	Jno° S. Webb			-
Danl Wilkins		-			Y	
Morris Wheeler		5-	Henry Young			5-
George Wythe	✓	2-	Amey E. Yeates			15-
John Wiley		19-			Z	
Ben. Welch		8-	Sarah Zuille			18-

The Roger Jones Family Papers, Mss 18063, Reel 6. Northumberland County. Manuscript Division, Library of Congress, Washington, DC, Presented after correspondence with the Library of Congress.

* * * * *

Reward For Desertion

150 Dollars Reward

Deserted from Camp Pendleton, Hanover county, three soldiers:

ISAAC CURTIS, five feet four inches high, dark eyes, dark hair, sallow complexion; by profession a farmer, and was enlisted in North Carolina.
THOMAS NANCE, five feet eleven inches high, dark blue eyes, light hair, and by profession a farmer, and was enlisted in North Carolina.
JOHN CARR, five feet ten inches high, 28 years of age, blue eyes, dark hair, fair complexion, was enlisted by Colonel Hamilton, North Carolina, Surry county; it is expected that the above deserters have gone the route towards North Carolina, and whosoever will apprehend the above deserters and deliver them to any officer, in the United States' army, shall receive the above reward — or **fifty** for either of them.

JOHN PENDLETON,
August 5 *Lieut. 3d Rifle Regt.*

Virginia Argus, Richmond, VA 3 Jan 1816. 4, 2.

Register of Free Blacks, 1810-1843
Essex County

Continued from Volume 7, Number 3, page 183.

This transcription is taken from a xeroxed copy of a bound and stitched book measuring 6½ x 6½ inches with the above heading; containing in all 167 pages, exclusive of a complete index of the names in the front of the book. Essex County Circuit Court Clerk's Office. This transcriber has a good knowledge of the names of the earlier (and long-time) residents of Essex County, and in fact many of these same names can still be found in the county. Even so, some names are difficult to read; if there are questions it is suggested that the originally xeroxed copy be consulted. VLHD

A Register of Free Negroes in the County
Essex County Circuit Court Office State of Virginia

[Note: until stated otherwise, each of the following entries were recorded with the following heading: *State of Virginia, Essex County Court Office, By virtue of an act of the General Assembly of this State passed 25th January 1803 entitled "and act more effectually to restrain the practice of negroes going at large". I have registered the bearer (who states herself to be a resident of this county) as follows....]*

No. 31 **Polly Rollins** daughter of **Jenny Rollins** born free it appearing by the statement of Thomas Brockenbrough in person that **Mary Soleleather** the mother of the said **Jenny Rollins** has always passed as a free born person colour dark Mulattoe about 1¾ years of age and about two feet four and ¼ inches — Given under my hand as Clerk of the said Court of Essex County 8th of Dec 1810. certified correct   John P. Lee

No. 32 **Nancy McGiven** affixed by Judgement of the Essex Court appeared by the records of said court colour bright Mulattoe about 34 years of age and Stature five feet ½ inches — Given under my hand as Clerk of the said Court of Essex County 8th of Dec 1810. certified correct   John P. Lee

No. 33 **Susan McGiven** born free daughter of **Nancy McGiven** which **Nancy** was freed by Judgt of Essex County Court colour bright Mulattoe about 7 years of age Stature 3 feet 10¾ inches — Under my hand as Clerk of the said Court of Essex County 8th of Dec 1810. certified correct   John P. Lee

No. 34 **Patrick McGiven** freed by Judgt of Essex County Court appearing by the records of the sd Court colour bright Mulattoe about 13 years of age and Stature 4 feet 11½ inches — Given under my hand as Clerk of the said Court of Essex County 8th of Dec 1810.

certified correct   John P. Lee

No. 35 **Laurence McGiven** free born son of **Nancy McGiven** who was freed by Judgt of Essex County Court colour bright Mulattoe about five years of age Stature three feet 2½ inches — Given under my hand as Clerk of the said Court of Essex County 8th of Dec 1810.

certified correct   John P. Lee

No. 36 **Lee** otherwise as **Leanner** emancipated by Moore Fauntleroy appearing by the Will of the sd Moore and the cert. of Rob. Fauntleroy the Exr endorsed an a copy therewith colour light black about 23 years of age & Stature five feet 3 inches and one half inch Given under my hand as Clerk of the said Court of Essex County 8th of Dec 1810.   John P. Lee

certified correct 17 Aug 1812   John P. Lee Clk

No. 37 **Joe Gilbert** emancipated appearing by a former register in the Clerks office of Essex County colour Black about 58 years of age & Stature five feet 7½ inches — Given under my hand as Clerk of the said Court of Essex County 8th of December 1810.

certified correct   John P. Lee

No. 38 **Harry Deckman** who states he was emancipated by Wm Williams ~~appearing~~ who has heretofore been registered and enrolled by the Comr of the Revenue and free person appearing by a cert. colour black about 37 years of age [illeg.] of the forefinger of the right hand and [illeg.] cut and a 5" scar five feet 7½ inches — Given under my hand as Clerk of the said Court of Essex County 8th of December 1810.

certified correct   John P. Lee

No. 39 **Maria McGuy** born free appearing by certificate of the Clerk of Richmond County dark Mulattoe about 27 years of age & Stature 5 feet 3¾ inches — Given under my hand as Clerk of the said Court of Essex County 8th of December 1810.

certified correct   John P. Lee

No. 40 **Samson Braxton** born free appearing by the statement of John P. Lee in person colour a dark Mulattoe about 27 years of age & Stature five feet 8¾ inches — Given under my hand as Clerk of the said Court of Essex County 8th of December 1810.

certified correct   John P. Lee

No. 41 **David Jones** born free appearing by a cert of the freedom of **Betsy Jones** his mother made out from the testimony of Jno B colour very dark Mulattoe about 16 years of age scars on his forehead Stature [added description illeg.] 5 feet 2 inche — Given under my hand as Clerk of the said Court of Essex County 8th of December 1810.

certified correct   John P. Lee

No. 42 **Nelson Charity** born free appearing by the testimony of George Loyde on oath colour ~~dark Mulattoe~~ shade lighter with a small scar on the left side of his upper lip and a turnfeet[?] on his right Ham occasioning him to limp Stature 5 feet 8½ inches — Given under my hand as Clerk of the said Court of Essex County 2nd of January 1811.

certified correct   John P. Lee

No. 43 **Nelson Satterwhite** born free appeaaring by the cert of Thos Pitts Just of the Peace filed colour dark Mulattoe about 21 years of age with scar in the right eyebrow occasioned by a cut and Stature 5 feet 6¼ inches — Given under my hand as Clerk of the said Court of Essex County 3nd of January 1811. certified correct   John P. Lee

No. 44 **Betsy Drake** born free appearing by the certificate of Newman Brock enterd and filed colour bright Mulattoe about 29 years of age with a blemish in her left eye & Stature 5 feet 2¾ inches — Given under my hand as Clerk of the said Court of Essex County 8th of January 1811.

certified correct   John P. Lee

No. 45 **Betsy Soleleather** appearing by Report of the Commissioner of the Revenue of this Cty colour Dark Mulattoe about twenty years of age and Stature 5 feet — Given under my hand as Clerk of the said Court of Essex County 20th of May 1811.

certified correct   John P. Lee

No. 46 **Betsy Braxton** born free appearing from information by J.P. Lee and Rd. Rouzee colour bright Mulattoe about 12 years of age with a scar on the joining of the left thumb and Stature 5 feet 4 inches — Given under my hand as Clerk of the said Court of Essex County 21th of May 1811.

certified correct   John P. Lee

No. 47 **Aggie Eli** free appearing by Report of free negroes adjd Mulattoes deposited in my Office by Comm of the Revenue a light Black about 47 years of age with a small win over the right Eye & Stature 5 feet 1½ inches — Given under my hand as Clerk of the said Court of Essex County 6th of June 1811.

certified correct   John P. Lee

No. 48 **Sally Eli** daughter of **Aggy Eli** appearing to be free by Report of Comm of the Revenue filed in my Office colour light black about 15 years of age and Stature 5 feet 1½ inches — Given under my hand as Clerk of the said Court of Essex County 6th of June 1811.

certified correct   John P. Lee

No. 49 **Rachel Mann** born free appearing by the info of Thomas Pitts colour Black about 50 years of age & Stature 5 feet 3¾ inches — Given under my hand as Clerk of the said Court of Essex County 19th of August 1811.
certified correct   John P. Lee

No. 50 **Betsy Mann** born free appearing by the info of Thos Pitts colour Black about 20 years of age & Stature 5 feet 9 inches — Given under my hand as Clerk of the said Court of Essex County 19th of August 1811.
certified correct   John P. Lee

No. 51 **William Lewis** born free appearing by the Certificate of Tunstall Banks colour Mulattoe about 33 years of age with a scar on the right temple and Stature 5 feet 9¾ inches — Given under my hand as Clerk of the said Court of Essex County 19th of Nov 1811.
Essex Quarterly Court held 19th Nov 1811   Teste Jno P. Lee
certified correct   John P. Lee

No. 52 **William Soleleather** son of **Mary Soleleather** who was free born appearing by the statement of Thomas Brockenbrough colour dark Mulattoe about 23 years of age middle finger upon the left hand crooked & Stature 5 feet 5¾ inches — Given under my hand as Clerk of the said Court of Essex County 14th of April 1812.
19 July 1813 cert correct by the Clk   John P. Lee

No. 53 **Milly Webb** daughter of **Nelly Webb** who was emancipated by the Will of Wm Fauntleroy app. by extract of Will filed bright Mulattoe about 16 years old & Stature 5 feet & ½ inch — Given under my hand as Clerk of the said Court of Essex County 13th of August 1812.
certified correct   John P. Lee

No. 54 **Moses Drake** born free appearing by Newman Brockenbroughs certificate colour very black Mulattoe aage 19 years of age with the first joint of the little finger on the left hand cutt off & Stature 5 feet 5⅜ inches — Given under my hand as Clerk of the said Court of Essex County 9th of Sept 1812.
1814 March 2nd Exd cert correct by the Clerk   John P. Lee

No. 55 **Rebecca Cole** born free appearing from info of Geo W Banks Esq colour bright Mulattoe about 14 years of age with a large mole on the left cheek & Stature 5 feet 1¾ inches — Given under my hand as Clerk of the said Court of Essex County 19th of Oct 1812.

John P. Lee Clk

20th August 1816 Examined by the Court and certified correct

W.B. Matthews Clk

No. 56 **Fauntleroy Cole** born free appearing by the info of Geo W Banks Esq colour bright Mulattoe about 13 years of age & Stature 4 feet 11½ inches — Given under my hand as Clerk of the said Court of Essex County 19th of Oct 1812.

John P. Lee Clk

No. 57 [complete entry crossed out] **Saul Bunday** born free appearing by the testimony of James L Cox colour very dark Mulattoe about 20 years of age & Stature 5 feet 8¼ inches — Given under my hand as Clerk of the said Court of Essex County 21st of December 1812.   Jno P. Lee

No. 57 **Jack Fields** born free appearing by the cert of the Clk of Hustings Court Office Lynchburg colour bright Mulattoe about 23 years of age with a mark on the point of his nose a small scar on the left eye & Stature 5 feet 4 inches — Given under my hand as Clerk of the said Court of Essex County 16th of July 1813.   Jno P. Lee

No. 58 **Wm Webb** born free appearing by cert of Thos Brockenbrough colour very dark Mulattoe about 19 years of age & Stature 5 feet 9½ inches — Given under my hand as Clerk of the said Court of Essex County 16th of July 1813.
16th August 1813 Certified correct by the court   Jno P. Lee

No. 59 **Harriett Adams** born free appearing by letter of James Webb Esq colour shade lighter than a dark Mulattoe about 14 years of age & Stature 4 feet 10½ inches — Given under my hand as Clerk of the said Court of Essex County 10th of Aug 1813.   Jno P. Lee

No. 60 **Dillard Gordon** born free appearing by certificate of John Jones Esq Colour bright Mulattoe about 26 years of age & Stature 5 feet 10¾ Inches — Given under my hand as Clerk of the said Court of Essex County 19th of Nov 1814.
1814 Nov 21st examd by the Ct & Wm B Matthews certified correct

W B Matthews Clk

No. 61 **Elisha Johnson** born free appearing by certificate of Geo W Lee a Justice of the peace Colour a dark Mulattoe about 27 years of age & Stature 5 feet 6¾ Inches — Given under my hand as Clerk of the said Court of Essex County 17th of Feb 1815.
1818 Aug 17th examd by the Ct & Wm B Matthews certified correct

W B Matthews Clk

To be continued

Henrico County Will Book 1, 1781-1787

Transcribed by Dr. Benjamin B. Weisiger, III
Contributed by Minor T. Weisiger

Continued from Volume 7, Number 3, page 190.

The entries from the Henrico Will Book 1, 1781-1787, as abstracted by Dr. Benjamin B. Weisiger (1924-1995), ended with page 199. His abstractions of county records were both meticulous and prolific. Your editor has continued the abstraction of this will book, hopefully, as accurately as Dr. Weisiger. These records, have been a continuing feature of Tidewater Virginia Families: A Magazine of History and Genealogy to the completion of Will Book 1.

p.341 Inventory of estate of **Hannah Harwood**, dec'd. 6 Mar 1787. Negro girl Jenny. Value est. £30. Appraised by **Joph Price, John Cock, John Price**. Returned 4 June 1787.

p.342 Will of **Thomas Watkins** Henrico Co
To three sons **Robert, Thomas** and **Claiborne** all land in Hanover Co, equally divided and son **Robert** to have plantation and houses as his part.
Item to son **George** land in Charlotte Co, Negroes Sam, Joe and Hannah.
Item to son **Andrew** lower part of land on which I live from Peach Island to **Ann Gathright**'s near Deep Bottom, including plantation Cloptons, three Negroes Bettie, Billy and Buster.
Item lend loving wife **Sarah** upper part of land I live on with mill and houses. Negroes Isham, David and Nathan, also Negroes Lyd and Ciss.
Item to son **Isaac** land I lent wife, four Negroes, Daniel, Phebe, Janey and young Charles.
Item to son **Robert** five Negroes, Old Charles, Old Amey, Young Amy, Agy and Rachel.
Item to son **Thomas** four Negroes, Dick, Sary, Fanny and Matt.
Item to son **Claiborne** three Negroes, Jack, Moll and Patty.
Item to daughter **Mary Hughes Watkins** three Negroes, Harry, Jude and Luce and £400.
Executors: father **Thomas Watkins** and brother **Francis Watkins**, friends **Smith Blakey** and **Stephen Pankey**.
7 Apr 1778   signed **Thomas Watkins, Jr**
Witnesses: **William Gathright, Thomas Bottoms, Susannah Freeman, Reuben Friend**.

Codicil: land left **George** he may have no part of his brother's land in case either die before they come of age. **Claiborne** to have Negro young Dick.
12 Apr 1778
Recorded July 1778 Oaths of **William Gathright** and **Thomas Bottoms** proved by **Jacob Carter** and **Jacob Childress**.
A Copy   signed **William White** D C Cl
Henrico Court 4 June 1787. Original destroyed by enemy.   **Adam Craig** C C

p.346 Inventory of Capt. **Michael Johnson**, dec'd. taken by **Benj. Johnson, Junr., David Johnson, John Miller**, Esq. Appraised by **David Bowles, Nathl Holman, John Ellis**. 29 Sep 1786.
Negroes Will, Lucy, Sue, Tom her child, Agness, Marsh, Patt, Forester, Sam, Moses, Sippier (boy), Dick, Joe, Jack, Will, Bob. No value given.
Returned 4 June 1787.

p.350 Will of **Mary Austin** Henrico Co, "sick and weak but perfect mind and memory".
Item to daughter **Mary Hatchel** Negro Rachel.
Item to son **William Austin** Negro Anthony.
Item to son **Archibald Austin** Negro Winney.
Item to son **Reuben Austin** Negro Nan (if he die, to son **Obediah**).
Item to daughter **Molly Bottom** sheep.
Item to daughter **Jenny Austin** feather bed and furniture.
Item to son **Obediah Austin** feather bed and furniture.
Item to son **William Austin** feather bed and furniture.
To sons **William, Archibald, Reuben** items.
Executors: sons **Archibald** and **William Austin**.
20 Dec 1786   **Mary X Austin**
Witnesses: **Ephriam Gathright, William Bethel, Isaac Echo**
Recorded 4 June 1787
Proved by **Ephriam Gathright, William Bethel**. Motion of **William Austin**, executor. Securities: **Ephriam Gathright** and **William Gathright**.
                                                   Adam Craig C C

p.352 Inventory and appraisal of estate of Colonel **Joseph Hutchings**, dec'd.
Negroes: Silvia, Pleasants, Betty, Norfolk, Bob Cudjee, Pomp, Violet, Cresser, Nell, Harry, Jeffry, Hager and child Jilpher, Jeffrey, Frances, Cobinner, Phillis and child Betty, John, Coidjoe, Will, Nedd, Libb, Sue and child Lucy, Old Lookup, Cabbinor. Value £882/16/6.

Paul Proby, Nathl Burch, Jonathan Calvert.

Returned 2 July 1787.

(ed. note: for correct spelling of above names, consult the original).

p.354 Will of **John Spear** Henrico Co and Parish, "perfect senses and sound memory".

Item give to loving wife **Patsy Spear** items, Negroes, Venus and Poll, lend Eleck and Philip.

Item to son **George Spear** items and remainder of estate at wife's death.

Executors: **Julius Allen, George Harwood, William Carter**.

signed John X Spear

Witnesses: **Ann Harwood, Rebecca Winston, Caty X Williams**

Recorded 3 Sep 1787

Proved by **Anne Harwood** and **Caty Williams**. Motion **George Harwood** and **William Carter**, executors.

Securities: **William Harwood, Robert Spear**

p.356 Inventory of **Benjamin Johnson**, late of Henrico co dec'd. Negroes Jack, Isaac, Ford, John, Harry, Doll, Poll, Bett, Jude, Woodrum, Charlotte, Chir, Pegg, Sall, Charles, Tom, Jesse, Milley, Harry, Lightfoot, Stephen, Amis. Value £1140/15. Appraisers **John Ellis, Hezekiah Henley, Jacob Smith, William Henley**.

Returned 3 Sep 1787.

p.360 Order to divide estate of **John Harwood, Sen.**, dec'd. 15 Jan 1787.

Negroes: Isham, Bristol, Bob, Jude, Jane, Moll and her child Rush.

To **James Harwood** Isham

To **Elisha Harwood** Bristol

To **William Harwood** Bob, Jude

To **Elizabeth Harwood** Moll and child Rush

To **Thomas Harwood** Jane   Value £292/5

Division of estate, each slave valued and each legatee to pay accordingly to others to equal value.

Appraisers: **Turner Southall, Jesse Williams, Reuben Coutt**

Returned 4 June 1787.

p.361 Estate of **John Williams** dec'd. with **Robert Pleasants** Executor. Value £132/12/7. Appraised by **John Pleasants, Bowler Cocke, Richard Sharp**. Sep 1778. Copy. Recorded 3 May 1787. Original destroyed by the enemy. Recorded 3 May 1787   **Adam Craig** C C

p.363 Court Henrico 2 July 1832. Motion of **Jacob Friend** with **Absolom Blackburn**, security. Certificate granted for administration *de bonis non* on estate of **William Friend**, dec'd. with will of **William Snead** annexed.
(ed. note: see will **William Sneed** page 70, *TVF* 6:98)

Teste **Loftin N. Ellett** CHC

Court Henrico 6 Feb 1843. Motion of **James Scott**, executor; **Joshua J Fey**, security. Certificate granted for administration *de bonis non* on estate of **Robert Braine**, dec'd. with will annexed in due form.
(see will page 193, **Robert Baine** *TVF* 6:253).   Teste **Loftin N. Ellett** CHC

We the subscribers appointed by the county court of Henrico County, on 13th January 1868 — commissioners to examine the transcript of Will Book Number 1 of the records of said court in obedience to its order and to certify as to the correctness of said transcript, do hereby certify, that we have examined said transcript and carefully compared it with the said original "Will Book" and with the original papers recorded in said book; and that the said transcript is a correct copy of the said book.

Given under our hands this 8th day of August 1868.

Concluded

St. John's Church Henrico Parish 1700s

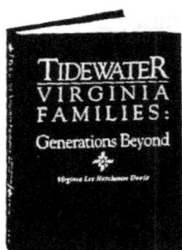

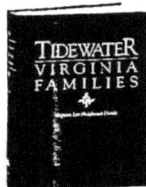

Dennis Ray Hudgins, ed., *Cavaliers and Pioneers, Volume VI, Abstracts of Virginia Land Patents and Grants, 1749-1762.* xxiv, 552 pp., comprehensive index, cloth. 1998. $40.00 ($32.00 to VGS members), plus $3.00 ship. first book, $1.00 ea. add. book. Volume VI is a continuation of the presentation and publication of Virginia's colonial patents. The first three volumes covering Land Patent Books 1-14 (1623-1732) were prepared by Nell Marion Nugent and published by the Virginia State Library. Volume IV, 1732-1741 (LP Books 15-19), Volume V, 1741-1749 (LP Books 20-28) were published by the Virginia Genealogical Society in 1994, following the format of Ms Nugent's work. Volume VI includes LP Books 29-34 and follows this same format. These patents reflect the extensive migrations into the lands of the Shenandoah Valley, the Piedmont and the Southside Virginia counties. The original format of naming the patentee, acreage, county, geographical features, adjacent landowners, cost and date of patent are continued as in Nugent. This volume completes the set to date, and is a must for serious researchers. Order from the Virginia Genealogical Society, 5001 W Broad St, #115, Richmond, VA 23230.

Constance K. Ring and Craig R. Scott, *Index to the Fairfax County, Virginia Register of Marriages, 1853-1933.* 208 pp., index, paper. 1997. $20.00, plus $3.00 ship. The surnames of the grooms are listed alphabetically with the full names of the brides indexed. There are more than 6,500 entries, giving the name of the groom, the bride, date of marriage, race (where indicated), marital status and the page where the entry can be found in the Marriage Register. The Register itself is to be found in the Fairfax Circuit Court Archives and the original entries include the place of birth and residence, occupation, names of parents, person performing ceremony and remarks. The entries were made by the court clerk at the time the license was returned to his office. Willow Bend Books, 2818 Ft Evans Rd, NE, #101, Leesburg, VA 20176.

M. Lee Minnis, *The First Virginia Regiment of Foot, 1775-1783.* 467 pp., index, appendix, biblio., cloth. 1998. $30.00, plus $4.00 ship. A comprehensive account of this Revolutionary War unit. It is an outstanding history of the unit; with muster rolls and biographies of each soldier. Mr. Minnis has included an explanation of terms used, a prologue to the formation of the unit, which was formed in Williamsburg in September 1775. He describes action in each of the unit's engagements and gives detailed biographical sketches of the members (listed in alphabetical order). His endnotes to the chapters are extensive, and he documents each of the biographical entries. He also lists patriots who died in service, and others who are belived to have been members of the regiment but have not been documented. This is truly a comprehensive, scholarly account of a valiant regiment that made a significant contribution to winning the Revolutionary War. Willow Bend Books, 2818 Ft. Evans Rd., NE, #101, Leesburg, VA 20176.
Note: for books published in Virginia, residents of VA must add 4.5% sales tax.

John W. Wayland, *The Washingtons and Their Homes.* 385 pp., illus., index, paper (1944), repr. 1998. $29.95, plus $3.50 ship. This book is a marvelous account of the

Washington family, not only from a genealogical standpoint, but by virture of their contributions to Colonial Virginia. Mr. Wayland has accomplished this through a tour of the homes and estates of the various Washington family members. He begins with *Wakefield*, George's father and the family of Westmoreland County. He continues by presenting *Mount Vernon* and other Washington family members' homes, along with a social history of their contributions to Virginia history and the era. There are over 400 biographical sketches of the Washingtons and a chronology of the Washington history. It is of excellent assistance in "putting together" the various relationships, and is enjoyable reading. #9481. Clearfield Company, 200 E Eager St, Baltimore, MD 21202.

Kip Sperry, *Reading Early American Handwriting.* 289 pp., 8½ x 11, illus., append., biblio., paperback. 1998. $29.99, plus $3.50 ship. This book is designed as an aid to understanding "what you see" in reading court records, documents, family letters, etc. The book begins with graphic illustrations of handwriting styles of the more legible nineteenth century style and works backward to the earlier and more difficult writing styles. Both upper and lower case alphabet styles are shown with many variations. Samples of alphabetic variations of the most difficult mid-seventeenth century county court records of Virginia are not represented, simply several examples of documents with their transcription. These are, unfortunately, the most difficult to transcribe. Of help to the researcher are the abbreviations and contractions commonly used, the Roman and Arabic numerals, and the dates and abbreviations of the calender in use at that time. This book and practice will make for proficiency in reading various handwriting styles of documents generally used in family research. #5513. Genealogical Publishing Co, 1001 N Calvert St, Baltimore, MD 21202.
Note: Clearfield or Genealogical Publishing, add $1.25, ship. each add. book.

Weynette Parks Haun, *Surry County, Virginia, Court Records, 1746-1748, Book IX.* 150 pp., comprehensive index, 8½ x 11, stapled soft cover. 1996. $25.00, plus $2.00 ship.
Weynette Parks Haun, *Surry County, Virginia, Court Records, 1749-1751, Book X.* 169 pp., comprehensive index, 8½ x 11, stapled soft cover. 1997. $25.00, plus $2.00 ship.
Weynette Parks Haun, *Sussex County, Virginia, Court Records, 1757-1759, Book II.* 165 pp., comprehensive index, 8½ x 11, stapled soft cover. 1997. $30.00, plus $2.00 ship. Once again, Ms. Haun has opened a door to the past. Because of her extensive experience in reading early records, and her knowledge of these people, her verbatim transcriptions are meticulous, accurate and complete. Ms Haun has continued her transcriptions of the Surry County records (county court records from 1718 to 1741 are missing from the courthouse). She has also continued her transcriptions of the Sussex County records (not all of the Sussex County Court Records have survived). Many ancestors have been found and relationships established because of her painstaking work. The County Court Order Books provide information that may not be found elsewhere, and also provide direction for further search in the more detailed records (wills, deeds, etc.). She has included the originial index that precedes the court order entries. In her index she has included places,

geographic entities and occupations as well as names. Ms. Haun has transcribed verbatim many of the early court records, including both Surry and Sussex counties, VA; **write for catalogue! Her books are a must.**
Order from North Carolina Research at Home, Attn Weynette Parks Haun, 243 Argonne Dr, Durham, NC 27704.
Note: NC Research at Home, add .$.50, ship. each additional book

S.A. Elliott, Pub., *The Washington Directory.* 108 pp., alphabetic, paper. (1827) repr. 1997. $8.00, plus $2.50 ship. This is a facsimile reproduction of the City of Washington, D.C. directory showing the name, occupation, and residence of each head of a family and person in business in the city. Also included is the Washington City charter and a listing of churches and public buildings and the location. #T1337. Family Line Publications, Rear 63 E Main St, Westminster, MD 21157.

F. Edward Wright, *Early Church Records of Rockingham County, Virginia.* vi, 122 pp., every name index. 1998. $10.50, plus $2.50, ship. Rockingham County was formed in 1778 from Augusta County. This book includes the marriage records as listed by the Rev. John Alderson and the Virginia Valley Records from county court. Records of the births and baptisms and in some cases marriages and deaths from the several early churches, beginning in 1750; Roder's, Peaked Mountain, Friedens, St. Michael's, Trinity, Smith's and Linville Creek churches are listed. Listings include all of those found through the 18th century. T1386. Family Line Publications, Rear 63 E Main St, Westminster, MD 21157.
Note: Family Line, add $.50 ship. each additional book.

Therese Fisher, A.G., *Marriages of Caroline County, Virginia, 1777-1853.* 272 pp., last name index, paper. 1998. $22.50, plus $4.00 ship. Marriage records are drawn from a number of sources and give the name of bride and groom, and where available, the minister and bondsman. Only the last names of the brides are given in the index; hardly acceptable with the desktop publishing techniques presently available. Of greater concern is the obvious mis-transcription of names. To anyone familiar with the names of Caroline County, this is a glaring deficiency. The information presented in the introduction further leads one astray concerning the loss of records, the terminology used and the recordation of information. The dates of marriages, as abstracted, must be checked against original sources also, when one is conducting family research and seeking accurate documentation. #3F378. Heritage Books, Inc, 1540-E Pointer Ridge Pl, #300, Bowie, MD.

ANNOUNCEMENTS:
Please submit your announcements at least three months in advance of publication.

SEARCH:
TRIPLETT, MARTIN, MILLER. Richmond Co, also seek info about Thomas Triplett, b England, m Elizabeth Martin, d 1698, Richmond Co. William Triplett m Isabella Miller, d King George Co 1758. Jim Burgess, 37 S Udall, Mesa, AZ 85204.

HAYNIE, TERRELL, WILKINS. William Wilkins, b 1746 VA, d 1807 SC (lived in Spartenburg, SC area), m Elizabeth Terrell, b 1756 VA or NC, d 1820 SC. Dau Jane Wilkins Austell, believed father was desc of Capt Richard Wilkins, Royal Navy, Welshman by birth. His sons John & Andrew settled in VA. John (p)m a dau of Richard Haynie. Seek evidence to support or refute this theory. Art Shepard, 4029 Quail Hollow Rd, Albany GA 31707.

ANDERSON, PROU, DONIPHAN, CARTER, ROSER. Seek info about following: Walter Anderson m dau of Cyprian Prou (will 1712), Richmond Co and Alexander Doniphan, will 1716, Richmond Co. John Lloyd m Elizabeth, d 1693, Richmond Co, dau of John Carter. David Roser m Sarah Sherwood by 1688, Richmond Co. Jim Burgess, 37 S Udall, Mesa, AZ 85204.

BASSETT, CLOPTON. Seek info on Catherine Bassett, w of Capt (Dr) Waldegrave Clopton, Jr b 1755, New Kent Co, lived Goochland Co, d GA 1832. Also info on her ancestors. A R Lemay, 8040 Stillbrooke Rd, Manassas, VA 20112.

NEALE, TOULSON. Seek descendants of Abner Neale (1696-c.1772), b Northumberland Co, d Craven Co, NC., m (1) (?), m (2) Judith Toulson, m (3) Elizabeth. Known children: Winifred Neale Thomas, William Neal, Daniel Neal, Abner Neal, Lucretia Neal, all born betw 1720-1731 in VA. Janet Pease, 10310 W 62nd Pl, #202, Arvada, CO 80004.

HARRIS, GAINES. Gainey Harris, d 1693, Lancaster Co, dau Ann m 1702, Henry Skipwith Carter. Ann Chowning was listed in his will as mother-in-law. Who were his parents and spouse, other family members? Catherine Gaines (d 1814, Essex Co) m Ambrose Howerton, s Robert Gaines Howerton, b 1796, d 1854. Who were her parents and siblings? Cora Lee Curtis, 1756 N Envoy Dr, Crystal River, FL 34429.

BURTON, John, d 1690, Henrico Co, m Elizabeth Elam. Dau m William Hatcher, who are other children? Are his parents Richard Burton and Katherine Christian? Janis Goodnow Taylor, 10619 N 96th St., Overland Park, KS 66214.

LEFTWICH, Ralph. Seeking names & addresses of cemeteries surrounding land patent of Ralph Leftwich (1658) in King & Queen County, as illustrated in TVF Aug-Sept 1998 issue. Bernard Leftwich Trippett, 417 Canterbury Dr, Kettering OH 45429

CLOSE/CLAUSE/CLOYS, Phettiplace, to Jamestown on *Starr*, 1608, age 15, LP on Warwicksqueqke R; s William LP on Poquoson R. Seek info about marriages, deaths, etc. Jim Clouse, 3054 Pineda Crossing Dr, Melbourne, FL 32940.

INDEX

Bottom
Molly 255
Bottoms
Thomas 254, 255
Bowles
David 255
Boyd
David 243
Bradeham
Robert 223
Bradenham
Edmund 223
Elizabeth 222, 223, 225
James 223
John 222, 223
Mary 222, 223
Robert 223
Sally 223
Susanna 223
William 223
Braine
Robert 257
Brame
family 213
Braughton
Job 243
Braxton
Betsy 251
Samson 250
Brazell
Henry 230
Brent
Hugh 243
Brock
Newman 251
Brockenbrough
Newman 252
Thomas 249, 252, 253
Bromfield
Bridget 208
John 208
Brookes
Robert 211
Broomfield
John 208
Brown
Benjamin 243
John 243
Buck
Benoni 207
Bermuda 207
Bridget 207
Elizabeth 207
Gercian 207
Gersham 207
Mara 207, 208

Buck
Peleg 207
Richard 207, 208
Bunday
Saul 253
Burch
Nathl 256
Burke
Mary 233, 235, 236
Burks
Mary 232
Samuel 232
Burras
Ann 207, 209
Burross
John 209-211
Burroughs
Anthony 209
Burrowes
Anthony 209
Grace 209
John 209, 210
Mary 209
Matthew 208
Robert 209
Burrows
Ann 208
Anthony 209, 210
Benoni 208
Bridget 207, 208
Christopher 208
John 207-209
William 208
Burruss
Charles 212, 213
Edmund 211-213
Elizabeth 213
Frances 213
Henry 213
Jacob 211-213
Jennings 213
John 210-213
Mary 213
Matthew 213
Samuel 213
Thomas 211-213
William 212
Burton
Betsy 237
Elizabeth 235, 262
John 262
Katherine 262
Richard 262
Bussell
Phillip 243
William 243

Byrd
Frances 217
Lucy 217
William 217, 232
Byrn
John 243
Cadzake
William 244
Calvert
Jonathan 256
Campbell
Collin 244
Cannon
Mary 231
Widow 232
Cap
William 244
Carleton
Benoni 210
Carr
John 248
Carter
Ann 262
Elizabeth 262
Giles 234
Henry 262
Jacob 255
John 262
Martha 234
Robert 244
William 256
Cary
Wilson 244
Chandler
James 223
Robert 223
Chapman
Ann 224
Annie 224, 225
Edwill 224
Edwin 219, 224, 225
Marrion 224
Richard 224
Robert 224
Walter 225
Charity
Nelson 251
Childress
Jacob 255
Chilton
Stephen 244
Chowning
Ann 262
Christian
Katherine 262

Christmas
  Edith 234
Chumbley
  Fr. 232
Clark
  Sarah 226
Clarke
  George 244
  John 244
  Mary 231
  Robert 244
Claughton
  Peme 244
Clause
  Phettiplace 262
  William 262
Clopton
  Catherine 262
  Waldegrave 262
Close
  Phettiplace 262
  William 262
Cloys
  Phettiplace 262
  William 262
Cock
  John 254
Cocke
  Bowler 256
  Elizabeth 230, 231, 236
  J. 232
  Jane 230, 236
  John 230
  Mary 230, 231, 233,
    236-238
  Richard 231
  Sarah 230, 231, 236
  Thomas 229
  William 230, 231, 236
Cole
  Fauntleroy 253
  Rebecca 252
Coles
  John 244
Collings
  Jane 211
Cop
  William 244
Copedge
  Charles 244
  Jesse 244
Corbell
  Spencer 244
Core
  Marshall 211

Cotrell
  Edwin 219
  Jennie 219
  Joseph 219
  Lula 219
  Marcus 219
  Samuel 219
  Willis 219
Cotterell
  Thomas 244
Coutt
  Reuben 256
Cox
  James 253
  John 244
  NFN 245
Craig
  Adam 255, 256
Craine
  James 244
Cralle
  John 244
  Kenner 244
Crawley
  John 244
Creek
  Richard 244
Croshaw
  Joseph 209
Curle
  Sarah 222
Curtis
  Isaac 248
Curtiss
  George 244
  Mary 244
Custis
  Frances 217
  John 217
Daft
  Hannah 230, 236, 238,
    239
  Joan 229, 238
  Joane 229
  Luke 239
  William 229, 230, 239
Dameron
  Aron 244
  Bartholomew 244
  George 244
  John 244
  Joseph 244
  Thomas 244
  William 244
Daughity
  James 244

Davenport
  William 244
Davis
  Bridget 208
  VLH 207
  William 208
Deckman
  Harry 250
Deforrest
  Cornelius 244
Dennis
  Sarah 230, 236
Denny
  John 244
  Richard 244
Dew
  William 244
Dixon
  C.C. 220
Doggett
  William 244
Doghead
  William 244
Doniphan
  Alexander 262
Douglas
  William 236
Downing
  Samuel 244
  Thomas 244
Downman
  Robert 244
  Travers 244
Drake
  Betsy 251
  Moses 252
  Viola 224
Dunaway
  Joseph 244
  Moses 244
Dunsford
  Mary 225
East
  John 232, 234
Echo
  Isaac 255
Edmonds
  Elias 244
  John 244
  Robert 244
Edwards
  Lula 219
  Mary 219, 225
  NFN 245
  Ozella 219
  Samuel 219

Harbert
Cuthbert 229
Joan 229
Harcum
Elisha 245
Ellis 245
Joseph 245
Will. 245
Harding
Exers 245
Hopkins 245
Mark 245
William 230
Harison
William 245
Harmon
Susanna 223
Harris
Ann 262
Betty 229
Gainey 262
Lucy 235, 237
Mary 231, 238
Peter 231, 238
Thomas 229
Harvey
Mungo 245
Onesepherus 245
Harwood
Ann 256
Elisha 256
Elizabeth 256
George 256
Hannah 254
James 256
John 256
Thomas 256
William 256
Hatchel
Mary 255
Hatcher
William 262
Haun
Weynette 260, 261
Haynie
Anne 245
Heze. 245
Isaac 245
John 245
Judith 245
Peter 245
Richard 262
Will. 245
Headen
George 245

Heath
John 245
Henderson
James 211
Henley
Hezekiah 256
Reynold 209
William 256
Hentley
Mary 235
Herbert
Cuthbert 229, 239
Hannah 239
Joan 229
Luke 229, 230, 239
Samuel 229
Hill
Charles 245
Ed 229
George 245
John 245
Hockaday
Abner 222
Bettie 222, 226
Cynthia 222
Edmund 221
Eliza 219, 220, 222, 224-226
Elizabeth 222, 223, 225
James 220-222
John 220-222
Judith 219, 222, 224-226
Lilly 224
Martha 221
Mary 221, 222
Millosentia 220
Philip 221
Rebecca 221
Sallie 226
Sarah 222, 226
Susan 222
William 216, 219-226
Holcombe
Hosea 238
Phoebe 238
Holland
Michael 232
Holman
Nathl 255
Hopkins
Isabella 234
Hornsby
John 245
Horton
James 230

Hosken
Millosentia 220
Howard
Nehemiah 238
Howerton
Ambrose 262
Catherine 262
Robert 262
Hudgins
Dennis 259
Hudnall
James 245
Richard 245
Sinah 245
Thomas 245
Hudson
Christopher 230
Hughlett
Samuel 245
Thomas 245
Hughs
Eliza. 211
Humphries
John 245
Hunt
George 245
Hunter
James 245
Hunton
John 245
Hurst
Henry 245
Hump. 245
John 245
Joseph 245
Spencer 245
Hutchings
John 245
Joseph 255
William 245
Indians
Pamunkey 210, 211
Ingram
George 245
Irons
John 245
Jackson
Benjamin 208
Martha 238
William 238
James
Robert 226
Jamison
Neil 245
Wattu 245

267

269

272

Heritage Books by Virginia Lee Hutcheson Davis:

Henrico County, Virginia Deeds, 1750–1774
Virginia Lee Hutcheson Davis and Gary Murdock Williams

Tidewater Virginia Families: A Magazine of History and Genealogy:

Volume 1, May 1992–February 1993

Volume 2, May 1993–February 1994

Volume 3, May 1994–February 1995

Volume 4, May 1995–February 1996

Volume 5, May 1996–February 1997

Volume 6, May 1997–February 1998

Volume 7, May 1998–February 1999

Volume 8, May 1999–February 2000

Volume 9, May 2000–February 2001

Volume 10, May 2001–February 2002

Volume 11, May 2002–February 2003

Volume 12, May 2003–February 2004